No

MILLERGATE
The Real Glenn Miller Story

BY THE SAME AUTHOR

AS DAVID GRAHAM

GRAVE OF SAND	Hale London 1963
OPERATION CLEANSWEEP	Hale London 1964
DOWN TO A SUNLESS SEA	Hale London 1980
	Simon & Schuster USA
	Verlag Ullstein Berlin
	Pan Books Paperback etc
	International Best Seller
SIDEWALL	Hale London 1981
SEVEN YEARS TO SUNSET	Hale London 1986

AS DONALD CARTER

HARD CASE	Hale London 1983
	Verlag Ullstein Berlin

WILBUR WRIGHT

CARTERS CASTLE	Century London 1985
	Verlag Ullstein Berlin
	Tor Paperbacks
	Readers Digest Condensed
	Literary Guild Choice
THREE PROUD DANCERS	Verlag Ullstein Berlin
KELLY'S RUN	Verlag Ullstein Berlin

Pending titles :

THE BELLS OF HELL
NOW,CENTURION
RIO BRAVO***
TIME - GATEWAY TO IMMORTALITY
FIRST IN,LAST OUT
BLUE SKIES

*** Part 1 of the Zimmermann Trilogy

MILLERGATE
The Real Glenn Miller Story

Wilbur Wright

Wrightway Publishing Limited
Allington Lane Southampton SO3 3HP

First published 1990

© Wilbur Wright 1990

Set in Times Roman

ISBN No. 0 9512547 0 7

Reproduced from Camera Ready Copy supplied and
Printed in Great Britain by Hobbs the Printers of Southampton

LIST OF CONTENTS

LIST OF ILLUSTRATIONS AND ACKNOWLEDGEMENTS

LIST OF ILLUSTRATIONS Cont.

Dustcover Seascape by kind permision of
Mr.Roy Westlake,A.R.P.S.

GLOSSARY

AA	Anti-aircraft		MACR	Missing Aircrew Report
AAF	Army Air Force		MIA	Missing in Action
ADC	Aide de camp		MOD	Ministry of Defence
ADRS	Air Depot Repair Squadron		NCO	Non-Commissioned Officer
AEFN	Allied Expeditionary Forces Network		NPRC	National Personnel Records Center
AF	Air Force		PDD	Presumed Dead by Drowning
AFB	Air Force Base		PR	Public Relations
AFSC	Air Force Service Command		QM	Quartermaster
AG	Adjutant-General		R.A.F.	Royal Air Force
Ala.	Alabama		RCAF	Royal Canadian Air Force
App.	Appendix		RN	Royal Navy
APO	Army Post Office		SAD	Strategic Air Depot
ARC	American Red Cross		SHAEF	Supreme Headquarters,Allied
ASR	Air Sea Rescue			Expeditionary Forces.
ATC	Air Traffic Control		TV	Television
BBC	British Broadcasting Corporation		TVS	Television South
Capt.	Captain		UK	United Kingdom
CID	Criminal Investigation Division		US	United States
CINFO	Central Office of Information		USA	United States of America
Col.	Colonel		USAAF	United States Army Air Force
DC	District of Columbia		USAF	United States Air Force
DFC	Distinguished Flying Cross		USAFE	United States Air Forces Europe
ETA	Estimated Time of Arrival		USFET	United States Forces,Euopean Theater
ETD	Estimated Time of Departure		USO	United Services Organisation
ETO	European Theater of Operations		Va.	Virginia
Fig.	Figure (Illustration)		VE	Victory in Europe
Gen.	General		VIP	Very Important Person
HQ	Headquarters		WAAF	Womens Auxiliary Air Force
LOC	Library of Congress		WO	Warrant Officer
Lt.	Lieutenant		WW2	World War Two
Lt Col.	Lieutenant Colonel			

ACKNOWLEDGEMENTS

This book could not have been completed without the help and encouragement of countless friends, acquaintances and others who simply wished to contribute to what may, in due course, become the definitive reference work on the Glenn Miller Mystery. They include the late Sqdn.Ldr Jack Taylor who first suggested the project, Mrs.Connie Richards who gave freely of her store of knowledge, photographs and her unique collection of Miller memorabilia. My gratitude too, to Ken Perfect of the Glenn Miller Society who contributed significantly, and to the late Herb Miller, as well as Dale Titler, Royal Frey, George W. Ferguson, Jean Pace, Bryan Murray, Bill McAllister, Mssrs George T.Simon and Geoffrey Butcher, Michael Harrison, Sheridan Morley and Charles Higham, who freely gave permission to quote from their own books. Not forgetting Hamish Hamilton Ltd. for permission to quote from the late David Niven's books.

I owe a debt of gratitude to Eddie Edmonds and his wife who were serving at Twinwood Farm on December 15 1944, and to George Reddy in Vancouver and the many other members of the 33rd R.A.F.Halton Entry who contributed not only their knowledge and advice but encouragement when the going got very tough. Thanks also to the various USAF Historical Agencies including Master Sergeant Schroeder, Mildenhall, who refused to be fazed by my flood of inquiries ! And most of all to the Departmental Heads of the American National Archives, the R.A.F. Museum and the MOD Air Historical Branch, John Edwards, Dennis Cottam, Clive Ward, Flt. Lt. French and his crew, Group Captain Tony Bartley, DFC & Bar, Colonel Tom Corrigan, Jack Donnelly, Mssrs Edward and David Pecora, and to Mr. Bowler, who was Air Traffic Controller at Twinwood Farm on the day Glenn Miller did not take off in Morgan's Norseman. A final word in gratitude to all those agencies who gave their permission to quote from their publications without charging any fee, and to HM Ordnance Survey - who did. . .

Wilbur Wright
Southampton
1990

PREFACE

WHEN I joined the Royal Air Force as an Aircraft Apprentice at No. 1 School of Technical Training, R.A.F.Halton in January 1936, little did I know that some 50 years later a colleague of mine would ask me to write a Preface for his latest book, which is entitled MILLERGATE. But with hindsight,it is predictable that one of the world's finest apprenticeship schemes,noted or perhaps notorious for nurturing a boy's natural curiosity and a craving for investigation and analysis, would produce a breed of men typified by Wilbur Wright.

The difficulties of researching and unravelling the events which led to the disappearance of Major Alton Glenn Miller in the cold foggy skies of wartime Britain in December 1944 was a challenge of astronomical proportions, demanding a special type of experience and motivation. I can think of no one with better qualifications : Wilbur has been at various times an engine and airframe fitter, flight engineer, a fighter pilot, air traffic and radar controller, flying instructor, flight safety officer, sales manager, company director, technical author and a writer of best-seller novels about flying.

The aptness of the book's title MILLERGATE becomes increasingly apparent as details emerge of the manifest cover-up and falsification of official documents. It was typical of Wilbur to approach the top level and ask the President of the United States to intervene, when he realised that some National Archives officials were being less than co-operative !

Whilst Wilbur stresses that the views and assumptions in the book are his alone, they are nevertheless backed by years of painstaking research and world-wide enquiries which have produced a wealth of new evidence on the mystery. Some of the disclosures in the book are startling : for example, a letter from the New Jersey State Registrar stating that `Glenn Miller died in Ohio in December 1944' - later disclaimed as a `typing error' ! It is clear that still more information must be available, and it is hoped that this book will persuade a number of people to come forward.

The book makes fascinating reading, and I know that millions of Glenn Miller fans all over the world will welcome this wide investigation and report into his untimely death, and I have no hesitation in recommending it to readers of all ages.

BILL SYKES
Air Vice Marshal
R.A.F. (Retd)

For Joyce, whose support made it all possible, and for David, who edited the audio tapes.

Fig. 1
The Noordyn UC64A Norseman

Fig. 2
Paul Dudley, Glenn Miller, Don Haynes

FOREWORD

ANY investigation into events which occurred almost half a century ago will encounter serious difficulties,not the least of which is that most of the individuals involved are long since deceased. Secondly, the period during which the events occurred coincides with the final convulsions of a World War involving millions of soldiers. All armies, it is said,travel on their bellies but the essential lubricant is paperwork - in such volume as to defy the imagination. So when such a conflict ends, there is a vast burning of files,documents, lists and photographs, of which only a tiny proportion can be preserved for posterity.

We may be sure,therefore, that any documents remaining in the files of deceased personnel have been reviewed and are considered valuable enough to be preserved. This is especially true of VIPs,and in the case of Glenn Miller, arguably the most popular bandleader of modern times (who vanished under mysterious circumstances in 1944) it seems certain that his personal file would be constantly under review. In the past 45 years there has been,in fact, a constant flow of inquiries on the Miller mystery - so many that the personal files of the three central characters are annotated `*KEEP ON TOP OF CABINET AT ALL TIMES'*...

As with all classic and intractable mysteries since the *Marie Celeste* was found under sail on December 5 1872 with no human soul aboard,speculative theories and rumours about the fate of Major Alton Glenn Miller have abounded, springing up like autumn mushrooms to cloud and distort the true facts. For any investigator there is a fine line drawn between logical justifiable conclusions based on corroborated evidence, and unjustified speculation in the absence of any evidence at all.

In the Miller saga there are three such issues : first, a possibility that Miller had not been a passenger on the C64 Norseman aircraft flown by pilot Johnny Morgan, but had been seriously injured and flown back to America for treatment - where he died soon afterwards. But we knew any investigation of that scenario might involve invasion of the privacy of the Miller family in California, and it was not undertaken lightly. Did the evidence we had accumulated justify an in-depth probe ? We thought so.

First,*the USAAF serial number on his travel orders for Paris was not his own, and could have led to a mis-identification.*

Second, that risk was enhanced because *Glenn did not wear his dog-tags,because of a skin infection.*

Third, researcher John Edwards received in 1973 a letter from a US WW2 veteran,*claiming that he was in the same ward in an Ohio military hospital as Glenn Miller in December 1944, and that the bandleader had died from his injuries.*

Fourth, we had conclusive evidence that *Miller was not aboard the missing Norseman aircraft. Fifth, a search of all US military cemeteries*

ies in Europe failed to produce any trace of Miller.

Sixth, we had substantial evidence to confirm *Glenn reached Paris on Thursday December 14 1944 and had thereafter vanished without trace.*

Seventh, evidence found in the Miller Burial File proved conclusively that *an extensive cover-up occurred in Paris,* confirming that SHAEF knew Miller was in France and was waiting for him to show up.

Eighth, we located evidence indicating that *Glenn was in Fred Paynes's British Bar in Paris on Friday December 15 - the very day he was supposedly lost in the Norseman.*

Ninth, *there was no trace of any of Glenn's personal effects*; none were returned to his widow Helen, suggesting strongly that he took his effects to France and they vanished with him. We believed that this mass of admittedly circumstantial evidence warranted an in-depth probe in America - an inquiry which, while failing to produce a satisfactory explanation, did pose several crucial questions.

The second issue concerned that extremely-popular movie personality David Niven. He was, *per se*, Glenn Miller's boss in the vital 6-month period before the bandleader vanished. Seconded to U.S Special Services, he was Associate Director of Troop Broadcasting from July to October 1944, and became Director when the incumbent, Col. Ed Kirby, returned home on October 1st. This period was the highlight of Niven's career outside show business, for which he was awarded the Legion of Honour after the war. He played an active part in planning the AAF Band concerts, and chaired a conference at SHAEF Versailles on November 15 1944, at which the Band concert in Paris commencing December 21st was approved.

Further, he and Glenn Miller were old friends from Hollywood days when the latter was making the movies *ORCHESTRA WIVES* and *SUN VALLEY SERENADE*. And their mutual friend Marlene Dietrich was in Paris performing in USO shows during the critical December period. Whenever possible the three would meet for dinner or lunch if they were in the same area. Indeed, of all people one might expect to be at Orly on Friday December 15 to greet Glenn Miller (if Haynes was to be believed) David Niven was favourite.

Yet, as he wrote himself after the war, on that day he was in Spa in Belgium, at US 1st Army HQ, visiting old friends. Even more remarkably, he made no mention at all in his post-war books of his lengthy association with Glenn Miller and the AAF Band, and omitted all references to the mysterious death of his old friend.

Inexplicably, Niven remained in the background during the eight tense days which elapsed before a public announcement was made, and did not appear at any of the AAF Band concerts - yet he was himself in charge of all arrangements ! It was essential in our view, to develop some kind of explanation for this strange behaviour, and we devoted a major part of our research to that end.

The third issue, and perhaps the most important - was the part played by

General Ray Barker, US Army, G-1 at SHAEF Paris and in charge of all US military personnel. He was the officer to whom Lt. Don Haynes reported on Tuesday December 19 1944, two days after arriving at Paris with the AAF Band and five days after he had `*seen Glenn Miller off from England in a C64 Norseman passenger plane'*, together with a staff officer Lt.Col.Norman F.Baessell.

It became obvious at an early stage in our investigation that the Don Haynes story was fatally flawed and unviable. Then we obtained confirmatory evidence that Glenn had flown from R.A.F.Bovingdon to Paris Orly on Thursday December 14, with a BBC engineer,the late Mr.Teddy Gower. The band leader vanished without trace, but the subsequent behaviour of General Barker, his staff and Haynes seemed to indicate that they were aware of the circumstances and had decided to wait until Major Miller showed up.

It was fortuitous that the UC64A Norseman aircraft flown by Flight Officer Johnny Morgan was reported missing on a ferrying flight to France on Friday December 15, for both Don Haynes and Miller had flown with Morgan previously in that aircraft.Further,Morgan's duties had included ferrying senior staff officers from 8th Air Force Service Command HQ at Milton Ernest (only a mile or two from the AAF Band base in Bedford) including Col.Baessell, with whom Miller was on friendly terms. Baessell was missing with Morgan.

At some time in the days that followed Haynes' arrival in Paris, his fabricated story emerged : he described driving Glenn and Baessell in atrocious weather to the R.A.F. base at Twinwood Farm, only one mile from Milton Ernest HQ,where they were picked up by Morgan in the Norseman. Haynes said they took off at 13.45 hours, bound for Orly,and the plane was never seen again.

That story,seemingly,was accepted by General Barker, who delayed all reporting procedures for nine days in the hope that Miller would turn up safely. But we are faced with a dilemma of huge proportions here. Our evidence confirms that Haynes' story was untrue : the question we must now ask is `*Did General Barker know this, but promulgated the report because even a false explanation was better than no explanation at all ?'* Or did he genuinely believe Haynes' story ? Barker died many years ago, but we were reluctant to state outright that he collaborated with Haynes in a major cover-up operation, designed to conceal the fact that SHAEF had no idea whatsoever what had happened to Miller,a VIP and serving USAAF officer under their care and jurisdiction. Yet all the evidence appears to confirm that this was the case.

We decided that we would assume, for the purposes of the investigation,that Barker assumed that Miller had arrived in Paris on Thursday 14 December and was out of touch. Further we suggest that he did not make this assumption until Lt. Haynes talked to him at SHAEF at 18.00 on Tuesday December 19 - by which time Glenn had been missing five full days. But we reserved judgement on his involvement with Haynes

3

and his fictitious story,   until all the evidence was to hand and fairly assessed. If that evidence uncovered some degree of collaboration and conspiracy to conceal the truth, so be it : the reader must draw his own conclusions, as we did. But for the purposes of the investigation we assumed, from the evidence presented, that General Barker was involved unless evidence to the contrary was obtained.

History must be the judge.

+   +   +

ONE

DEATH OF A VIP

1. FOUNDATIONS

THE mysterious disappearance of Major Alton Glenn Miller on December 15 1944 passed within a few decades into legend, generating countless rumours, theories and scenarios. From the time of the Press Release (Fig.42) on December 24,which like most wartime reports was subject to censorship giving a minumum of information, there was widespread belief that this was no ordinary loss of a small passenger aircraft in icy foggy weather. Further, Glenn Miller was a VIP of the day and millions of his fans were dissatisfied with the meagre amount of information released, and the unexplained delay in making the news public.

That dissatisfaction increased after the war, when it became clear that no formal statement was going to be issued, when no attempt was made to question the sole witness, Lt.Don Haynes, and when the few documents which were released were suspect, to say the least. The Release was timed significantly for 18.00 hours, just one hour before a scheduled AAF Band broadcast to America. It was as brief as it was vague :

`*Major Alton Glenn Miller, Director of the famous United States Army Air Force Band which has been playing in Paris is reported missing while on a flight from England to Paris. The plane in which he was a passenger left England on December 15 and no trace of it has been found since its take-off. Major Miller, one of the outstanding orchestra leaders in the United States, lived at Tenafly, New Jersey, where his wife presently resides. No members of Major Miller's band were with him on the missing plane.'*

When a US Army aircraft was lost in the ETO, a Missing Aircrew Report(MACR) was compiled by the operating unit within 48 hours and sent to the War Department, Washington. It was rarely possible in combat zones to institute an inquiry, for planes were lost every day from enemy action, aircrew error and technical defects;there were days when 200+ planes were lost. One might reasonably expect that an incident involving a VIP would receive special attention - but documents found in the secret Miller Burial File in Washington confirm that no search was made for the missing aircraft, and that no investigation was initiated at the time.

Yet we discovered conclusive evidence that an extensive search was mounted in Paris, not for all three of the men alleged to have been in the plane,or for the aircraft - but for Major Glenn Miller in person.Units involved in the search included the US Provost Marshal Department, the

Criminal Investigation Division of the US Army, and Special Services Division at SHAEF. Haynes himself spent his first two days in Paris searching hotels and restaurants for Miller, before reporting to General Barker, as recorded in his diary.

The only possible conclusion we can draw is that staff at SHAEF and Haynes himself believed that Glenn Miller had arrived safely in Paris, and had therefore not been aboard the missing Norseman. Indeed, the first official mention of the Norseman story emerged on Wednesday December 20 (Fig.46) in a confirmatory signal from 8th AFSC at Milton Ernest to General Barker at Versailles - a full week after Glenn was last seen outside a Mayfair nightclub heading for his hotel at Marble Arch.

But why, we may ask, did Haynes and others search Paris hotels and restaurants for Miller, when his plane had been reported crossing the English coast at Dymchurch and had not reached the French coast ? Did they think he had swum ashore and walked to Paris ?

Even more puzzling, Haynes had spent that fatal weekend at Milton Ernest,Headquarters of the Command which operated the Norseman. The Air Traffic reporting procedures ensured that 8th AFSC would learn of the Norseman's loss no later than Saturday morning (a surviving witness in Brussels Control Tower that morning recalls telephone calls requesting information. Yet Haynes always insisted that his first intimation of disaster was on reaching Orly on Monday afternoon !

Again, only one conclusion is possible - he was not informed because he did not `need to know'. Glenn was not aboard the aircraft.If he had been,a major search would have been mounted and Haynes informed.

After a fruitless search, Lt. Don Haynes reported to General Barker at 18.00 on Tuesday evening. According to his diary he described driving Glenn Miller and Baessell from Milton Ernest to R.A.F.Twinwood Farm (Fig.5) and putting them aboard Morgan's Norseman. He was, Haynes maintained, the last person to see Glenn Miller alive and the sole witness of the take-off.

At that time,as the war's end drew near, there seemed no firm reason to disbelieve Haynes. Official secrecy prevented release of the full story until after the war - but as time went on, it became clear that no public statement was to be made at all, and that fuelled the flames of suspicion. It was not until November 1948 that a Missing Aircrew Report was released (Fig.12/13) although it was `security-declassified' two years earlier in March 1946).

It caused consternation among all serious investigators. It was remarkable more for its omissions than its contents, and generated a search for the truth which is ongoing today all over the world. Inexplicably, it contained no statement by Haynes - nor was he named as `*the person with last knowledge of the aircraft'*. The route was `Abbotts Ripton (the home base) to Twinwood Farm-A42-Bordeaux'. In fact many people assumed that base A-42 was Bordeaux ! But it was Villacoublay, south of Paris. Haynes, on the other hand, said Morgan came to Twinwood Farm from R.A.F. Honington in Suffolk, and was bound for Orly ! There was worse to come. The `unknown' local weather on 15 December was on record in the Meteorological Office. The C64 engine number, essential for identification, was `unknown' - but on record in an office near that of the unit Adjutant who compiled the Report. The MACR was indubitably suspect. There was no reason why Haynes could not give an eyewitness statement, even if he was in Paris. It could have been recorded on oath by the AG Department, and there was plenty of time to send it back to Abbotts Ripton - the MACR was delayed for 9 days. Indeed, his whole story rested upon his meeting with General Barker (of which no official record exists), his unviable diary account 25 years later, and a single word in the MACR - `*TWINWOOD*'.

From the day the MACR appeared, two questions preoccupied the researchers. First, if as seemed probable, Glenn Miller was not aboard the missing Norseman, what really happened to him in France ? And second, what became of the aircraft and what route did Morgan take ? Some quite extraordinary theories emerged to account for Glenn's mysterious disappearance. His C47 Dakota had been shot down by German fighters over the Channel. He had been killed by bombs jettisoned by returning Lancaster bombers, died of cancer in a London hospital, shot dead by Lt.Col. Baessell because of the latter's black market activities. And most outrageous of all, he had been killed in a street brawl in Pigalle, the Paris red light district.

But there was no real evidence, no witnesses, and while a score of researchers pursued the case for more than forty years, the mystery seemed insoluble. Yet in considering the viability of Haynes' story, there was one disturbing factor. Miller, at 40 years of age, had always disliked flying. Often he referred to premonitions of an early death, and only a week or two before he vanished, he wrote to brother Herb in America :

> `*By the time you get this, I will be in Paris - barring a nose-dive into the Channel...*'

On another occasion he told a band-member :

> `*I don't think I'll make it home with the boys. I'll get mine in some beat-up old airplane...*'

His problems were exacerbated by sinus trouble and a persistent neck rash; Haynes related that his boss would get up from his seat in flight and walk around the aircraft nervously.

It is extremely difficult in the face of this evidence to understand why Glenn Miller opted to fly to Paris in a tiny single-engined passenger plane with no navigational or de-icing aids and an obsolescent radio, flown by a rookie pilot on a day when, quoting Haynes, the weather was so bad all UK flying was at a standstill and Paris shuttle flights had been grounded for three days !

The truth, of course, was that the weather was not as bad as Haynes would have us believe on Friday December 15 1944. (See Figs.39/40). Thousands of R.A.F. and American aircraft flew that day,and USAAF shuttle flights into Orly continued until 15.00 on a restricted basis; considerably more flew on the previous day, Thursday December 14. Further, Morgan was inexperienced, a poor instrument pilot, and he would never have been given clearance to fly in the atrocious weather Don Haynes described.

How then did Haynes explain Glenn Miller's extraordinary decision to accept Col.Baessell's offer of a lift to Paris in the Norseman ? First,he wrote after the war that Glenn had a `social engagement' in Paris and didn't want to disappoint his hosts. But that certainly did not warrant taking such risks. Second, Haynes said that Glenn insisted on changing plans and travelling to Paris ahead of the Band instead of Haynes,to finalise transport and accommodation.

But Haynes had spent three days in Paris less than two weeks previously,for that very purpose ! And third, while weather conditions were bad enough to ground everyone else, Morgan would have no difficulty in landing at Twinwood Farm, being `*a very experienced pilot who had recently completed a tour of 34 heavy bomber missions'*.

This however was totally untrue. At the time of his death John Morgan had flown less than 600 hours, none of it on operations, and had a poor grade in bad-weather instrument flying. Further, Haynes was aware of this, having flown with the pilot on several occasions. He had socialised with Morgan and according to his diary knew him well.

Finally, the radio producer Cecil Madden was quoted as saying he had tried to dissuade Glenn from flying to Paris - but when ? Haynes had booked him onto a Thursday December 14 shuttle flight before Don returned to Bedford on Wednesday. The same day, Glenn had his baggage taken round to the Old Quebec Street Air Terminal, spending Wednesday evening at the Milroy Club, Mayfair with Battle of Britain ace Tony Bartley,DFC and Bar, leaving at 2.30 am to return to his Marble Arch hotel. Madden was not among the party - and Glenn was never seen alive again.

The final piece of evidence is startling. We learned that Haynes did not return to Bedford on Wednesday night until a late hour, spending the evening at the Milroy Club with Tony Bartley, Lt.Tony Pulitzer USAAF, Glenn Miller and a so-far unidentified girl singer. Also in the party was John Morgan, who had come down from Abbotts Ripton to see the final UK Band performance in the Queensberry Club.

Thanks to the evidence of a still-surviving witness, we can trace the precise moment at which Don Haynes abandoned the truth and began to fabricate his story. It was Wednesday afternoon on December 13, when he said he drove back alone to Bedford in thick fog.

Fig. 3
Flight Officer John R.S. Morgan

Fig. 8
Brig.Gen. Donald R.Goodrich

Fig. 4
Lt.Col. J.D.Niven,LM Rifle Brigade.

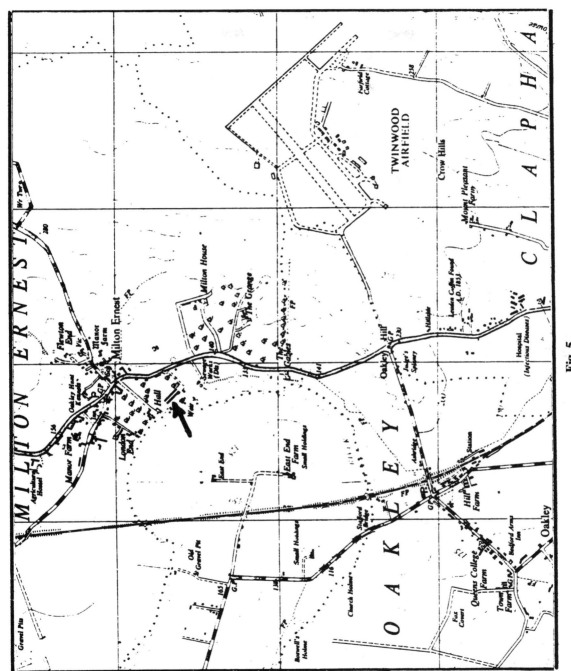

Fig. 5
Twinwood Farm and Milton Ernest

Fig.6
Milton Ernest Hall, 1944

Fig. 7
Mount Royal Hotel, London

Fig. 9
Lt.Col. Norman F. Baessell

From that moment, he told no one the true facts, and when we examine his diary, we shall find that it too was unviable.

2. **MILLER COMES TO BRITAIN**

Glenn had an elder brother Deane; when Herb the youngest died in Dulwich,London in 1987, we were among those who attended his funeral. Their parents Lewis Elmer and Mattie Lou Miller lived at 601 South 16th Street, Clarinda Iowa, where Glenn was born on March 1 1900. They were a musical family; Mattie Lou played the organ and the young Glenn sang in the church choir. His parents gave him a mandolin, which the boy promptly traded for a trumpet, emulating Deane, who played in the Town Band. Then a bandleader friend Jack Mossberger gave Glenn a trombone and from that moment no other instrument existed for the young musician.

Graduating on May 20 1921, Glenn began playing in small nomadic jazz combinations all over the Mid-West, including Holly Mayer,Max Fisher, Tom Watkins and finally Ben Pollack and his band in the Venice Ballroom, Los Angeles. In October 1928, Glenn married his childhood sweetheart Helen Dorothy Burger from Boulder, Colorado and they settled in New York. By 1935, Glenn had his own band but things went badly; they closed down after playing their final date in York,Pennsylvania. Glenn went back to New York tired and disillusioned,to earn a living playing in Broadway theatre orchestras, studying music and composition in his spare time.

In spring 1938 Glenn began to put together the orchestra with which he became famous for the next four years. His income rocketed and they lived in a spacious apartment in Byrne Lane,Tenafly,New Jersey until he was inducted into the US Army as a volunteer on November 23 1942.

The famous Miller band was broken up but Glenn kept in contact, having no intention of remaining buried indefinitely in the arid field of marching music. Having miscarried badly, Helen Miller was unable to bear children,but they adopted two; Steve was a year old in 1944 and a girl Jonnie came along soon afterwards. Glenn escaped eventually from military band music, forming the American Air Force Band, known as the 2001st Base Unit (Radio) based in New Haven,Conn. comprising 62 musicians,many from his old outfit. Glenn had his Band Manager Don Haynes appointed as Executive Officer with the rank of Lieutenant.

Don was a one-time band booking agent who joined Glenn and his band as manager, during their residency at the Cafe Rouge in the Hotel Pennsylvania in New York City. But Glenn's burning ambition was to entertain the troops overseas, and he went to Washington to see a friend,Col. Ed. Kirby in Special Services Division. Kirby pulled strings to good effect; the Band received orders for overseas and Glenn flew to England on June 18 1944. The Band followed a week later in the Queen Elizabeth I, and found their new billets in Sloane Square,London.

But this, as Miller ruefully said, was right in the middle of Bomb Alley with V1 'doodlebugs' coming in frequently. On their second morning Miller, Haynes and Sgt. Paul Dudley went to SHAEF REAR at Bushey Park, London, to talk to Col. Ed. Kirby (at that time Director of Troop Broadcasting) about finding safer billets. To Miller's delight, the Associate Director was his old friend Lt.Col. David Niven, who immediately took over administration of the Band and became, *per se*, Glenn's Commanding Officer. Niven drove the three musicians out to Bedford, a quiet town 50 miles north of London to which most of the BBC had been evacuated during the Blitz. David Niven was to play an important part in the events which would ensue.

3. **BEDFORD AND MILTON ERNEST (Fig.5)**

Careful consideration and planning went into the integration of the AAF Band into the existing framework of Forces entertainment. Only two weeks previously Allied troops had landed on the Normandy beaches and radio programmes were an essential factor in maintaining morale. As well as giving live concerts before Service audiences, the Band would make live and recorded broadcasts on both the BBC and AEF networks. Adequate billeting and messing arrangements for the Band were provided in houses forming an annexe to the ARC Club in Ashburnham Road,Bedford, while Miller, Haynes and Lt. Paul Morden used the ARC Officers Club at the intersection of Kimbolton and Goldington Roads. Glenn also had a small apartment in Bedford which he used infrequently, but worked mainly in London at his office in the Langham Hotel, living in rooms at the Mount Royal Hotel, Marble Arch.

There were many USAAF units round Bedford and the ARC Officers Club was invariably crowded; Glenn and Haynes began to use the Club at 8th Air Force Service Command at Milton Ernest Hall, three miles out of Bedford. For administrative purposes the Band was under 8th AFSC, but their parent unit was HQ Training Command; for that reason Glenn Miller did not appear on any 8th Air Force Casualty List.

In the course of time, both Glenn and Don Haynes became friendly with the Commanding Officer Officer, Brig. General Donald R. Goodrich (Fig.8) and his Special Assistant Lt.Col.Norman F.Baessell. (Fig.9). Goodrich was a homely mild-mannered old man whose Army career had begun in the WW1 trenches; he was affectionately known to his subordinates as 'Poopsie'. But in December 1944, Goodrich was terminally ill with cardiac problems, spending most of his time in his house `The Bury' across the river from Milton Ernest Hall. Army engineers had thrown up a Bailey Bridge for access, and Goodrich delegated most of the work to his Executive Officer Col.Early. Within days of Miller's disappearance, the General was evacuated to Maxwell AFB in Alabama,where he died shortly afterwards. He was never interrogated on the Miller affair.

4. **THE AIRFIELDS IN THE MYSTERY.(Fig.10).**

(a) **R.A.F.Twinwood Farm (Fig.5)**

Eighth AFSC was responsible for the supply, repair,general servicing and modification of all 8th AF aircraft in the UK and on the Continent after D-Day. Twinwood Farm was located one mile from Milton Ernest Hall, convenient for air uplifts of the Band to concert venues at other bases. Originally intended as a municipal airport for Bedford, Twinwood became a typical wartime station on which domestic accommodation was dispersed at remote sites against attack from the air. The main technical site was located just south of the triangle of runways,with a main gate on the south side of the base. The Air Traffic Control Tower was located next to the main technical site, and a secondary gate near the end of Runway 09 linked the base with Milton Ernest village near Oakley crossroads.

In December 1944 the base housed No. 51 Night Fighter Operational Training Unit equipped with Bristol Beaufighters and some Mosquitos. Station Flight located near the Control Tower was responsible for receiving visiting aircraft, which were parked near the Tower. Visiting pilots were obliged to report to ATC after landing. Four people who were stationed at Twinwood Farm in December 1944 were traced, an aircraft engineer, two WAAFs and an Air Traffic Controller, Mr.Bowler. In addition to a Control Officer in the Tower, all R.A.F. airfields deploy a Runway Controller (usually an N.C.O.) in a caravan at the threshold of the duty runway, to monitor traffic and initiate emergency signals. The runway caravan is not manned when the airfield is closed for flying, and the Tower is manned by a skeleton staff maintaining a radio watch on emergency channels only. A signals square outside the Tower will indicate that the airfield is closed and no radio contact is possible while flying is suspended : there would be no fire or rescue vehicles on standby and no pilot would risk a landing there, save in dire emergency.Further, the standard method of controlling the descent of an aircraft through cloud was ground VHF radio linked to a radio DF facility, enabling the Controller to guide the aircraft down into visual contact with the airfield (but not necessarily aligned with the runway). In conditions of low overcast and minimal visibility such as Haynes described as prevailing at Twinwood Farm on December 15, no pilot could descend through cloud and reach the airfield without radio assistance from the ground, that is to say, from an open and fully-manned Control Tower.

All R.A.F. stations, including Twinwood Farm, maintained a daily diary of events (Form 540) many of which have been preserved in the Public Records Office at Kew, London. In the Form 540 for Twinwood Farm for Friday December 15 1944, the date on which Don Haynes claimed he put Glenn Miller aboard Morgan's Norseman, the entry reads :
`No flying today. Airfield closed.'

(b) **Alconbury and Abbotts Ripton**

Eighth AF Service Command operated several Air Depot Groups on suitable R.A.F. bases including Honington, Wattisham and Burtonwood. The 44th Strategic Air Depot at Wattisham ran a number of subsidiary Depots and Servicing Squadrons based within the perimeters of operational airfields, including the 35th Air Depot Repair Squadron at Abbotts Ripton, inside the perimeter of R.A.F.Alconbury 30 miles north of Twinwood Farm. While 44 SAD Wattisham specialised in the servicing and repair of fighter aircraft such as the P38 Lightning, P47 Thunderbolt and P51 Mustang, Abbotts Ripton worked on heavy bombers including the B17 Fortress and B24 Liberator. The 35th ADRS also operated a communications flight using a Percival Proctor and Airspeed Oxford, to ferry personnel and spares.

Soon after D-Day, the 44th SAD at Wattisham took delivery of four brand-new Noorduyn UC64A Norseman aircraft (Fig.1), one of which was Serial No. 44-70285. The `44' prefix indicates the year of manufacture, and two surviving pilots, George W. Ferguson (Fig.11) and Jean Pace flew 70285 on several trips to the Continent with Lt.Col.Baessell. His task as a Special Assistant to General Goodrich was the location,provisioning and commissioning of Advanced Repair Depots in France and Belgium.

But in September 1944, George Ferguson was detached to Brussels, taking one Norseman with him, while 44-70285 was transferred to the communications flight at Abbotts Ripton,together with a young noncommissioned ex-R.C.A.F pilot, John Robert Stuart Morgan (Fig.3).

By December 1944, 44-70285 had flown not more than 500 hours *in toto*.Morgan's Form 5 (flight time record) shows that it flew only seven times in November and twice in December,the last being the fatal December 15 mission to France. Based on a Repair Squadron,70285 probably received optimum servicing and the possibility of mechanical failure on its final trip would seem minimal. However,we established that the aircraft had an endemic history of hydraulic leaks in the propeller constant-speed system; on one flight to Paris with Baessell Jean Pace aborted the mission after landing at Bovingdon and returned to Wattisham for repairs.

All USAAF ETO bases were assigned code numbers,including :

Station 101 - Camp Lynn, Air Signals Depot, Medmenham.
112 - R.A.F.Bovingdon, USAAF Troop Staging Post.
470 - 44 SAD, Wattisham, Suffolk.
506 - 8th AFSC, Milton Ernest, Bedford.
525 - R.A.F.Heston, Middlesex. USAAF Transport.
595 - R.A.F.Honington/Troston Air Depot, Suffolk.

After the invasion, British Continental bases were given a `B' prefix

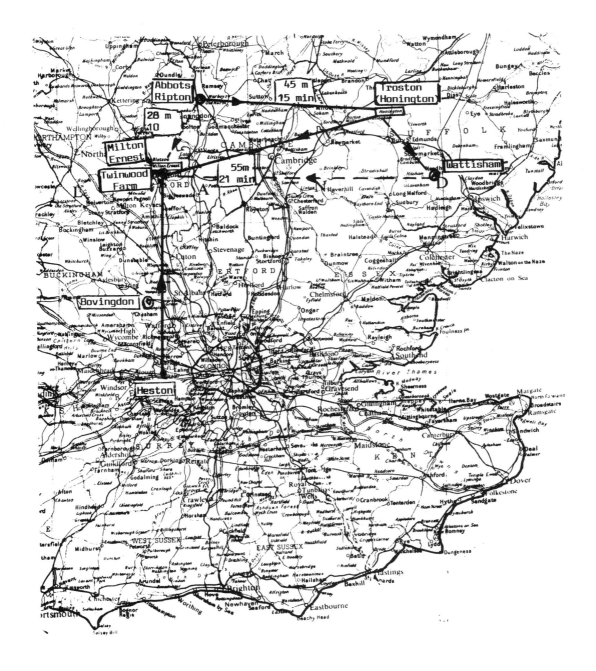

Fig. 10
Airfields in the Miller Mystery

Fig. 11
Lt.Col. George W. Ferguson, USAF Ret.

and number (for example `B42' Beauvais), while American bases used `A' plus a number,e.g. `A42' Villacoublay.

(c) **R.A.F.Bovingdon**

After June 1944, Bovingdon became the main departure and arrival field for USAAF Continental flights. (R.A.F. Northolt served a similar purpose for R.A.F.Transport Command). There were no resident transport squadrons at Bovingdon : aircraft were provided for shuttle runs by squadrons based elsewhere and came into Bovingdon to pick up passengers. All flight allocations were handled at the Air Transit Booking Centre in the Langham Hotel, on production of travel orders, and all heavy baggage was deposited at the Old Quebec Street Terminal in London 24 hours before the flight. At Bovingdon the seating allocation was handled on a number basis working on the flight number: for example,a passenger might be told at the Langham Hotel he was booked on Flight Number 2 from Bovingdon to Orly next day.On arrival at Bovingdon, he would be allotted a seat number, boarding the correct flight when it was called.

All passenger lists compiled at the Langham Hotel, therefore, were ephemeral documents and destroyed once the flight had landed safely. This system is important in the general context, in that Major Glenn Miller or any other passenger would not be called by name to board his flight. The announcement would simply state `*Flight 2 for Paris Orly boarding now'*. In effect, he would be travelling incognito and unrecognised by the other passengers. In Glenn's case, some six days elapsed before it was finally established that he was missing : the passenger lists for flights the previous week would have been destroyed. As a general rule, passengers bound for SHAEF Versailles were routed via Villacoublay, while those heading for Paris took the Orly flights. If, as we now believe, Glenn caught a C47 shuttle flight on Thursday December 14,he would not need to report to SHAEF until Monday morning,since the Band were to travel on Saturday and spend the weekend settling into the billet at the *Hotel des Olympiades* in Montmartre. It seems certain that Glenn would fly into Orly - and in fact, Haynes wrote in his diary that on arrival, he found that `*Glenn's plane had not arrived at Orly'*. Bovingdon also operated Customs and Immigration Controls.

Air Regulations required all Continental flights to land at Bovingdon for clearance, and to file a flight plan if the aircraft was outbound. The plan forms an essential part of all cross-country flights, especially those involving sea crossings. A mission from Abbotts Ripton to Paris would be cleared initially to Bovingdon, where further clearance was given to Paris after approval of a flight plan. The system involved firstly, operational orders issued by the parent organisation; secondly, submission of a written flight plan by the pilot;thirdly, final approval of the plan by Air Operations and flight clearance by Air Traffic Control. In this way, it was ensured that the pilot was duly authorised and capable of carrying out the mission; that the aircraft had sufficient fuel for the mission with a safety reserve and carried the appropriate navigation/communication equipment needed for the flight. Further, that the forecast weather was acceptable with suitable diversion airfields available, and that the destination airfield could accept the aircraft. After take-off, the departure airfield would inform the destination airfield by telephone or teleprinter, advising the aircraft ETA. Similarly, the destination field informed the departure airfield when the aircraft landed, providing a positive control.

Procedures for dealing with any overdue or missing aircraft were laid down. After 1 hour, a flight was listed as 'overdue' and the destination field would contact the departure field and all other possible landing points along the route. After 2 hours the aircraft would be listed as 'Missing' and the HQ of its parent Command would be notified at that time.

Here we must cover the subject of searches for missing aircraft. Any decision to launch an air or sea search depended directly upon whether or not an emergency radio 'Mayday' call had been received. Such a call would include the aircraft's position, altitude, airspeed, heading and the nature of the emergency. If no position report was received, it was futile to launch a search, unless the route and last known position were known. In cases of nonscheduled flights like the Norseman, the various landing points were stipulated on the flight plan, but the pilot had considerable latitude in selecting the route between these points. For example, if he was flying under low cloud to remain in visual contact with the ground, he might opt to divert to avoid high ground. Extensive search of the available records revealed that only one 'Mayday' call was received on December 15 1944, and that was from a USAAF aircraft far away in the North Sea. (The term is derived from the French 'M'aidez'). In the absence of any position report, an air or sea search was out of the question. As it happened, Morgan's aircraft was seen by a local Dymchurch resident crossing the coast outbound, but at such low level that the viewer deemed it advisable to notify the Royal Observer Corps. The report did not reach SHAEF until the following week, but the sighting (mentioned in Don Haynes' post-war diary) is of considerable interest when assessing the route Morgan took.

Was the 'clearance' procedure always followed strictly ? Col. George Ferguson and Jean Pace say 'no' categorically. It was not unusual, they say, for senior staff at Milton Ernest to obtain clearance by telephone from Bovingdon. We know this was the case with the Morgan flight. In a letter from the Adjutant General to Mrs. Helen Miller on February 8 1946 (see Fig.32) the writer Colonel Donnell states Morgan was cleared directly to France from Abbotts Ripton. He would not, therefore, be required to land at Bovingdon, or even overfly the airfield, taking the long way round west of London. Morgan's route is discussed at length in a subsequent chapter.

(d) **Villacoublay (A42)**

In 1986, Villacoublay was a heavily-guarded French Air Force base which has been in continuous use since 1917, including the German occupation from 1940 - 1944. After the Liberation,it became a 9th AF Advanced Air Depot and a terminal for USAAF shuttle flights from Bovingdon. It assumes minor importance as the incorrect destination given in the MACR.

(e) **Beauvais (B42)**

This was a large USAAF medium bomber base some 42 miles to the north of Paris (see Fig.49). It was finally identified as Morgan's true destination when we found his Service Record Card from Abbotts Ripton (Fig.27). The similarity of `B42' and `A42' is significant : if the MACR route had been stated as `Abbotts Ripton-B42-Bordeaux' and the word `Twinwood' omitted, the MACR would have been correct.

(f) **Bordeaux-Merignac (Y37) (Fig.48)**

There has been constant speculation on the inclusion of Bordeaux as final destination in the MACR. First, it checks with Morgan's Operation Orders on his Record Card - meaning that the MACR compiler saw the Card, the Orders or a flight plan at the time. There is no other source. Second, those same orders specified the sequence of destinations as `B42 (Beauvais) Bordeaux' with no mention of Twinwood Farm or `A42' Villacoublay'. Third, it is quoted in the `Findings of Death' documents of Miller and Baessell as the only destination in France. Fourth, Bordeaux was Station Y37, indicating a non-operational and unused airfield,because it was too far from the battle zones. Fifth, there is a letter in the Miller File in Washington referring to a `crash and bodies' at Bordeaux (Fig.33). But we evolved a satisfactory explanation why Col.Baessell was bound for Bordeaux, given in a later chapter.

5. **THE DON HAYNES STORY**

According to Haynes, he was the sole witness to the Norseman's departure from Twinwood Farm, and this is quite remarkable. It was a busy training unit : if it was open there would be other air traffic in the vicinity. Even if flying was suspended one would assume that at least one more person would report seeing a single aircraft land and take off again. But no one has ever come forward to support Haynes' story : on the contrary - three of the four ex-R.A.F. Twinwood Farm personnel we located insisted that no Norseman landed on December 15 1944,while the

the fourth confused her dates. The three insisted that no Norseman landed on December 15 1944. They learned of Miller's disappearance from a BBC news bulletin issued simultaneously with the SHAEF Press Release in Paris. And we have the evidence of the Form 540 in the Public Records Office in Kew, London.

Incredibly, we have only two documents containing the Don Haynes story : the first is the confirmatory signal (Fig.46) sent from 8th AFSC to General Barker, but as we shall show, the information it contained originated in Paris with Don Haynes, and was signalled back to Barker. The second is the Miller Casualty Report dated December 22 1944. Further, all official references to the account can be traced directly back to Haynes' discussions with Gen. Barker in Paris, which were revealed in Haynes' diaries after he died in 1971. The issue is simple :

If the story can be disproved beyond any shadow of doubt,we can be certain that Glenn Miller was not a passenger on Morgan's aircraft, that he left England by some other means and disappeared without trace after his arrival in Paris.

So what was the tale that Don Haynes told ? It was simple,brief and he used real events in the past to add authenticity.

At a conference at SHAEF on November 15 chaired by Lt. Col. David Niven, a 6-week AAF Band concert tour in Paris was approved,subject to the Band prerecording sufficient programmes to cover their absence from Saturday December 16 1944. That stint was completed by December 10,a Sunday, and the AAF Band performed its final UK concert in the Queensberry Club,London, on Tuesday December 12. That day SHAEF issued orders for the Band to proceed to Paris `on or about Saturday December 16'.Haynes said he had planned to go over two days earlier on Thursday December 14, to finalise transport and accommodation for the Band in Paris. But walking back to the Mount Royal Hotel together on Tuesday December 12 Glenn told Haynes he wanted to go over early himself because `he had a social engagement'. Don Haynes agreed, saying he would change Glenn's orders the next day and book him on a Thursday flight to Orly from Bovingdon. On Wednesday afternoon Haynes left Glenn in London and drove to Bedford in thick fog to pack for the Band flight on Saturday morning.

On Thursday morning, Haynes ran into Col.Baessell in the 8th AFSC Officers Club. Baessell said he was flying out to Paris next morning in Morgan's Norseman - would Don like a ride ? Haynes refused, saying he was flying with the Band on Saturday - but Glenn was in London waiting for a flight and was grounded by the bad weather. At the Colonel's suggestion Haynes telephoned Glenn, who accepted the offer of a lift; after lunch Haynes drove down to London,picked up Glenn who was already packed, and brought him back to Milton Ernest. Next morning (Friday December 15) Haynes picked up Glenn and Baessell and drove them out to Twinwood Farm to wait for the arrival of Morgan in his Norseman from Station 595, Honington, Suffolk. He landed about 13.40, stayed on the runway with engine running until Glenn and Baessell boarded, and took off for Orly at 13.45. The aircraft and occupants were never seen again. Haynes visited the Band billet in Bedford, packed his own effects and kept a dental appointment that afternoon at 8th AFSC HQ. He spent the rest of the weekend there because the flight was delayed until Monday morning by bad weather. When the Band finally landed at Orly his first intimation of trouble was when Major Miller failed to meet them. Haynes spent Monday and Tuesday searching various Paris hotels and restaurants or Glenn; at 18.00 on Tuesday, he reported to Gen. Barker at SHAEF and during that interview the Norseman story emerged. Barker telephoned General Goodrich at Milton Ernest, and Lt. Haynes repeated the story : Barker instructed Goodrich to check it out and signal back confirmation to him as soon as possible. But unwilling to accept that Glenn was dead, Don Haynes and Gen. Barker suspended all reporting action for 5 days, until Barker released the Casualty Report (Fig.20) on December 22 and notified Mrs.Miller in New Jersey by telegram next day. At 18.00 hours on Christmas Eve, just an hour before a scheduled AAF Band broadcast to America, the news was released - and the rest is history.

Haynes said the Band played their first concert in the *Palais de Glace* on Thursday December 21, but no announcement was made about Glenn being missing - only that `*Major Miller could not be with the Band that evening'*. Barker cancelled the following two concerts for blatantly-puerile reasons, but a scheduled Christmas Eve broadcast was a `must' ! If Glenn had not turned up with an hour to go, the news would have to be released.

This was the story that Don Haynes told to a select few at SHAEF in December 1944; the public was given only the snippets of information in the Press Release, and gradually the story faded into obscurity. The Band returned home in August 1945 and was disbanded, but the War Department never published a formal account of Miller's disappearance. Haynes was never questioned or interrogated (a 1946 inquiry proved that no investigation took place at all - see Fig.43). Many researchers wrote to the US Army Defense Department postwar but no additional information was released; until 1988 the National Archives and Personnel Records Centers denied the existence of personal Burial Files for the three men, and in a 1973 letter from NPRC St.Louis Mo., Mr.John Edwards was told that `*The Files were probably destroyed in the fire...'*. In the absence of any alternative, the Don Haynes story was generally accepted until the early Seventies when he died, after working as an insurance salesman and an official in the US Postal Service. He was interviewed several times on radio and TV but adhered to his story, albeit with several embellishments as time went on.

Indeed, there seemed to be no reason why he should lie about such a personal matter.In the early days after the war Haynes worked briefly for the Miller organisation. Herb Miller told us before he died that he heard there had been a controversy of some sort which involved among other individuals the Miller family attorney David Mackay, who was ordered by a court in 1979 to repay a sum approaching $800,000 to the Miller children - royalties and interest wrongfully deducted under a `sweetheart' contract. He had talked them into paying him one-third of all Glenn's royalties. But we found no evidence of Haynes being involved at all.

6. ANALYSIS OF THE HAYNES ACCOUNT

The events which followed Glenn Miller's disappearance were extraordinary, even for wartime. The SHAEF Press Release (see Fig.41) was typical, giving the absolute minimum of information. Miller was not a combat officer : the plane was a passenger type, unarmed, on a ferrying mission, and Miller was a famous VIP - yet the Release omitted all details of the aircraft, pilot,route, departure and destination airfields. Even more remarkable, it omitted any reference to Lt. Haynes seeing the aircraft off. The general public knew nothing of this, while the military's desire to avoid a breach of security would account for some but not all of these omissions. The only document released at the time was Miller's Casualty Report (Fig.20),a copy of which was sent to Helen Miller in New Jersey. It too omitted any information which might shed light on the mystery, such as the type of plane, departure airfield and destination.The `Band officer' who saw the plane depart was not named, but an amended Casualty Report dated March 1948 states that the aircraft left Twinwood Field for Paris. This was the first public reference to the Haynes story.

We know why no sea search was mounted to find the Norseman,and no wreckage was located on land : we believe that no inland search was made because Morgan had been seen crossing out to sea at Dymchurch, at a time well in keeping with a departure from Abbotts Ripton at 13.25 (evidence in the Miller Burial File). His was the only small single engined passenger aircraft reported that day. There are several serious inconsistencies in the Haynes story :

* Miller's Orders for Paris (Fig.19)

Dated December 12 1944, the orders were produced,typed and distributed in 56 copies by SHAEF REAR in three days between December 10 (end of the prerecording session) and December 12. If Haynes,as he said,had Glenn's orders cut afresh on Wednesday December 13,they could not have been distributed by Saturday December 16. Further, the orders authorised Glenn to travel by Air Transport `on or about December 16' : they were valid for any flight a few days before or after that date. On Wednesday 13, one day after Glenn's orders were issued, Haynes booked him on a flight from Bovingdon next day ! There was clearly no need for any change - Glenn could travel any day he chose. Additionally, Don Haynes said that Glenn had an engagement in Paris on Friday evening : if this was so, Miller would have arranged to fly over on Thursday in the first place ! This is why Haynes booked him on a Thurday flight - and never changed that arrangement.

* **Weather Conditions (Figs.39/40)**

Haynes described the weather at Twinwood Farm as `200 foot cloud-base, heavy rain and fog', explaining that John Morgan was able to land because he was very experienced. The true weather was quite good : 3000 foot cloudbase, visibility more than 1 mile, light winds and no rain. But John Morgan was an inexperienced pilot who had never flown on air operations - and Haynes knew this.

* **Destination Airfield**

Throughout his diary account, Haynes insisted that the Norseman was bound for Paris Orly. We shall examine this anomaly later, but it suggests he never saw an MACR (which gives the destination as A42 Villacoublay) and did not know that Morgan's Record Card survived, confirming the true destination as `B42' Beauvais. Nor did he know that Baessell, after night-stopping at Beauvais, was bound for Bordeaux on the west coast of France. Evidence ? In his diary, describing his last conversation with Morgan, he says to the pilot `*See you in Paris tomorrow.'* Finally, Haynes did not know that Twinwood Farm was closed for flying on Friday December 15 1944.

* **Departure Airfield**

As we shall see, there were two Haynes diaries. In one, referred to as the Library of Congress version, he wrote that Morgan flew from *Station 525* (Heston, Middlesex) to pick up his passengers at Twinwood Farm. In the MINUS ONE version, he states that Morgan flew down from *Station 595* (Honington,Suffolk) ! Neither is true : Morgan's Form 5,a record of flight times, shows no positioning flight to either Heston or Honington. He flew only twice in December - on the 2nd returning from Paris with Baessell, and on his last mission on the 15th. Note that the MACR includes an intermediate landing at Twinwood Farm, while Morgan's own orders and Col.Donnell's letter to Mrs. Miller states Morgan was cleared from *Abbotts Ripton to Bordeaux* with no mention of a Paris stop-over !

* **Take-Off Time**

In his postwar diaries Haynes wrote that the Norseman left Twinwood Farm at 13.45 hours. He also wrote that the ADC to General Barker,

Major May, queried that time and made some telephone calls to England. The MACR compiled four days later at Abbotts Ripton changed the take-off time from Twinwood Farm to 13.55, but Haynes had never seen an MACR. So why did May advise 8th AFSC to change the time ? Morgan's recorded take-off time at Alconbury was 13.25 and Orly Operations would know that. But Haynes said Morgan landed at Twinwood at 13.40, leaving five minutes later at 13.45. This gave Morgan just 15 minutes to take off from Abbotts Ripton, fly 30 miles to Twinwood, land and take his passengers on board ! Major May knew it was impossible, and he advised 8th AFSC to add 10 minutes to Haynes' time, i.e. 13.55 departure from Twinwood Farm.

Now, this is a vital point. May, checking on Morgan's take-off time from Abbotts Ripton, would certainly be informed of his true route (which included neither Twinwood Farm nor A42 Villacoublay). May would telephone Twinwood and learn that the airfield had been closed to flying on December 15. He may even have checked on Haynes' weather report for that day - and found it wildly inaccurate. Why, in that event, did Major May not advise General Barker of the facts and reveal the Haynes story as fictitious ? We can draw only one conclusion : *Barker and Major May must have known that already.* One final item : Gen. Barker asked Haynes where Morgan had obtained flight clearance, to which Don replied `*From Station 595,Honington'*. Sir Walter Scott had it right :

`Oh what a tangled web we weave...'

7. AFTERMATH

Helen Miller, according to the evidence in Glenn's Burial File, disbelieved the Haynes story *in toto*, and spent several years searching European war cemeteries and running down every rumour, no matter how far-fetched (see Fig.32). In November 1948, she moved west to join her parents in California and while several Miller documents were released at that time, this may have no significance. Hostilities ended in May 1945 and the AAF Band performed at many venues in Europe until they came home in August for demobilisation. In theory, there was ample time for Haynes to be interrogated at length, or a full-scale inquiry launched. After returning to civilian life he could have been called to provide a statement as a material witness - but American military and governmental authorities remained inactive.

We have to ask why this was so, and why no official version of the story was ever released. We have to ask why no immediate investigation was ordered. Some of the answers emerged when we gained access to the Miller Burial File : first, we found definitive evidence that the MACR (No.10770) was a fraudulent document,and the real `ORIGINAL' Report was in the File. Second, there was hard documentary proof that the AG's Department had deliberately withheld much vital information from Helen

Miller. From all this, we were able to construct a timetable of events in 1946 culminating in the first official but cursory investigation. Helen Miller wrote persistently to the AG Department to ask for information but the US authorities made no effort to initiate an investigation until 1946 as follows :

Jan 14   The Finding of Death document (Fig.22) was released after a full year and a day, on December 16 1945. It stated that the Norseman's destination was Bordeaux, and omitted all reference to both Twinwood Farm and Villacoublay. It contradicted the Haynes story in every respect.

Jan 15   Helen Miller wrote to the Adjutant General in Washington.

Jan 30   The AG instructed USFET (US Forces European Theater) to investigate. USFET passed on the order to USAFE (US Air Forces Europe).

Feb 2   USFET signalled to Washington (Fig.47) confirming that no investigation took place in 1944, that the MACR omitted any weather information or type of radio equipment carried, and if de-icing equipment was fitted. The route was confirmed as A42 Villacoublay/Bordeaux as in the MACR but no departure airfield was specified.

Feb. 6   Colonel Donnell replied to Mrs. Miller (Fig.32). Morgan, he wrote, was cleared direct from Abbotts Ripton to Bordeaux, France, via Twinwood Farm, but omitted all reference to a stop-over at Paris to drop Glenn - surely the most important factor to Helen Miller.

Mar 25   The fraudulent MACR 10770 was compiled at Maxwell AFB, Alabama.

The vital connection between Donnell's reply and fabrication of Report 10770 can be demonstrated as follows. Up to February 1946 no MACR had been released, protected by the security classification. The ORIGINAL MACR N-19 (Figs.14/15) was in Miller's file in Washington, but for certain reasons it could not be released. Nor had the `confirmatory' signal (Fig.46) been published. USFET, in the February 2 signal to Washington, referred to the `ORIGINAL' MACR, but that document was suppressed in the military archives ! USFET could have obtained a copy of the text only from 8th AFSC - and those details had originated with Don Haynes. But the AG knew Helen would not give up easily : further, many researchers were now asking for further information; eventually, an MACR would have to be released. When we found the

`ORIGINAL' MACR in Glenn's Burial File, we were astounded to find that it was unsigned by the Abbotts Ripton Adjutant, Captain Ralph S.Cramer ! We did evolve finally an explanation for this. But why had this apparently worthless document been preserved for 44 years ? Primarily, because it revealed starkly the invalidity of Haynes' story. Much vital information was omitted : there was no eyewitness statement from Haynes, nor was he named as the last person to see the aircraft. By protecting him from all interrogation and ensuring he published no written account, the cover story had remained viable. But publication of a flawed and unsigned document would precipitate an in-depth investigation - and this could not be contemplated.

There was only one possible solution. A reasonable facsimile of the MACR, properly signed by the Abbotts Ripton Adjutant, had to be produced, declassified and released. After one false start (see Fig.16) MACR 10770 was fabricated, and circulated by National Archives in Washington for the next 44 years as the `sole original and genuine article'.

We doubt if this satisfied Mrs. Helen Miller in November 1948, and it instantly denounced by researchers in all parts of the world. USFET,USAFE and Washington made no attempt to initiate an official inquiry, but routine military procedures had to be followed.

In 1947 a Board of USAAF Officers was convened in the USA to determine the non-recoverability of the remains of the three men who were supposedly in the missing Norseman. At this point, the story takes on a strange twist.

The Board members, presumably, had access to the personal files of Miller, Morgan and Baessell. There, they would find :

(a) The `ORIGINAL' genuine MACR.
(b) The fabricated MACR 10770.
(c) Miller's orders with travel date.
(d) Morgan's Service Record Card with route details.
(e) Morgan's Forms 5 (flight times record).
(f) Col.Donnell's letter to Helen Miller.
(g) `Findings of Death' documents showing Bordeaux as destination.

We now know that at least four of these documents were abstracted from the Files. Three were eventually located by researchers : Glenn's orders exhibiting an incorrect serial number, and Morgan's documents, none of which were included in the File sent to us by National Archives. All three were diametrically opposed to the Haynes story. We can safely assume that the Board were shown the fraudulent MACR 10770, and not the `ORIGINAL'. That unsigned document was withheld from the Board, and whatever the omissions and deficiencies in Report 10770, it was accepted by the Board and quoted in their Findings. But why did they not subpoena Don Haynes to supplement the information in the

MACR, perhaps to provide at last a written statement of the facts as he knew them ? We must not shy away from the implications. The Board was a creature of the AG's Department - and the AG had already gone to extreme lengths to discourage further investigation of the case. There were many more surviving witnesses, who no doubt had a tale to tell, but who were not called for interrogation (at least,if they were, they never talked about it) :

  * Capt.Ralph S.Cramer and his staff at Abbotts Ripton.
  * Air Traffic Control staff and ground crew at Twinwood Farm.
  * Duty personnel at Milton Ernest that fatal weekend.
  * Operations and Air Traffic staff at Abbotts Ripton.
  * The officer who wrote Morgan's orders at HQ 2nd SAD.
  * Operations and ATC personnel at Orly Airport.
  * Special Services Division at SHAEF.
  * The Adjutant General's department in Paris.
  * General Barker and Major May at SHAEF.
  * Lt.Col.David Niven, Glenn Miller's immediate superior.

Yet no effort was made to interrogate these personnel in 1944, 1946 or 1947. It seems clear that in December 1944, only a handful of people were privy to the Norseman story :

  * General Ray Barker, G-1 at SHAEF.
  * Major May,his ADC.
  * The Adjutant-General in France, General T.J.Davis.
  * General Goodrich and Col.Early at Milton Ernest.
  * The SHAEF Chief of PR Division, Col.Dupuy.
  * Don Haynes himself.

The Band were not informed at once of the tragedy : after two days Haynes told them the Norseman story, but most of the Band musicians we contacted were reluctant to talk at all of events so long ago. One, Mr. Nat Peck, refused categorically to discuss them. In the Miller File we found a curious letter from General Davis to the Commander-in-Chief, Gen. Dwight D.Eisenhower (Fig.34). We can safely assume that Ike, who liked to be kept informed of all significant developments, had been told Glenn Miller was missing by Monday December 21. General Davis was probably briefed by Gen.Barker the same day and the letter dated December 22 has some strange undertones. They were all aware that Miller had been missing for five days. If Haynes was to be believed, all three men in the plane had been dead since Friday December 15 and there was no real justification for suspending all casualty procedures as General Barker had done. Those procedures included :

  * The Miller Non-Battle Casualty Report.

* The Press Release.
* Notification of the next of kin, Helen Miller.
* Compilation of the Missing Aircrew Report.
* Explaining Glenn's absence at a December 21 concert.
* Notifying the War Department in Washington.

Haynes' diaries reveal that he and the SHAEF staff were convinced Glenn Miller had arrived safely in France and was simply out of touch, probably enjoying his first break in six months of hard work.To avoid further disquiet, Gen. Barker had cancelled further performances on December 22 and 23, giving as a reason the black-out and the danger that Col. Skorzeny's American-speaking raiders might penetrate Paris and injure Band members ! But now a deadline loomed - a scheduled broadcast by the AAF Band to America at 18.00 hours on Christmas Eve. If Glenn had turned up as little as an hour before the concert, he could have been rushed to the Olympia Theatre - but the delay could not extend beyond 18.00 hours on December 24. A Press Release was prepared (Fig.42) and scheduled for issue at that time. But two days previously,Gen.Davis wrote his letter to Eisenhower. It reported Haynes' story briefly but did not identify him or the departure airfield by name. Yet it does name Baessell and Morgan ! Davis requested that an immediate radio casualty report should be despatched to the War Department `*in view of the circumstances set forth in paragraph 4 below...*'.

He was referring, of course, to the Christmas Eve broadcast, to which considerable publicity had been given in the U.S.A. In addition, he specified clearly the time the news should be released - at 1800A (i.e.19.00 Paris time). The broadcast to America was scheduled for 20.00 hour Paris time). Gen. Davis wrote his letter on Friday December 22 immediately after Gen.Barker released the Casualty Report and instructed 8th AFSC to compile their Missing Aircrew Report. Mrs. Helen Miller received a telegram on Saturday December 23, the same day that Capt.R. Cramer began compiling his MACR at Abbotts Ripton.

But why did Gen. Davis write the letter in the first place ? As Adjutant General of American Forces in Europe, it was his task and duty to inform next of kin and the War Department of casualties. He needed no permission from General Eisenhower to carry out normal reporting procedures. Miller's Casualty Report, prepared that same day, would not reach Washington for at least four days,even if sent by air. It was possible to cancel the Christmas Eve broadcast,but it would necessitate an explanation of Miller's absence : the primary difficulty lay in explaining the week-long delay between Miller vanishing and the War Department being told. The MACR should have been compiled by Sunday December 17 and the War Department should have received it by Wednesday 20th. Instead, it was despatched on December 23 and reached Washington on January 22 1945 ! Finally, we know that General Eisenhower liked to receive briefing sheets every morning containing the main items of news and he knew (unofficially at least) of Miller's loss by Tuesday December 19. In a tape-recorded interview, Ike said much about the loss and its effect on morale, but nothing about the date and time he was informed.

The evidence, we submit, suggests strongly that an official cover-up took place, backed by deliberate delays in the reporting procedures.It confirms also that Major Miller arrived safely in Paris, probably on Thursday December 14, and vanished without trace. We should remember that such occurrences are much more frequent than is generally believed : some are easily explained in terms of domestic quarrels,financial problems, amnesia or foul play. There is a vast bibliography of inexplicable disappearances. We are not suggesting there was any element of the paranormal in Glenn Miller's disappearance. But every year some thousands of people vanish without trace, and not all of them are victims of foul play.

What did concern us was the deliberate and ongoing efforts to cover up the truth in this case and we discovered much evidence in the documents sent us by other researchers, supplementing the data found in the three Burial Files in 1988.

+   +   +

TWO

THE DOCUMENTS IN THE MYSTERY

1. BEGINNINGS

When the late Sqn.Ldr. Jack Taylor approached us with the suggestion that an investigation of the Miller saga could prove fruitful,he had obtained only three documents in five years of research : the MACR 10770 (Figs.12/13), the Casualty Report (Fig.20) and the Confirmatory Signal dated December 20 1944. At that time, we accepted the MACR as genuine but full of inconsistencies; further,the signature was illegible and the typed identification details beneath it were badly blurred. (That problem alone has preoccupied researchers for a quarter of a century...). Written inquiries produced more items : an amended Miller Casualty Report dated March 1948, and `Finding of Death' documents for Miller and Col.Baessell. We obtained all three `Reports of Death' documents and we learned that no search was made and no investigation was initiated in 1944.

Making contact with a fellow researcher John Edwards, we learned that he had made every effort in 1973 to obtain copies of personal Form 201 files for Glenn Miller, Baessell and Morgan which he believed existed somewhere in America, but Washington had denied all knowledge of them. Edwards had written several times to National Personnel Records Center, St.Louis,Mo. but they could only suggest the files had been lost in some fire. What they didn't tell Edwards is that all files for deceased personnel held by Casualty and Memorial Affairs Division in Alexandria Va., with access via the Washington National Personnel Records Center !

The history of our own efforts to obtain these Files is extraordinary, covering a period of almost two years during which, sadly, Jack Taylor passed away, as did Herb Miller.

But our broad front of inquiry took in not only personnel documents and reports but an active search for the missing UC64 Norseman itself. Correspondence with US departments, even by air mail, was very time-consuming, but in 1986 we began our search for any accident report available on Norseman 44-70285, or indeed any Norseman lost in 1944.

Our first interest was in Morgan's aircraft :

May 8   Request to USAF Inspection and Safety Center, Norton AFB California, for an accident report on Norseman 44-70285. Their reply : `We have searched our files. We have no record of a December 15 1944 Norseman mishap'.

Jun 14   A further letter to Norton AFB for details of the mishap to Norseman 43-5367 on December 26 1944 (as mentioned in detail in the Air Historical Branch Report (Fig.45).

Aug 7   A reply from Norton AFB. `*We have searched thoroughly through our records to identify the December 26 mishap. None of the mishaps reported during this period was reported as "missing". Only if we can identify a mishap are we able to provide an engine number'.*

Now, Norton AFB normally records all cases of destroyed, damaged or missing aircraft - yet we were able to identify from the Cumulative Loss Listing new fewer than eight UC64A Norseman aircraft which were reported `missing' in December 1944 ! We could find no reasonable explanation for this apparent refusal to provide information, especially in what was arguably the most intriguing incident in WW2 !

Jul 25   A letter to the Military Field Branch in the National Archives Washington asking if a personal Miller File existed, requesting further information on the MACR, the flight plan if it existed, a list of personnel who were based at Abbotts Ripton in December 1944, and details of the Norseman engine number. The reply, predictably, lacked any useful information.

Aug 5   `*We contacted the Department of the Army, Casualty and Memorial Affairs Division, Alexandria Va. and enquired about the Burial File for Major Miller...They are unable to locate the File. We contacted Air Force History and enquired about documentation pertaining to the loss of this plane. They were unable to supply the information you requested. Additionally, they were unable to provide any information pertaining to the 35th Air Depot Group that may have been of value. Finally, we contacted Military Reference Branch of National Archives. Although they have several files relating to the loss of the Miller plane, none of these contain the engine number.'*

While totally negative in content, this letter opened one or two doors for us. It forms the first documentary evidence confirming a deliberate policy of obfuscation and delay in certain Government departments : the Casualty and Memorial Affairs Division were, in fact, custodians of all files which related to deceased personnel, but certain files of specific interest such as those of Miller, Morgan and Baessell which were the subject of constant inquiries were handled by the Washington National Personnel Records Center, with the tacit approval of Casualty and Memorial Affairs. Their statement that they were `*unable to locate the file' was manifestly incorrect and misleading.* (Personal `Burial' Files, incidentally, were opened for all personnel, including those listed as `missing' with no known grave).We wrote to the Casualty and Memorial Affairs Division,Alexandria,asking for details of the Miller Burial File. The reply from Alexandria was astounding !

Nov 6   `*We have made repeated attempts to retrieve the individual (Miller) deceased File from Washington NRC. Requests for his File have been ongoing for years.These attempts and our current attempts have met with negative results. This Agency is merely the custodian for individual deceased personnel files, which are stored at Washington National Personnel Records Center'.*

Nov 15   Letter to National Personnel Records Center at St.Louis,Mo. reference Morgan and Col.Baessell,quoting John Edwards' approach in 1973.

Dec 15   Reply from St.Louis : `*The records... are not in our files. If they were here on July 12 1973,they would have been in the area which suffered most damage in the fire on that date and may have been destroyed'.*

The fact is that the Burial Files were not, and never had been in St.Louis, which housed millions of files for what we may term `non-sensitive' cases. Sensitive files were sent to Alexandria but controlled as a matter of policy by the NPRC in Washington. But they are all part of the national US Archival system. We wrote at once to the National Personnel Records Center, Washington. Meanwhile, we had discovered that the MACR 10770 (Figs.12/ 13) was a fraudulent document.This is a remarkable story in its own right, as we shall see, and we hastened to advise the National Archives,asking if any other Report existed.

Aug 27   A letter to the Military Field Branch (which maintains files on Missing Aircrew Reports). We informed them that the MACR 10770 was a fabricated and unviable document,enc-losing a copy of the Ansell Report (Appendix `A') and asking for an enlarged `first copy'.

We were extremely anxious to identify the compiler of the Report,but the signature was undecipherable and his printed identification below had been roughly obliterated. The enlarged copy arrived on September 18, but was of no help in identifying the signatory. There was no men-tion of any other Report on file for 44-70285. But the writer did advise that any Burial Files would be in the custody of the Department of the Army, accessible through Alexandria - which pointed us towards Casualty and Memorial Affairs.

By this stage we were becoming increasingly frustrated with being constantly shunted from one department to another.

Sep 18   A note to the Military Reference Branch demanding access to all Miller and associated documents which were on file, under the Freedom of Information Act,1979 - including Casualty Reports, any flight orders issued to John Morgan and records of air movements between Bovingdon and Paris on December 15 1944.

Oct 15   Mr.Reese of the MRB listed the available documents (presumably in the Miller File) including MACR 10770, Casualty Reports and Reports of Death (all of which we possessed already) and some minor papers.

Oct 15   A letter to Military Reference Branch enclosing evidence that MACR 10770 was a fraudulent document, suggesting that the Archives should cease circulating it.In retrospect we believe that Mr.Reese should have provided a copy of the `ORIGINAL' MACR N-19, which was in the same File from which he extracted those documents he provided. It does not seem possible that he was unaware of its existence, in view of the continuous flow of inquiries on the Miller case (so many that the File had to be kept on top of the cabinet at all times ! At that time we had not obtained a copy of the `ORIGINAL' but we were certain it existed,if only as a template for fabricating MACR 10770.

Oct 23   Letter in the strongest possible terms to Alexandria with copies of all previous correspondence,in which we complained bitterly about blatant delaying tactics such as `mis-laying' files !

And this finally broke the log-jam. We received Fig.38, the November 6 letter which revealed details of the inter-departmental squabbles about custodianship of the various Burial Files. We sent an immediate and peremptory demand to the National Personnel Records Center in Washington DC for the urgent and unconditional release of the various Files. Naively, we thought we were home free - but we did not allow for the stubbornness of the last-ditch opposition.

Dec 19   The National Personnel Records Center reply states : `*The records...are not in our files."*

By now, we were totally frustrated. Even our request for data under the Freedom of Information Act had been ignored.

Dec 23 A letter to President Ronald Reagan, describing our battle with the bureaucrats, asking him to intervene in person on our behalf.

Dec 23 A letter to the Military Field Branch (Mr.Boylan) enclosing a copy of the November 6 Alexandria letter. We said it was clear that a calculated cover-up operation was in train to deny us access to the Burial Files. If something was not done immediately, we would fly to Washington for a personal confrontation. And so 1986 ended in impasse : we knew the Files existed but we could not break down the bureaucratic barrier. At the turn of the year we reopened hostilities.

Jan 2 A furious letter to the Records Center, Washington. We asked three specific questions : (a) *Do you hold the Files as Alexandria says ?* (b) *Under the Freedom of Information Act, will you mail us copies ?* (c) *What is their present security classification ?*

Two long weeks passed. It was perfectly clear that some drastic action was now unavoidable : the only way we would reach the Files was via a Watergate-style burglary ! So I made a telephone call to Washington.

"National Archives ?"
"Yes,sir.How may we help you ?"
"My name is Wright," I said."Calling from England. Can you give me the name of the top man in the Archives ?"
"Uh...you mean the Acting Archivist of the United States himself,sir ?"
"That's the chap," I said cheerfully.
"That would be Doctor Frank W.Burke,sir."
"Okay," I said. "Put me through to him."
A long silence. Then -
"You mean right now,sir ? He's... uh, he is not available right now.It might be best to speak to a Departmental Head. What is the nature of your inquiry ?"
"Major Glenn Miller," I said shortly.
"Major... Right,sir ! Putting you through to Mr.Chalou."
Waiting, I switched on my tape recorder.
"Mr.Wright ? This is George Chalou.How can I help you ?"
"I am a professional author," I told him. "I'm having a great deal of trouble obtaining access to the Glenn Miller Burial File."
Another lengthy pause.
"Have you written us,sir ?"
"Frequently. Repetitively. Fruitlessly. You want more ?"
Mr Chalou coughed delicately. "I get the picture,sir."

"Good. Here's the position.I learned of the existence of the Burial Files from Alexandria and traced them to the National Personnel Records Center in Washington.The last we heard,they had misplaced them. Seems they borrowed the Files from Alexandria - and refuse to give them back."

"Right," said Mr.Chalou. "And no way they'll get them back either ! Those files have been under lock and key for years - and that's how they'll stay !"

+   +   +

I stared at the telephone,astounded. **Here was the first direct confirmation we sought, of a deliberate official policy to suppress the Miller Files !**

"In that case," I said slowly, "we have a problem. We have reason to believe the File may contain vital evidence that Miller was not aboard the missing Norseman, and perhaps there is a death certificate of some kind. We've written to you people repeatedly and all we got was the runaround. Now, we want to see that File and we'll come to Washington if necessary."

Mr.Chalou hesitated. "Uh - that won't do any good. Even if we had the File..."

"No ?" I said nastily. "Well, I think you should know, Mr. Chalou, that we wrote to President Reagan a week ago with the full story, asking him to intervene."

"YOU DIDN'T !"

"Oh,yes we did. So next time your phone rings - *guess who* ?"

A third long silence.

"Okay, Mr.Wright. Give me an address and phone number.I'll get right back to you."

"When ?"

"Uh - within fourteen days."

"Fine," I said. "I am flying over to Pasadena soon to check something out. I can call in on you if necessary."

"Well," George Chalou said cautiously, "let's see what we can come up with."

"Thank you very much," I said - and meant every word.

+   +   +

Nothing of note happened for a week. Then -

Jan 2   Mr. Reese wrote to us from the Military Reference Branch :
          `*This is a follow-up to your conversation with Mr. George Chalou of this office. The information on the Major Alton*

31

Glenn Miller Burial File was included in Mr.Boylan's letter.' (True : it was the minor documents which we already had on file). `*Also enclosed, a copy of our reply to your `Freedom of Information' letter dated September* (which contained nothing of real value). `*Over the years we have received numerous inquiries concerning the fate of Major Glenn Miller. With the exception of the documents we have listed in our replies, we have not located any other documentation in our Files.'*

This was a serious and important statement. Mr. Reese was saying, in effect, that the only documents existing in his files were the minor examples he had sent. All of them, as we determined later, were copied from the originals in the File - with which Mr.Reese was evidently extremely familiar...*We have had numerous inquiries...over the years.'* Yet when the File did eventually arrive, it contained no less than 36 items, some of paramount importance in the context of the cover-up operation ! Further, we have no real assurance that it was a complete package...

Jan 16   We wrote to Mr. Reese again in desperation, asking him to check once more the File contents...

Jan 30   A mind-boggling reply from the National Archives : `*The Director of the National Records Center had a staff member conduct an extensive search for the Miller Burial File. He was able to inform Memorial Affairs that the File had been located. When you visit,we will make available to you for examination the original MACR. We are unable to hire experts to examine the document as you requested.'*

The `original' MACR ? They were talking about Report No. 10770 - which we knew beyond doubt to be a forgery ! And if the File had been `*misplaced'*, how had they managed to copy the minor documents we had been sent, from a File so frequently used it was kept on top of the storage cabinet ? One thought struck us instantly : according to Alexandria, they had been trying for years to recover the File from NPRC,who said they'd mislaid it. Was it not remarkable that, within ten days of our last-ditch telephone call, it was `*found'* ? Most disturbing of all, they were *still* suggesting that MACR 10770 in the File was the real and only `original' - yet it was certain they had seen the true `ORIGINAL' MACR N-19 in that same File ! Can there be any doubt at all that an official policy to suppress the data in the Burial Files was in train ?

Feb 12   A quite plaintive letter from Memorial Affairs in Alexandria to

WAR DEPARTMENT
HEADQUARTERS ARMY AIR FORCES
WASHINGTON

Classification changed
~~to RESTRICTED~~
by R. A. BRADUNAS, Lt. Col., AC
by P. M. MUENCH, Capt., AC
Date... MAR 15 1946

MISSING AIR CREW REPORT

IMPORTANT: This Report will be compiled in triplicate by each Army Air
Forces organization within 48 hours of the time an air crew
member is officially reported missing.

Ripton
1. ORGANIZATION: Location, by Name Abbotts ; Command or Air Force VIII Air Force Svc
   Group 35th ADG ; Squadron Repair ; Detachment 2d Strategic Air Depot
2. SPECIFY: Place of Departure Abbotts Ripton Course Bordeaux Via A-42
   Target or Intended Destination Bordeaux; A-42 Type of Mission A
3. WEATHER CONDITIONS AND VISIBILITY AT THE OF CRASH OR WHEN LAST REPORTED:
   Unknown
4. GIVE: (a) Day 15 Month Dec Year 44 ; Time 355 ; and Location Twinwood
   of last known whereabouts of missing aircraft.
   (b) Specify whether aircraft was last sighted ( ); XXXXXXXXXXXXXXXX
   XXXXXXXXXXXXXXXXXXXXXXXXXXXXXXXXXXXXXXXXXXX Information not Available ( )
5. AIRCRAFT WAS LOST, OR IS BELIEVED TO HAVE BEEN LOST, AS A RESULT OF: (Check
   only one) Enemy Aircraft ( ); Enemy Anti-Aircraft ( ); Other Circumstances
   as Follows: Unknown

6. AIRCRAFT: Type, Model and Series UC-64A ; AAF Serial Number 44-70285
7. NICKNAME OF AIRCRAFT, If Any Norseman
8. ENGINES: Type, Model and Series Radial - 1340 P&W ; AAF Serial
   Number (a) Unknown ; (b) ; (c) ; (d)
9. INSTALLED WEAPONS (Furnish below Make, Type and Serial Number); None
   (a) ; (b) ; (c) ; (d) ;
   (e) ; (f) ; (g) ; (h) ;
   (i) ; (j) ; (k) ; (l) ;
   (m) ; (n) ; (o) ; (p) ;
10. THE PERSONS LISTED BELOW WERE REPORTED AS: XXXXXXXXXXXXXXXX
    XXXXXX Non Battle Casualty
11. NUMBER OF PERSONS ABOARD AIRCRAFT: Crew 1 ; Passengers 2 ; Total 3
    (Starting with Pilot, furnish the following particulars: If more than 11
    persons were aboard aircraft, list similar particulars on separate sheet
    and attach original to this form.)

Crew Position	Name in Full (Last Name First)	Rank	Serial Number	Current Status	
1. Pilot	Morgan, John R.S.	F/O	T-190776	Missing	,AC
2. Passenger	Baessell, Norman F.	Lt Col	O-905387	Missing	,AC
3. Passenger	Miller, Alton G.	Major	O-505273	Missing	,AC
4.					
5.					
6.					
7.					
8.					
9.					
10.					
11.					

12. IDENTIFY BELOW THOSE PERSONS WHO ARE BELIEVED TO HAVE LAST KNOWLEDGE OF AIR-
    CRAFT, AND CHECK APPROPRIATE COLUMN TO INDICATE BASIS FOR SAME:-

Check Only One Column.

Name in Full (Last Name First)	Rank	Serial Number	Contacted by Radio	Last Sighted	Saw Crash	Saw Forced Landing
1. Unknown						
2.						
3.						

Fig. 12
Missing Aircrew Report No. 10770 - Page 1

13. IF PERSONNEL ARE BELIEVED TO HAVE SURVIVED, ANSWER YES TO ONE OF THE FOLLOWING STATEMENTS: (a) Parachutes were used ___; (b) Persons were seen walking away from scene of crash ___; or (c) Any other reason (Specify)
_____Unknown_____

14. ATTACH AERIAL PHOTOGRAPH, MAP, CHART, OR SKETCH, SHOWING APPROXIMATE LOCATION WHERE AIRCRAFT WAS LAST SEEN OR HEARD FROM.

15. ATTACH EYEWITNESS DESCRIPTION OF CRASH, FORCED LANDING, OR OTHER CIRCUM- STANCES PERTAINING TO MISSING AIRCRAFT.

16. GIVE NAME, RANK AND SERIAL NUMBER OF OFFICER IN CHARGE OF SEARCH, IF ANY, INCLUDING DESCRIPTION AND EXTENT ____None_____

_____

_____

Date of Report __23 December 1944__

For the Commanding Officer:

(Signature of Preparing Officer)

17. REMARKS OR EYEWITNESS STATEMENTS: None

JAN 22 1945

RECEIVED

Fig. 13
Missing Aircrew Report No. 10770 - Page 2

MISSING AIR CREW REPORT NO.... L-19

1. ORGANIZATION: Location __Abbotts Ripton__ ; Command or Air Force __8th AF__ Depot
   Group __35th ADG__ ; Squadron __Repair__ ; Detachment __2d Strategic Air__
2. SPECIFY: Point of Departure __Abbotts Ripton__ ; Course __Bordeaux via A-42__
   Intended Destination' __Bordeaux A-42__ Type of Mission __A__
3. WEATHER CONDITIONS AND VISIBILITY AT TIME OF CRASH OR WHEN LAST REPORTED
   __unknown__
4. GIVE: (a) Day __15__ ; Month __Dec__ ; Year __44__ ; Time __1355__ and
   location __Twinwood__ of last known whereabouts of missing aircraft
   (b) Specify weather; ( ) Last Sighted; ( ) Last contacted by Radio; ( )
   Forced Down; ( ) Seen to Crash; or Information not Available. (x)
5. AIRCRAFT WAS LOST, OR IS BELIEVED TO HAVE BEEN LOST, AS A RESULT OF: (Check
   only one ( ) Enemy Aircraft; ( ) Enemy Anti-Aircraft; ( ) Other Circumstances
   as follows __unknown__
6. Aircraft: Type, Model and Series __UC-64A__ ; A.A.F. Serial Number __44-70285__
   Aircraft Nickname __Norseman__
7. ENGINES: Type, Model and Series __Radial 1340 P&W__ A.A.F.Serial Number (a)_____
   (b) __unknown__ ; (c)_____ ; (d)_____
8. INSTALLED WEAPONS (Furnish below Make, Type and Serial Number) :
   (a)_____ ; (b)_____ ; (c)_____ ; (d)_____
   (e)_____ ; (f)_____ ; (g)_____ ; (h)_____
9. THE PERSONS LISTED BELOW WHERE REPORTED AS: (a) Battle Casualty_____
   or (b) Non-Battle Casualty_____
10. NUMBER OF PERSONS ABOARD AIRCRAFT: Crew __1__ ; Passengers __2__ ; TOTAL __3__
    (Starting with pilot, furnish the following particulars: If more than 10
    persons were aboard aircraft, list simular particulars on separate sheet
    and attach original to this form).

	CREW POSITION	NAME IN FULL (Last Name First)	RANK	SERIAL NUMBER	PRESENT STATUS
1.	PILOT	Morgan John R	F/O	T-190776	MIA PDD
2.		Baessell, Norman F	Lt Col	O-905387	MIA PDD
3.		Miller, Alton G.	Major	O-505273	MIA PDD
4.					
5.					
6.					
7.					
8.					
9.					
10.					

11. REMARKS: PLOTTED BY:

    GEOGRAPHICAL COORDINATES_____   DULAG LUFT_____
    GRID COORDINATES_____   ISOLATED BURIALS_____
    NEAREST TOWN_____   MACR INFORMATION_____
                                        OTHER INFORMATION_____

ORIGINAL

Fig. 14
'ORIGINAL' Missing Aircrew Report No. L-19 - Page 1

WD, Hq AAF, Washington, Missing Air Crew Report

Name in Full (Last name first)	Rank	Serial Number	Contacted by Radio	Last Sighted	Saw Crash	Saw Forced Landing
1. Unknown						
2.						
3.						

13. IF PERSONNEL ARE BELIEVED TO HAVE SURVIVED, ANSWER YES TO ONE OF THE FOLLOWING STATEMENTS: (a) Parachutes were used: ___; (b) Persons were seen walking away from scene of crash_____; or (c) Any other reason (Specify)___
        Unknown

14. ATTACH AERIAL PHOTOGRAPH, MAP, CHART, OR SKETCH, SHOWING APPROXIMATE LOCATION WHERE AIRCRAFT WAS LAST SEEN.

15. ATTACH EYEWITNESS DESCRIPTION OF CRASH, FORCED LANDING, OR OTHER CIRCUMSTANCES PERTAINING TO MISSING AIRCRAFT.

16. ATTACH A DESCRIPTION OF THE EXTENT OF SEARCH, IF ANY, AND GIVEN NAME, RANK AND SERIAL NUMBER OF OFFICE IN CHARGE HERE____None

For The Commanding Officer:

Date of Report_____23 December 1944.

_____
(Signature of Preparing Officer)

RALPH S. CRAMER
Capt-AC
Adjutant

REMARKS:

NICKNAME OF AIRCRAFT:- "Norseman"

Fig. 15
'ORIGINAL' Missing Aircrew Report No. L-19 - Page 2

qualify their November 6 `bombshell' letter. They had not meant that `*NPRC were holding onto the File against their will...only that NPRC had been unable to locate it...'* A copy of the File, they said, was enclosed.

Well, it was much too late to close that stable door - and needless to say, nothing was enclosed with the letter. Things were looking very black now.

Feb 20   A letter to the US Attorney General suggesting an investigation elicited the reply that there was `*insufficient evidence on which to act...*

Feb 20   A letter to Chief Archivist Frank W.Burke. No reply.

Mar 12   A frantic letter from John Manning of Memorial Affairs in Alexandria,Va.**They had mailed us a complete copy of the Glenn Miller File on February 5 1987.**

This was baffling. We received their February 5 letter, in an airmail envelope 9 inches by 4. We had a premonition they were going to claim that the File had slipped out of the envelope flap en route... Nothing else happened, and on March 15 1987, we held a final conference; the project was closed down. We had done everything possible, but it was not to be : in the end,the system had beaten us.

+   +   +

Mar 19   A buff envelope arrived, containing 36 items which,a covering letter assured us, comprised the entire Burial File of Major Glenn Miller. It had been sent (as Mr.Manning said) six weeks earlier on February 4 1987.

Surface mail.

+   +   +

2. MISSING AIRCREW REPORT 10770 (Figs.12/13)

From the time MACR No. 10770 entered into general circulation in 1948, it was believed to be the genuine original document and was universally accepted, despite the widespread unease about its many inconsistencies. We were the first to note the typeface anomalies (Figs.17,18) and we commissioned a New Scotland Yard expert Michael Ansell to examine the document and prepare a report on its authenticity (App.A). His assessment, that the Report had been typed on two quite different machines on different occasions, confirmed all our suspicions. We wrote, as previously noted, to the Washington National Archives. To our utter astonishment, they insisted that MACR 10770 was the sole, genuine and original document, and further, that no other Report existed ! But the evidence supporting fabrication was overwhelming : the immediate need was to identify when and where it had been substituted for the real MACR, and by whom the document had been prepared. Undoubtedly, a genuine MACR had been used as a reference source, which could only be that compiled by the Abbotts Ripton Adjutant on December 23 1944. But where was that original ? At that point, we were extremely uneasy and pessimistic. Everything pointed to the probability that the genuine document had been destroyed after the facsimile had been made. By extrapolation, the `original' must have contained something the US government or Archives did not wish to reveal,and we believed that it might contain either a statement by an independent witness (other than Haynes) or a deposition by the so-far unidentified officer who had compiled the Report. But there was one intractable problem to which we had no answer. Despite all its errors, in-consistencies and anomalies it had been signed apparently, by someone in authority ! No wonder his typed personal details had been carefully obliterated... Assessing the Report, we came to the conclusion that it was fabricated at Maxwell AFB, Alabama, at about the same time it was de-classified,ie. March 23 1946. Somehow, the persons involved had per-suaded the unknown compiler to countersign the forgery - or perhaps the signature itself was forged.

Our first clue came when we saw that a capital `B' in `Bordeaux' was slightly depressed,whereas the `B' in `Baessell' was not. Second, the figure `2' in `A42' was twisted slightly clockwise, whereas that in Mill-er's serial number was not. Third, misalignments in the crew list sug-gested that the names of Baessell and Miller had been inserted at a different time to that of John Morgan. Further, we noted that a capital `B' in `Bradunas' in the Declassification Certificate exhibited a characteristic depression similar that in `Bordeaux', from which we and Mr. Ansell concluded that one of the machines used to type the MACR (supposedly compiled in 1944) had been used to complete the Declassi-fication Certificate in 1946. We believe this evidence is unassailable. Our next task was to analyse the MACR entries, several of which gave cause for great concern.

(a) **Compilation Date - December 23 1944**

This was some 9 days after Glenn Miller, Morgan and Col. Baessell had vanished. A date stamp on P.2 purports to say that it arrived in Washington on January 22 1945 - 40 days after the incident,having apparently been sent by sea mail. This would appear unusual for a document reporting the loss of a VIP, and which had already been the subject of an urgent Radio Casualty Signal between SHAEF and the War Department. Remarkably, the `ORIGINAL' MACR N-19 in the File does not have an arrival-time stamp but we believe it was, in fact, despatched by air carrier to the US War Department following the General Davis letter (Fig.34) and the radio message it requested. We do not know the contents of that signal - but reason suggests that it contained the gist of Haynes' account. The MACR had not yet been compiled, and Glenn's Casualty Report (Fig.20) was brief to the point of curtness. All MACRs were to be despatched *within 48 hours of crew members being officially reported `missing'.* The operative word is `*officially'* : Glenn Miller was not missing,*per se*, until his Casualty Report was issued on 22, 8 days after he was last seen alive, and that Report was delayed on the direct instructions of General Barker him- self. Indeed, had there been no Christmas Eve broadcast at all, one must ponder how long that delay might have been extended !

But in true Army fashion, SHAEF took care to ensure that the record was straight : Miller had been officially reported missing on Wednesday December 20 (Fig.46) but the signal was not circulated,while Gen.Davis notified Eisenhower `officially' the same day the Casualty Report was released. We believe these timings were significant and planned.

(b) **The Norseman Route Details.**

Always a source of intense speculation, we shall analyse the relevant factors in a later chapter, but the details in the MACR are confusing,to say the least. For example, `A42' is not qualified as `Villacoublay' by name, as are Abbotts Ripton and Twinwood. It appears in both `Course' and `Intended Destination' sections, and apart from the word `Twin- wood' it is the sole entry which corroborates the Haynes story. Now, Morgan and Col.Baessell, on their trips to Paris, invariably landed at Orly; the Colonel was fond of the night life and had little or no reason to visit SHAEF. Why, and by whom, was Villacoublay chosen ? Haynes himself always believed Morgan was bound for Orly : our assumption was that the similarity of `A42' to Morgan's real destination `B42' Beauvais was at once coincidental and attractive.

After 46 years it is difficult to establish who instructed the compiler to include Villacoublay. Certainly not Don Haynes, who was in Paris and never saw an MACR. Not the compiler himself, who had access to Morgan's orders, flight plan and Service Record Card. Not Gen.Barker at SHAEF, who gave instructions to General Goodrich and got on with fighting the war in the Ardennes. Our best guess would be Major May, Barker's ADC who worked closely with Haynes in the days following the tragedy. We know already that May, recognising that the 13.45 time of take-off Haynes gave for the Norseman was unrealistic, had passed the amended time of 13.55 to 8th AFSC : it would be simple to add that Haynes said Morgan was bound for Villacoublay to drop

Glenn Miller.

It all fits in, and now we see the personal dilemma of Captain Ralph S. Cramer,the Adjutant at Abbotts Ripton. He had been ordered on Tuesday December 19 by 8th AFSC to delay compilation of the MACR after General Barker spoke to Goodrich. But Capt.Cramer had known his Norseman was missing since Saturday, when Beauvais Air Traffic Control notified Alconbury and Milton Ernest. We have no doubt that Cramer conducted his own local inquiry as per regulations,including the impounding of the aircraft documents. When instructions came in on December 22 to compile the MACR, he already knew quite a lot about the case. While 8th AFSC had told him Morgan had made an unscheduled landing at Twinwood Farm and was bound for A42 Villacoublay, he was aware that :

* Morgan was cleared direct to B42 Beauvais, with final destination.
* Bordeaux, and had departed Abbotts Ripton at 13.25 hours.
* This was confirmed by his orders and flight plan.
* Baessell boarded the C64 at Abbotts Ripton,not Twinwood Farm.
* Twinwood was closed to all flying on December 15 1944.
* The weather was reasonable, with no rain or fog, totally different to Lt.Haynes' account.
* No one at Twinwood had reported a Norseman landing.

Possibly, Cramer had been instructed to omit all details of the weather, the engine number and both Haynes' name and his eyewitness statement.The question which springs at once to mind is this : did Cramer telephone Haynes in Paris to check the story and perhaps ask for a statement ? There are two alternatives. One,that he called,but Haynes said he had been told to say nothing - or two, that Cramer was told to obey General Goodrich's orders - and no sane captain argues with a General. Whatever the case, Cramer was obliged to omit the most important detail of all - an eyewitness statement by the last and only man to see the aircraft and occupants.

(c) **Engine Number**

If the remains of the fabric-covered Norseman were ever discovered, the fabric and airframe number 44-70285 would have rotted away,and the sole remaining means of identification was the engine number stamped on a metal plate on the front crankcase at 5 o'clock, looking at the front of the engine. That would survive as long as the engine itself,and we were assured by the manufacturers Pratt & Whitney that they could identify the aircraft in which an engine was installed,given the engine number. That number was recorded in several of the aircraft documents including the servicing schedule; when 44-70285 was transferred to 35 ADRS Abbotts Ripton from Wattisham in September 1944, all the documents went with it and were held,probably, in the same office block where Capt.Cramer was located.

So why was the number shown as `unknown' ?

There are but two possible explanations : one, that Cramer was instructed to omit it, or two, that the documents were unavailable. When an aircraft was reported missing, the usual procedure was to impound the documents locally,against a possible inquiry to determine negligence where applicable. Once the aircraft was confirmed as lost, the documents were despatched to Norton AFB California,where our story began - but not until it was included in the Cumulative Loss Listing. For some reason we were unable to determine, the Norseman 44-70285 was not included until 1947 - but the documents in that event were still at Abbotts Ripton ! As a serving Air Force officer, Capt.Cramer could not refuse to compile the MACR. But there are two disturbing side-issues in regard to the engine number. First, we found in the Burial Files a Press cutting and a Memo from CINFO (PR Division) relating to the discovery of a Norseman in the sea off the French coast in 1973. A check on the engine number had confirmed that it was 44-70285. No other information was available. Second, in 1987 we were collaborating with TVS television in Southampton on an exploratory dive to a Norseman which had been located in 1980 by ex-RN captain Clive Ward, master of his own marine survey vessel. The intention was to obtain the engine number plate, and we telephoned every possible US source to trace the engine number, including Maxwell AFB in Alabama. There, we spoke to Mr. Rodd, who stated cheerfully that we were too late with our dive : `*someone had already been down to the wreck and removed the brass number plate, which was now in the National Archives in Washington'* !

We were flabbergasted, but naturally telephoned the Archives at once, speaking to a cooperative lady called Elaine Everley. After we repeated Mr.Rodd's story, she refuted it flatly. There were no artifacts in National Archives : only documents. But she agreed to speak to Mr.Rodd and call us back. When she did so it was to report that Rodd had confessed the story wasn't true, that he'd told it `*just for a laugh'*. But some weeks later we learned that the engine number plates were in fact made of brass.

How did Rodd know that ?

Initially, we took that statement at face value, but with the discovery of the cutting in the File, it seemed to us that it had been sent to Washington from the Maxwell AFB Historical Center and inserted in the sensitive Miller File - but why ? Rodd, clearly, had seen the cutting and in good faith told us about it. Why, therefore, had Elaine Everley told us it was done `*for a laugh'* and omitted all reference to the cutting ? It was extremely tempting to assume that the US Government knew the Norseman had been located and identified, but there was no concrete evidence to that effect. Yet the suspicions remained, and we were to encounter situations like this throughout the investigation.

(c) **Search and Investigation (MACR Para.16)**

We know that, in the lack of a Mayday call and a Position Report, any physical search for the Norseman was problematical - southern England in 1944 was a very crowded locality and reports of a crash would have emerged quickly. But the deciding factor was the sighting of a Norseman heading out to sea from Dymchurch, a report which reached SHAEF on Tuesday December 19. This served not only to eliminate all possibility of a crash on land, but to confirm the aircraft had been lost at sea. It is possible that a sea search could have organised between Dymchurch and the French coast - but realistically it was a non-starter. The aircraft presumably ditched about 14.40 on Friday December 15, five days earlier - and survival time in the English Channel was measurable in minutes, not hours or days. Further, it could have flown inland from the French coast, crashing in some remote area - and with hundreds of aircraft being lost each day, reports would be unlikely. There was also an element of *laisser faire* about such missions as Baessell's : George Ferguson relates that he and the Colonel would vanish for days at a time on the Continent, sometimes taking along a mechanic to refuel and service the aircraft. Baessell would authorise each flight, telling his pilot where to go. John Edwards received a letter from a F/Sgt Fox, skipper of an R.A.F. search and rescue launch based at Ramsgate,who described spending two days searching the eastern Channel for the Norseman, but the facts say otherwise. The Morgan aircraft was not offically listed as missing for 5 days,and a search of all available wartime records failed to reveal any ASR search for the aircraft between December 16 and 31.

But we obtained confirmation from several sources that a major search was mounted in Paris for Glenn Miller himself, which began on Tuesday December 19 and continued until the Christmas Eve broadcast. Despite various reports, Haynes was not questioned or asked for a statement while he was based in Europe, and the AG Department records confirm that there was no 8th AF inquiry into the crash. The Records of Death documents for all three men confirm that no investigation took place in 1944 - but did this refer to the aircraft, or the occupants ? In 1988 we obtained a copy of a letter signed 'Peter',in papers provided by a member of the Glenn Miller Society. We dismissed it initially as a hoax, but there is an odd air of authenticity about it. The name of the addressee had been removed to protect his identity, and the letter was signed simply 'Peter'. The text was as follows :

`Responding to your letter dated February 10 1984,be advised that I was a Criminal Investigation Division Agent assigned to the Glenn Miller case. After rather extensive investigation, we could find no evidence that, indeed, Glenn Miller and his plane was lost in the English Channel on a flight to France. We could uncover no criminal or illegal* *evidence which would indicate other than the kind of tragedy reported. We explored the possibilities of foul play or some distortions in the life of Glenn Miller. Of course the investigation was suddenly halted because of VE Day and the haste to return home. What did and has bothered me greatly was our inability and that of professional researchers to find any wreckage of the plane or the bodies. This one single matter makes one question the entire incident. But again, we could find no one who was concealing or otherwise thwarting the investigation. It is, in my opinion, unreasonable to assume that both the plane and the bodies could not have been recovered or at least that this kind of accident could have occurred. Indeed, this has all the elements of a mystery, yet I must admit that I could find no contrary evidence. But deep down in my heart I have never accepted the finding as a plane lost in the Channel...'*

We were never able to identify the writer;he was clearly intelligent and well-educated,and if the letter is genuine, it confirms that an investigation was initiated in 1944, no matter what official reports said (Fig.46). We thought that the date,1984, was significant : there were many active researchers at work, but what concerned us was why this writer had not come forward earlier, particularly in the Seventies when Miller Mystery Fever was at its height - at that time John Edwards actually flew over the assumed route of the Norseman with TV presenter Angela Rippon ! Quite possibly, the writer had read Mr. George T. Simon's book *GLENN MILLER AND HIS ORCHESTRA (Bigbee Promotions 1973)* - why had he not contacted the author ?

Suppose, we thought, that this extraordinary document may have been an exercise in disinformation initiated by some United States Government department with a vested interest in suppressing the true facts of the matter ? Reading the letter in that context,certainly it takes on a different image. If we accept the Report of Death document confirmation that no investigation took place, why was this letter produced ? Most of the content is negative in effect, but one sentence appeared to be significant - `*We could find no one who was concealing or otherwise thwarting the investigation'.*

The concept of a cover-up had not emerged in 1944-1945 at all. It was not until the MACR 10770 was released in March 1948 that any suspicions arose. Why, we asked ourselves, had a US Army CID agent considered the possibility of a cover-up at the time of the incident ? The idea was untenable. But if such a letter was circulated deliberately, to encourage the idea that a cover-up had been suspected,investigated and eliminated in 1945, the benefits to its originators were manifest,and would serve to deflect suspicions on the part of researchers.

Readers must reach their own conclusions, as did we.

(c) **The Anonymous Compiler**

The central difficulty when assessing MACR 10770 was the fact that some individual, presumably in authority, had signed in March 1946 at Maxwell AFB a fraudulent and forged document. Identification was impossible because of the undecipherable signature and the partially-obliterated details beneath it. We spent many months on that signature, using blown-up versions and experts in calligraphy, and we learned too late that the compiler, Capt. Ralph S.Cramer, died in the Seventies. Also (as far as we could ascertain) he had never been identified or interrogated. Whoever erased his identification details had achieved his aim in delaying the inevitable for 44 years; the name of Capt. Ralph S.Cramer appeared for the first time on the `ORIGINAL' MACR N-19 (Figs.14/15) with full rank and identification in 1987 - but minus his signature !

This was most extraordinary. Why, we pondered, had Captain Cramer not signed the `ORIGINAL' in 1944, but agreed to sign the fabricated version in 1946 ? Or had he ? We obtained copies of several documents bearing his signature, routine papers from 35 Air Depot Repair Squadron at Abbotts Ripton, and performed an experiment using black carbon paper and a sharp hard pencil. We were able to produce excellent facsimile signatures. Long before this, in July 1986, we wrote to the National Archives in Washington enclosing the Ansell Report. On August 5 they replied :

> `We double-checked the MACR 10770 microfiche against the origi-nal copies in that file. The fiche is complete. We are unaware of any additional information pertaining to that Report.'

And on September 19 1986 :

> `Enclosed are the copies of MACR No. 10770 as requested. You may ex-examine the original at any time. As a matter of policy, we do not comment on the content of files.'

On January 30 1987 :

> `We have forwarded to you copies of all material we have been able to locate relating to the loss of Major Miller. As stated... we will gladly make original copies of the MACR 10770 available to you...'.

`Original copies'...? Really ? There could be but one `original' - and thereafter copies as required. And all the time, the real `ORIGINAL' MACR was in Glenn Miller's File ! We had only ourselves to blame for failing to note at the outset that MACR 10770 was, for a wartime docu-ment, much too neat, well-formulated, with no typographical or spelling errors and meticulously laid out. It was much too good to be true; when we compared it with the `ORIGINAL' MACR, we were humiliated.

3. **THE 'ORIGINAL' MACR N-19 (Figs.14/15)**

The remarkable feature of MACR N-19 is that it is not a true 'original' document, but an extract from an original, which we were never able to locate. It is not in the Register of MACRs in Military Reference Branch, National Archives. The document heading, instructions for compilation and possible reclassification certificate seen in 10770 are missing. Now, the Miller File arrived in March 1987 but contained only Page 1 of the 'ORIGINAL' MACR L-19. Further, the section identifying the 'person with last knowledge of the aircraft' was missing. If Haynes made an eye-witness statement, it would be on Page 2. We wrote immediately to the Military Reference Branch in Washington asking for the missing page. They replied :

> '*The reverse of enclosure B...is blank and there is no Page Two.'*

End of story, we thought glumly. But encouraged by our success, we demanded and received the Burial Files for John Morgan and Colonel Baessell some weeks later. Lo and behold ! Page 2 of the 'ORIGINAL' MACR L-19 was in the Morgan File ! (See Fig.15). This was a major victory and we began to assess the N-19 Report in depth. There are several obvious anomalies, such as the irregular paragraph numbering compared with the 10770 Report, in which paras. 6,7 and 8 in Report 10770 have been contracted to 6 and 7 in Report N-19. Also, a new 'REMARKS' paragraph is seen - yet there is a second 'REMARKS' section on Page 2 ! The 'occupants' entry was interesting : there was no misalignment as seen in MACR 10770, but the typed annotation 'MIA'(missing in action) had been deleted and 'PDD'inserted (we could find no official translation but assumed that it meant 'Presumed Dead by Drowning'.

But the 'MIA' made us think very hard. Had Flight Officer Morgan's Norseman really been shot down by German aircraft over the Channel ? In his Burial File we found an amended Report of Death dated November 6 1952, which corrected this to 'Non-Battle Casualty'. There was also a copy of the 'ORIGINAL' MACR in the File, but whereas Miller's copy was amended to 'PDD' by hand, Morgan's was unamended. It was very strange but we could afford no more time on speculation. We were drawn back time and time again to Page 2 of MACR N-19, which included full typed identification of Capt. Ralph S. Cramer - but no signature. *What did this mean* ?

It was essential to make a reasoned and sensible evaluation of this document, avoiding speculation and conjecture. It is axiomatic that an unsigned document is worthless - so why had MACR N-19 been preserved for almost half a century in a secret file in the Washington National Archives ? Why had those same Archives insisted repeatedly that Report 10770 was the sole, genuine and original Report, when a copy of the `ORIGINAL' MACR lay in two of the three Burial Files kept on top of the cabinet for easy access ?

There was no doubt in our minds that senior officials in the National Archives knew of the existence of this unsigned Report N-19 - yet they had tried desperately to keep it hidden from the public eye.

* *Why was a fraudulent Report 10770 prepared at Maxwell AFB ?*
* *Why were Capt.Cramer's identification details erased ?*
* *Why had only parts of the 'ORIGINAL' MACR been extracted ?*
* *What was so important that it had to be deleted ?*
* *Why did Archives refuse an expert examination of Report 10770 ?*
* *Why had they denied there was a Page Two for MACR N-19 ?*
* *Why had Pages 1 and 2 been kept in two separate Files ?*
* *Why had they said that Miller's File was misplaced,yet had extracted documents from it to send to us ?*

To bring these facts into perspective, it is necessary to retrace our steps back to SHAEF on Friday December 22,1944. Gen. Barker had autho-rised the issue of Miller's Casualty Report, conferred with Gen. Davis and agreed the text of the letter to Gen.Eisenhower. A Radio Casualty Signal was on its way to the War Department, a telegram to Mrs. Miller in New Jersey. Major May telephoned General Goodrich at 8th AFSC Milton Ernest and later, his Executive Officer Colonel Early told Cramer at Abbotts Ripton to complete the MACR as soon as possible. Major Miller, he explained, was now officially reported missing.

Ralph Cramer now faced a terrible dilemma, as a serving USAAF officer pledged to do his duty and obey the commands of his superiors - he could do either but not both. In the past several days he had become certain that the story Lt. Haynes had told in Paris wasn't true. Cramer was sure that Twinwood Farm had been closed to flying on December 15, and the weather Haynes described was all in his imagination. He knew Morgan was bound for Beauvais/ Bordeaux and had been cleared direct to France on the telephone by Baessell, who had boarded the Norseman at Abbotts Ripton. Cramer knew the Norseman's engine number, but had been told to omit it - and most serious of all, he had not been permitted to obtain a statement from Lt. Haynes in Paris.

In short, Cramer was being ordered to compile (and sign) an incorrect, incomplete and misleading report concerning a VIP of the day - and reason suggested there was going to be a lot of hassle and publicity before this thing was over. Cramer's career, in fact, was on the line, and we believe he took the only course open to him. He would complete their damned Report - exactly as he had been instructed. But no way he was going to sign it !

So Capt. Ralph S. Cramer, in his capacity as Adjutant, had the MACR N-19 typed out and roneoed in several copies. One he despatched to Washington direct by air; there were aircraft leaving for America every

R E S T R I C T E D

<u>COPY</u>

WAR DEPARTMENT
HEADQUARTERS ARMY AIR FORCES
WASHINGTON

MACR No. ___10770___
COPY

MISSING AIR CREW REPORT

IMPORTANT: This report will be compiled in triplicate by each Army
Air Forces organization within 48 hours of the time an
aircraft is officially reported missing.

1. ORGANIZATION: Location: Abbotts Ripton ___ Command or Air Force VIII Air Force SVC
   GROUP 35th ADG ___ ; SQUADRON Repair ___ ; DETACHMENT 2d Strategic-

2. SPECIFY: Point of Departure Abbotts Ripton ; Course Bordeaux Via A-42(Air Dep(?)
   Intended Destination Bordeaux A-42 ; Type of Mission A

3. WEATHER CONDITIONS AND VISIBILITY AT TIME OF CRASH OR WHEN LAST REPORTED:
   Unknown

4. GIVE: (a) Date 15 Dec 44 Time 1355 ;And Location of Last
   known whereabouts of missing aircraft Twinwood
   (b) Specify whether ( ) Last sighted; ( ) XXXXXXXXXXXXXXXXXXXXXX
   XXXXXXXXXXXXXXXXXXXXXXXXXXXXXX Information not available.

5. AIRCRAFT WAS LOST, OR IS BELIEVED TO HAVE BEEN LOST, AS A RESULT OF (Check
   only one: ( ) Enemy Aircraft; ( ) Enemy Anti-Aircraft; ( ) Other Circumstances as follows ___ Unknown

6. AIRCRAFT: Type, Model and Series UC-64A : AAF Serial No. 44-70285

7. ENGINES: Type, Model and Series R-1340 P&W ; AAF Serial No. (a)___
   ___Unknown___(b)___(c)___(d)___

8. INSTALL WEAPONS (Furnish below Make, Type and Serial Number)
   (a)___(b)___(c)___(d)___
   (e)___(f)___(g)___(h)___

9. THE PERSONS LISTED BELOW WERE REPORTED AS: XXXXXXXXXXXXXXXXXX
   XXXXXXXXXX Non-Battle Casualty

10. NUMBER OF PERSONS ABOARD AIRCRAFT: Crew 1 :Passengers 2 : Total 3
    (Starting with pilot, furnish the following particulars: If more than 11
    persons were aboard aircraft, list similar particulars on separate sheet
    and attach original to this form).

	Crew Position	Name in Full (Last Name First)	Rank	Serial Number	Status
1.	Pilot	Morgan, John R. S.	F/O	T-190776	DED
2.	Passenger	Baessell, Norman F.	Lt. Col	O-905387	DED
3.	Passenger	Miller, Alton G.	Major	O-505273	DED
4.					
5.					
6.					
7.					
8.					
9.					
10.					
11.					

12. IDENTIFY BELOW THOSE PERSONS WHO ARE BELIEVED TO HAVE LAST KNOWLEDGE OF
    AIRCRAFT, AND CHECK APPROPRIATE COLUMN TO INDICATE BASIS FOR SAME:

1.

R E S T R I C T E D

C6-60498,AF

Fig. 16
The `SAMPLE' Missing Aircrew Report

.. .   -   --- Ripton
.on, by Name Abbotts   ; Command or Air Force VIII Air
Squadron Repair   · ; Detachment 2d Strategic Air D
parture Abbotts Ripton, Course Bordeaux Via A-42
Destination Bordeaux ; Type of Mission   A
) VISIBILITY AT THE OF CRASH OR WHEN LAST REPORTED

arting with Pilot, furnish the following particulars: I
sons were aboard aircraft, list similar particulars on s
attach original to this form.)

| | Name in Full | | Serial |
Crew Position	(Last Name First)	Rank	Number
1. Pilot	Morgan, John R.S.	F/O	T-190776
2. Passenger	Baessell, Norman F.	Lt Col	O-905387
3. Passenger	Miller, Alton G.	Major	O-505273
4.			
5.			
6.			
7.			

Fig. 17
Typescript Blow-Up - MACR No. 10770

HEADQUARTERS ARMY AIR FORCES
WASHINGTON

MISSING AIR CREW REPORT

Classification changed
t...
by B. A. BRADURAS, Lt. Col.,
by F. J. WUENCH, Capt., AC
Date MAR 26 1946

This Report will be compiled in triplicate by each Army Air
Forces organization within 48 hours of the time an air crew
member is officially reported missing.
.. .   -   --- Ripton

Fig. 18
Classification Certificate Blow-Up - MACR No. 10770l

C O N F I D E N T I A L

SUPREME HEADQUARTERS
ALLIED EXPEDITIONARY FORCE
REAR HEADQUARTERS
APO 413

AG-201-AGF ÷ Miller,Alton G. (Off)   12 December 1944

SUBJECT : Orders.

TO : Major ALTON G. MILLER, 0606271 G-1 Division, Supreme HQ

    1.   You will proceed by military aircraft (ATC) on or about
16 December 1944 from present station to SUPREME HQ,ARMY AG-TM
on the Continent to carry out the instructions of the A.C. of S
G1,SUPREME HQ AEF,and on completion thereof return to present
station.

    2.   Travel by military aircraft is directed. Baggage allowance
limited to sixty-five (65) pounds.

               By command of General Eisenhower

Fig. 19
Glenn Miller's Orders for Paris.
Note the incorrect Serial Number
`0606271' instead of `0505273'

NON —BATTLE CASUALTY REPORT

NAME	SERIAL NUMBER	GRADE	ARM OR SERVICE	REPORTING THEATRE
MILLER ALTON GLENN	O5C5273	MAJ	AC	ETO

PLACE OF CASUALTY	DATE OF CASUALTY			FLYING OR JUMPING STAT	TYPE OF CASUALTY	SHIPMENT NUMBER
	DAY	MONTH	YEAR			
ENROUTE ENGLAND TO PARIS, FRANCE	15	DEC	44		MNG	358007-CC-1X

NAME AND ADDRESS OF EMERGENCY ADDRESSEE

THE INDIVIDUAL NAMED ABOVE DESIGNATED THE FOLLOWING PERSON AS THE ONE TO BE NOTIFIED IN CASE OF EMERGENCY, AND THE OFFICIAL TELEGRAPHIC AND LETTER NOTIFICATIONS WILL BE SENT TO THIS PERSON. THE RELATIONSHIP, IF ANY, IS SHOWN BELOW. IT SHOULD BE NOTED THAT THIS PERSON IS NOT NECESSARILY THE NEXT-OF-KIN OR RELATIVE DESIGNATED TO BE PAID SIX MONTHS' PAY GRATUITY IN CASE OF DEATH

MR.-MRS.-MISS—FIRST NAME—MIDDLE INITIAL—LAST NAME	RELATIONSHIP	DATE NOTIFIED
MRS. HELEN D. MILLER	WIFE	23 DEC 44 lmb
NO. AND NAME OF STREET—CITY—STATE		

REMARKS: AG 201 (22 Dec44)   ☐ CORRECTED COPY

Paris, E-77699 cas msg 3028. Was taken to airfield by off. of AAF
Band who witnessed takeoff. No trace of airplane can be found.

ACTION BY PROCESSING AND VERIFICATION SECTION: REPORT VERIFIED ____ FORM 45 ____ AG 201 REQ ____

CASUALTY BRANCH FILE ATTACHED ____ OR CHARGED TO _____ DATE ____

PREVIOUSLY REPORTED   NO ✓   YES ____ (AS INDICATED BELOW):

FILE NO.	MESSAGE NO.	TYPE	DATE AND AREA	E. A. NOTIFIED

FORWARDED TO ▶

SPEC. IDEN.	TELEGRAM	WOUNDED	LETTER	CORRES.	S. R. & D.	CERTIF.	M. & M.	NON-DEL.

REPORT NOT VERIFIED ____ NO FORM 45 ____ NO CAS. BR. FILE ____ CHECKED BY ____ 23 Dec 44 REVIEWED BY ____

THIS SPACE FOR USE OF MACHINE RECORDS BRANCH, A.G.O.

ACCT. AREA	CASUALTY STATUS	ORIGINAL CAS. DATE			MESSAGE NO.	LATEST CAS. DATE			REFERENCE AREA	CAS POS.	RESIDENCE		COMP	RACE
		DAY	MO.	YR.		DAY	MO.	YR.			STATE	COUNTY		
34	35	36	37	38	39 40	41 42	43 44	45	46 47	48 49	50 51	52	53 54	55 56 57	58 59

DISTRIBUTION "A" ☐ 37 COPIES

(ALL TYPES OF CASUALTIES PERTAINING TO MILITARY PERSONNEL, EXCEPT WOUNDED.)
COPIES FURNISHED: SEE CASUALTY BRANCH MEMORANDUM NO. 48, 1944.

DISTRIBUTION "B" ☐ _____ COPIES

(ALL WOUNDED MILITARY PERSONNEL AND ALL TYPES OF CASUALTIES PERTAINING TO CIVILIANS WHO ARE W. D. EMPLOYEES, EMPLOYEES OF W. D. CONTRACTORS AND OTHERS SUBJECT TO MILITARY LAW.)
COPIES FURNISHED: SEE CASUALTY BRANCH MEMORANDUM NO. 48, 1944.

W.D. A.G.O. FORM NO. 895
16 JUNE 1944

Fig. 20
Casualty Report - Glenn Miller

NON —BATTLE CASUALTY REPORT

NAME	GRADE	DATE CAS. REPORT RECEIVED
MILLER ALTON G	MAJ	
ASN 0505273	HUS	

| NAME AND AD- DRESS OF E. A. | MRS HELEN D MILLER BYRNE LANE TENAFLY NEW JERSEY | DATE TELEGRAM SENT 19 MAR 48 |

THE INDIVIDUAL NAMED BELOW DESIGNATED THE ABOVE PERSON AS THE ONE TO BE NOTIFIED IN CASE OF EMERGENCY, AND THE OFFICIAL TELE- GRAPHIC AND LETTER NOTIFICATIONS WILL BE SENT TO THIS PERSON. THE RELATIONSHIP, IF ANY, IS SHOWN BELOW. IT SHOULD BE NOTED THAT THIS PERSON IS NOT NECESSARILY THE NEXT-OF-KIN OR RELATIVE DESIGNATED TO BE PAID SIX MONTHS' PAY GRATUITY IN CASE OF DEATH.

THE SECRETARY OF ~~WAR~~ HAS ASKED ME TO EXPRESS HIS DEEP REGRET THAT YOUR   HUSBAND

GRADE	NAME	SERIAL NUMBER	ARM OR SERVICE	REPORTING THEATRE	F OR J STATUS	SHIPMENT NUMBER
MAJ.	MILLER, ALTON GLENN	0505273	AC			072013 U-2

TYPE OF CASUALTY	PLACE OF CASUALTY	DATE OF CASUALTY			CASUALTY CODE
		DAY	MONTH	YEAR	
DIED	IN ENGLISH CHANNEL	15	DEC	44	

REMARKS: AG 704 /11 MAR 48/   [ ] CORRECTED COPY REPORT OF DEATH ISSUED 23 MAR 48

MEMO S.R. AND D. UNIT. APPROVED BY OIC. CAS. SEC. PA. BR.   DIED WHEN PLANE CRASHED SOMEWHERE IN THE ENGLISH CHANNEL WHILE ON MISSION FROM TWINWOOD FLD, ENGLAND TO PARIS, FRANCE. IN PAY AND DUTY STATUS AT TIME OF DEATH, NOT RESULT OF OWN MISC. FINDING DEATH ISSUED PREVIOUSLY UNDER SEC.5, PUBLIC LAW 490, 7 MAR. 42, AS AMENDED, SHOWING PRESUMED DATE DEATH 16 DEC. 45. RPT DEATH BASED ON INFO REC'D SINCE THAT DATE, IS ISSUED IN ACCORDANCE WITH SEC.9 OF SAID ACT, AND ITS EFFECT ON PRIOR PAYMENTS AND SETTLEMENTS IS AS PROVIDED IN SEC.9. VIVID. Home Add: Tenafly, Bergen Co., New Jersey.

PROCESS IN ACCORDANCE WITH PAR. 2B, OPER. BUL. 35, 1945.

ACTION BY COMPOSITE SECTION: REPORT VERIFIED ✓ FORM 43 AG 201 REQ
CASUALTY BRANCH FILE ATTACHED ___ OR CHARGED TO ___   DATE ___
PREVIOUSLY REPORTED NO ___ YES ___ (AS INDICATED BELOW):

FILE NO.	MESSAGE NO.	TYPE	DATE AND AREA	A. NOTIFIED
Public Law-490		DED	16 Dec 45, ETO	

FORWARDED TO →	SPEC. IDEN.	C. & P.	TELEGRAM	LETTER ✓	CERTIF.	F. REL.	CORRES.	REPAT.	S. R. & D.	NON-DEL.

REPORT NOT VERIFIED ___ NO FORM 43 ___ NO CAS. BR. FILE ___ CHECKED BY ___ REVIEWED BY ___

DISTRIBUTION "A" [ ] 29 COPIES   DISTRIBUTION "B" [ ] 31 COPIES

WD AGO FORM 0365
1 MAY 1945   EDITION OF : JAN. 1945 MAY BE USED.

Fig. 21
Amended Casualty Report - Glenn Miller

WAR DEPARTMENT   4902

THE ADJUTANT GENERAL'S OFFICE

WASHINGTON 25, D. C.

FINDING OF DEATH OF MISSING PERSON

Pursuant to the provisions of Section 5 of the Act of 7 March 1942 (Public Law 490 77th Cong.) as amended, upon direction and delegation by The Secretary of War, The Chief, Casualty Branch, The Adjutant General's Office, finds Major Alton G. Miller, Army Serial Number 0505273, Air Corps,

to be dead. He was officially reported as missing ~~in action~~ *as of the* 15th *day of* December 194 4. *For the purposes stated in said Act, death is presumed to have occurred on the* 16th *day of* December , 194 5.

BY ORDER OF THE SECRETARY OF WAR

George F. Herbert

ADJUTANT GENERAL
CHIEF, CASUALTY BRANCH

SUMMARY OF INFORMATION

AREA		FLYING STATUS	JUMP STATUS	LINE OF DUTY	OWN MIS-CONDUCT	ON DUTY STATUS	ABSENCE AUTH'D
	European	No	No	Yes	No	Yes	

PREVIOUS REVIEWS	
None	

DATE OF BIRTH.	HOME ADDRESS	DATE OF ENTRY ON CURRENT ACTIVE SERVICE	LENGTH OF SERVICE (AS OF PRESUMED DATE OF DEATH)		
			YEARS	MONTH	DAYS
1 Mar 1904	Tenafly, New Jersey.	8 Dec 1942			

EMERGENCY ADDRESSEE

NAME	RELATIONSHIP	ADDRESS
Mrs. Helen D. Miller	Wife	Byrne Lane Tenafly, New Jersey

BENEFICIARIES

NAME	RELATIONSHIP	ADDRESS
Helen Dorothy Miller Steven Davis Miller	Wife Child	Byrne Lane Tenafly, New Jersey
Mattie Lou Miller	Mother	1740 Sherman Street Denver, Colorado

REMARKS

Distribution 56

Circumstances of Disappearance: The aircraft in which he was a passenger failed to arrive at its destination, Bordeaux, France, on a transport mission from England.

No record of service as an enlisted man.

Fig. 22
Finding of Death Document - Glenn Miller

REPORT OF DEATH   DATE 24 MARCH 1948 ekm

FULL NAME	ARMY SERIAL NUMBER	GRADE
MILLER, ALTON G.	O 505 273	MAJOR

HOME ADDRESS	ARM OR SERVICE	DATE OF BIRTH
Tenafly, New Jersey	AC	1 Mar 1904

PLACE OF DEATH	CAUSE OF DEATH	DATE OF DEATH
European Area	Airplane crash	15 Dec 1944

STATION OF DECEASED	DATE OF ENTRY ON CURRENT ACTIVE SERVICE	LENGTH OF SERVICE FOR PAY PURPOSES		
		YEARS	MONTHS	DAYS
European Area	8 Dec 1942			

EMERGENCY ADDRESSEE (Name, relationship, and address)

Mrs. Helen D. Miller, Wife, Byrne Lane, Tenafly, New Jersey

BENEFICIARY (Name, relationship, and address)
Mrs. Helen Dorothy Miller, Wife, Bryne Lane, Tenafly, New Jersey
Steven Davis Miller, Child, Bryne Lane, Tenafly, New Jersey
Mrs. Mattie Lou Miller, Mother, 1740 Sherman Street, Denver, Colorado

INVESTIGATION MADE		IN LINE OF DUTY		OWN MISCONDUCT		WAS DECEASED ON DUTY STATUS		AUTHORIZED ABSENCE		IN FLYING PAY STATUS		OTHER PAY STATUS (Specify below)	
YES	NO X	YES X	NO	YES	NO X	YES X	NO	YES	NO	YES	NO X	YES	NO

ADDITIONAL DATA AND/OR STATEMENT   [ ] BATTLE   [X] NON-BATTLE

Finding of death has been issued previously under Sec 5 Public Law 490, 7 Mar 42,
as amended, showing presumed date of death as 16 December 1945. This report
of death, based on information received since that date is issued in accordance
with Sec 9 of said act, and its effect on prior payment and settlements is as
prescribed in Sec 9.

In accordance with the provisions of Section 2 and 7 of the Act of 7 March 1942
(56 Stat. 145) as amended the records show that this officer completed 2 years,
and 8 days of active service at the time of his death.

BY ORDER OF THE SECRETARY OF THE ARMY
~~XXXXXXXXXXXXXXXXXX~~

ADJUTANT GENERAL

WD AGO FORM 52-1
1 JUN 1945   EDITION OF 1 FEBRUARY 1945 MAY BE USED.

Fig. 23
Report of Death Document - Glenn Miller

WAR DEPARTMENT
THE ADJUTANT GENERAL'S OFFICE
WASHINGTON 25, D. C.

351600

R C 11 JANUARY 45   NON—BATTLE CASUALTY REPORT

NAME	SERIAL NUMBER	GRADE	ARM OR SERVICE	REPORTING THEATRE
MORGAN JOHN R. S.	T 190 776	F/O	AC	ETO

PLACE OF CASUALTY	DATE OF CASUALTY			FLYING OR JUMPING STAT	TYPE OF CASUALTY	SHIPMENT NUMBER
	DAY	MONTH	YEAR			
ENGLAND	16	DEC	44		MNG	006037-14-C-1X

NAME AND ADDRESS OF EMERGENCY ADDRESSEE

THE INDIVIDUAL NAMED ABOVE DESIGNATED THE FOLLOWING PERSON AS THE ONE TO BE NOTIFIED IN CASE OF EMERGENCY, AND THE OFFICIAL TELE-GRAPHIC AND LETTER NOTIFICATIONS WILL BE SENT TO THIS PERSON. THE RELATIONSHIP, IF ANY, IS SHOWN BELOW. IT SHOULD BE NOTED THAT THIS PERSON IS NOT NECESSARILY THE NEXT-OF-KIN OR RELATIVE DESIGNATED TO BE PAID SIX MONTHS' PAY GRATUITY IN CASE OF DEATH

MR.-MRS.-MISS—FIRST NAME—MIDDLE INITIAL—LAST NAME	RELATIONSHIP	DATE NOTIFIED
MRS. W. MORGAN	MOTHER	9 JANUARY 1945

NO. AND NAME OF STREET-CITY-STATE		
11716 MEMORIAL AVENUE	DETROIT	MICHIGAN

REMARKS: AG 704 (2 Jan 45)   ☐ CORRECTED COPY   LMB

ETO Ship 002. F/O took off from Abbotts Ripton having cleared for
Twinwood and having operation orders for A-42, Bordeaux, left Twinwood
in C-64 #285, and has not been heard from since.

ACTION BY PROCESSING AND VERIFICATION SECTION: REPORT VERIFIED ___ FORM 43 ___ AG 201 REQ. ___

CASUALTY BRANCH FILE ATTACHED ___ OR CHARGED TO ___ DATE ___

PREVIOUSLY REPORTED   NO ___ YES ___ (AS INDICATED BELOW)

FILE NO.	MESSAGE NO.	TYPE	DATE AND AREA	E. A. NOTIFIED

FORWARDED TO →

SPEC. IDEN.	TELEGRAM	WOUNDED	LETTER	CORRES.	S. R. A. D.	CERTIF	M. & N.	NON-DEL.

REPORT NOT VERIFIED ___ NO FORM 43 ___ NO CAS. BR. FILE ___ CHECKED BY ___ REVIEWED BY ___

THIS SPACE FOR USE OF MACHINE RECORDS BRANCH, A.G.O.

ACCT. AREA	CASUALTY STATUS	ORIGINAL CAS. DATE			MESSAGE NO.	LATEST CAS. DATE			REFERENCE AREA	CREW POS.	RESIDENCE		COMP	RACE
		DAY	MO.	YR.		DAY	MO.	YR.			STATE	COUNTY		
34	35	36	37	38	39	40	41	42	43	44	45	46	47	48	49	50	51	52	53	54	55	56	57	58	59

DISTRIBUTION "A" ☐ ___ COPIES

(ALL TYPES OF CASUALTIES PERTAINING TO MILITARY PERSONNEL, EXCEPT WOUNDED.)
COPIES FURNISHED: SEE CASUALTY BRANCH MEMORANDUM NO. 48, 1944.

DISTRIBUTION "B" ☐ ___ COPIES

(ALL WOUNDED MILITARY PERSONNEL AND ALL TYPES OF CASUALTIES PERTAINING TO CIVILIANS WHO
ARE W. D. EMPLOYEES, EMPLOYEES OF W. D. CONTRACTORS AND OTHERS SUBJECT TO MILITARY LAW.)
COPIES FURNISHED: SEE CASUALTY BRANCH MEMORANDUM NO. 48, 1944.

W.D., A.G.O. FORM NO. 0365
16 JUNE 1944

Fig. 24
Casualty Report - John Morgan Fig. 25

WAR DEPARTMENT

4902

THE ADJUTANT GENERAL'S OFFICE
WASHINGTON 25, D. C.

FINDING OF DEATH OF MISSING PERSON

Pursuant to the provisions of Section 5 of the Act of 7 March 1942 (Public Law 490 77th Cong.) as amended, upon direction and delegation by The Secretary of War, The Chief, Casualty Branch, The Adjutant General's Office, finds Flight Officer John R. S. Morgan,
Army Serial Number T190776, Air Corps,
to be dead. He was officially reported as missing ~~IXIXXIX~~ *as of the* 15th *day of* December 1944 . *For the purposes stated in said Act, death is presumed to have occurred on the* 16th *day of* December , 1945.

BY ORDER OF THE SECRETARY OF WAR

George F. Herbert

**ADJUTANT GENERAL
CHIEF, CASUALTY BRANCH**

SUMMARY OF INFORMATION

AREA		FLYING STATUS	JUMP STATUS	LINE OF DUTY	OWN MIS-CONDUCT	ON DUTY STATUS	ABSENCE AUTH'D
European		Yes	No	Yes	No	Yes	

PREVIOUS REVIEWS		
None		

DATE OF BIRTH	HOME ADDRESS	DATE OF ENTRY ON CURRENT ACTIVE SERVICE	LENGTH OF SERVICE (AS OF PRESUMED DATE OF DEATH)		
			YEARS	MONTH	DAYS
14 Jun 1922	Detroit, Michigan	25 May 1943			

EMERGENCY ADDRESSEE

NAME	RELATIONSHIP	ADDRESS
Mrs. W. Morgan	Mother	11716 Memorial Avenue Detroit, Michigan

BENEFICIARIES

NAME	RELATIONSHIP	ADDRESS
Beneficiaries not of record		
NAME	RELATIONSHIP	ADDRESS

REMARKS

Distribution _56_

Circumstances of Disappearance: The aircraft which he was piloting failed to arrive at its destination, Bordeaux, France, on a transport mission from England.

Appointed from Royal Canadian Air Force.

THIS FORM SUPERSEDES WD AGO FORM 0353, 1 NOVEMBER 1944, WHICH MAY BE USED UNTIL EXISTING STOCKS ARE EXHAUSTED.

**Fig. 25
Finding of Death Document - John Morgan**

DEPARTMENT OF THE ARMY
~~WAR DEPARTMENT~~
THE ADJUTANT GENERAL'S OFFICE
WASHINGTON 25, D. C.

NON—BATTLE CASUALTY REPORT

	NAME	GRADE		DATE CAS. REPORT RECEIVED
AG 201	MORGAN JOHN R S	F/O		
	ASN T190776	SON		
NAME AND AD- RESS OF E.A.	MRS W MORGAN 11716 MEMORIAL AVENUE DETROIT MICHIGAN			DATE ~~TELEGRAM~~ SENT 19 Mar 48

THE INDIVIDUAL NAMED BELOW DESIGNATED THE ABOVE PERSON AS THE ONE TO BE NOTIFIED IN CASE OF EMERGENCY, AND THE OFFICIAL TELE-GRAPHIC AND LETTER NOTIFICATIONS WILL BE SENT TO THIS PERSON. THE RELATIONSHIP, IF ANY, IS SHOWN BELOW. IT SHOULD BE NOTED THAT THIS PERSON IS NOT NECESSARILY THE NEXT-OF-KIN OR RELATIVE DESIGNATED TO BE PAID SIX MONTHS' PAY GRATUITY IN CASE OF DEATH.

THE SECRETARY OF ~~WAR~~/HAS ASKED ME TO EXPRESS HIS DEEP REGRET THAT YOUR SON

GRADE	NAME	SERIAL NUMBER	ARM OR SERVICE	REPORTING THEATRE	F OR J STATUS	SHIPMENT NUMBER
F/O	MORGAN, JOHN R.S.	T 190776	AC		K	U-3X
						072019-

TYPE OF CASUALTY	PLACE OF CASUALTY	DATE OF CASUALTY			CASUALTY CODE
		DAY	MONTH	YEAR	
DIED	IN ENGLISH CHANNEL	15	DEC	44	

REMARKS:
AG 704 /11 MAR 48/   ☐ CORRECTED COPY   REPORT OF DEATH ISSUED 23 MAR 48 ckm

MEMO S.R. AND D. UNIT. APPROVED BY OIC. CAS. SEC. PA. BR.   DIED WHEN PLANE CRASHED SOMEWHERE IN THE ENGLISH CHANNEL WHILE ON MISSION FROM TWINWOOD FLD, ENGLAND TO PARIS, FRANCE.   IN PAY AND DUTY STATUS AT TIME OF DEATH, NOT RESULT OF OWN MISC.   FINDING DEATH ISSUED PREVIOUSLY UNDER SEC.5, PUBLIC LAW 490, 7 MAR. 42, AS AMENDED, SHOWING PRESUMED DATE DEATH 16 DEC. 45. RPT DEATH, BASED ON INFO REC'D SINCE THAT DATE, IS ISSUED IN ACCORDANCE WITH SEC.9 OF SAID ACT, AND ITS EFFECT ON PRIOR PAYMENTS AND SETTLEMENTS AS PROVIDED IN SEC.9.
                Home Add: Detroit, Wayne Co., Michigan.
PROCESS IN ACCORDANCE WITH PAR. 2B, OPER. BUL. 35, 1945.

ACTION BY COMPOSITE SECTION: REPORT VERIFIED ____ FORM 43 ____ AG 201 REQ ____

CASUALTY BRANCH FILE ATTACHED _____ OR CHARGED TO _____ DATE ____
PREVIOUSLY REPORTED ____ NO ____ YES ____ (AS INDICATED BELOW):

FILE NO.	MESSAGE NO.	TYPE	DATE AND AREA	E. A. NOTIFIED
Public Law 490		DED	16 Dec-15 Feb	16 Dec 45

FORWARDED TO →	SPEC. IDEN.	C. & P.	TELEGRAM	LETTER	CERTIF.	F. REL.	CORRES.	REPAT.	S. R. & D.	NON-DEL
				✓						

REPORT NOT VERIFIED ____ NO FORM 43 ____ NO CAS. BR. FILE ____ CHECKED BY ____ REVIEWED BY ____
                                                        15 Mar 48

DISTRIBUTION "A" ☐ 29 COPIES   DISTRIBUTION "B" ☐ 31 COPIES
WD AGO FORM 0365
1 MAY 1945 ~~ITION OF~~ JAN 1945 MAY BE USED.

Fig. 26
Amended Casualty Report - John Morgan

REPORT OF DEATH

DATE 23 MARCH 1948 ekm

FULL NAME	ARMY SERIAL NUMBER	GRADE
MORGAN, JOHN R. S.	T 190 776	F/O

HOME ADDRESS	ARM OR SERVICE	DATE OF BIRTH
Detroit, Michigan	AC	14 Jun 1922

PLACE OF DEATH	CAUSE OF DEATH	DATE OF DEATH
European Area	Airplane crash	15 Dec 1944

STATION OF DECEASED	DATE OF ENTRY ON CURRENT ACTIVE SERVICE	LENGTH OF SERVICE FOR PAY PURPOSES
		YEARS. / MONTHS / DAYS
European Area	25 May 1943	

EMERGENCY ADDRESSEE (Name, relationship, and address)

Mrs. W. Morgan, Mother, 11716 Memorial Avenue, Detroit, Michigan

BENEFICIARY (Name, relationship, and address)

Beneficiaries not of record

INVESTIGATION MADE		IN LINE OF DUTY		OWN MISCONDUCT		WAS DECEASED ON DUTY STATUS		AUTHORIZED ABSENCE		IN FLYING PAY STATUS		OTHER PAY STATUS (Specify below)	
YES	NO X	YES X	NO	YES	NO X	YES X	NO	YES	NO	YES X	NO	YES	NO

X BATTLE ☐ NON-BATTLE

ADDITIONAL DATA AND/OR STATEMENT

Appointed from Royal Canadian Air Force.

Finding of death has been issued previously under Sec 5 Public Law 490, 7 Mar 42, as amended showing presumed date of death as 16 December 1945. This report of death, based on information received since that date is issued in accordance with Sec 9 of said act, and its effect on prior payments and settlements is as prescribed in Sec 9.

In accordance with the provisions of Section 2 and 7 of the Act of 7 March 1942 (56 Stat. 145) as amended the records show that this officer completed 1 year, 6 months and 21 days of active service at the time of his death.

XC-6-036-049

3-25-48

BY ORDER OF THE SECRETARY OF THE ARMY

ADJUTANT GENERAL

WD AGO FORM 52-1
1 JUN 1948

EDITION OF 1 FEBRUARY 1948 MAY BE USED.

Fig. 27
Report of Death Document - John Morgan

F/O   Morgan   John R.S.   35th Dep Rep Sq.

AC   T-190776

Asgd & jd with Primary T/O Dy as Asst Engr O and Add M/R
Dy as Asst Flt Test & Flt Line O, per par 8, SO 226, Hq
2nd SAD.
Above Asgd O fr Dy to DS Paris, per par 1, SO 227, Hq
VIII AFSC. 8 Nov 44   approx 15 days.
fr TD Patts to Dy as of 18 Nov 44.
Tr Dy to TD Bordeaux France B42 for purpose of ferrying
personnel per Operations Order #5, Hq 2d SAD, Office cf
th Operations Officer. 15 Dec 44
   Fr TD to absent missing ɤX(Non Battle) on ferrying
flight over English Channel enroute to B42, 15 Dec 44.
   fr Absent missing to dropped from rolls of orgn

Fig. 28
Service Record Card - John Morgan

WAR DEPARTMENT
THE ADJUTANT GENERAL'S OFFICE
WASHINGTON 25, D. C.

NON
—BATTLE CASUALTY REPORT

RC 10 JAN 45

NAME	SERIAL NUMBER	GRADE	ARM OR SERVICE	REPORTING THEATRE
BAESSELL NORMAN F	0 905 387	LT COL	AC	ETO

PLACE OF CASUALTY	DATE OF CASUALTY DAY	MONTH	YEAR	FLYING OR JUMPING STAT	TYPE OF CASUALTY	SHIPMENT NUMBER
ENGLAND	15	DEC	44		MNG	006037-1-C-1X

NAME AND ADDRESS OF EMERGENCY ADDRESSEE

THE INDIVIDUAL NAMED ABOVE DESIGNATED THE FOLLOWING PERSON AS THE ONE TO BE NOTIFIED IN CASE OF EMERGENCY, AND THE OFFICIAL TELE-GRAPHIC AND LETTER NOTIFICATIONS WILL BE SENT TO THIS PERSON. THE RELATIONSHIP, IF ANY, IS SHOWN BELOW. IT SHOULD BE NOTED THAT THIS PERSON IS NOT NECESSARILY THE NEXT-OF-KIN OR RELATIVE DESIGNATED TO BE PAID SIX MONTHS' PAY GRATUITY IN CASE OF DEATH

MR.-MRS.-MISS—FIRST NAME—MIDDLE INITIAL—LAST NAME	RELATIONSHIP	DATE NOTIFIED
MRS AMANDA L BAESSELL	WIFE	8 JAN 45 bhl
NO. AND NAME OF STREET—CITY—STATE		
615 K STREET NORTHWEST	WASHINGTON D C	

REMARKS.
AG 704 (2 JAN 45)   ☐ CORRECTED COPY

ETO Ship #002.   Airplane No 44-70285 departed Twinwood Field for France, plane missing and unreported since departure. Passenger.

ACTION BY PROCESSING AND VERIFICATION SECTION: REPORT VERIFIED._____ FORM 43._____ AG 201 REQ._____

CASUALTY BRANCH FILE ATTACHED_____ OR CHARGED TO _____ DATE _____

PREVIOUSLY REPORTED   NO_____ YES_____ (AS INDICATED BELOW:)

FILE NO.	MESSAGE NO.	TYPE	DATE AND AREA	E. A. NOTIFIED

FORWARDED TO →   SPEC. IDEN.   TELEGRAM   WOUNDED   LETTER   CORRES.   S. R. A. D.   CERTIF.   M. & M.   NON-DEL.

REPORT NOT VERIFIED_____ NO FORM 43_____ NO CAS. BR. FILE_____ CHECKED BY _____ REVIEWED BY _____

THIS SPACE FOR USE OF MACHINE RECORDS BRANCH, A.G.O.

ACCT. AREA	CASUALTY STATUS	ORIGINAL CAS. DATE DAY	MO	YR	MESSAGE NO.	LATEST CAS. DATE DAY	MO	YR	REFERENCE AREA	CREW POS.	RESIDENCE STATE	COUNTY	COMP	RACE
34	35	36 37 38	39	40 41 42	43 44 45	46 47	48	49	50 51 52	53	54 55 56 57		58	59

DISTRIBUTION "A" ☐ _____ COPIES
(ALL TYPES OF CASUALTIES PERTAINING TO MILITARY PERSONNEL, EXCEPT WOUNDED.)
COPIES FURNISHED. SEE CASUALTY BRANCH MEMORANDUM NO. 48. 1944.

DISTRIBUTION "B" ☐ _____ COPIES
(ALL WOUNDED MILITARY PERSONNEL AND ALL TYPES OF CASUALTIES PERTAINING TO CIVILIANS WHO ARE W. D. EMPLOYEES, EMPLOYEES OF W. D. CONTRACTORS AND OTHERS SUBJECT TO MILITARY LAW.)
COPIES FURNISHED: SEE CASUALTY BRANCH MEMORANDUM NO. 48. 1944.

W.D., A.G.O. FORM NO. 0365
16 JUNE 1944

Fig. 29
Casualty Report - Lt.Col. Baessell

WAR DEPARTMENT

THE ADJUTANT GENERAL'S OFFICE
WASHINGTON 25, D. C.

4902

FINDING OF DEATH OF MISSING PERSON

Pursuant to the provisions of Section 5 of the Act of 7 March 1942 (Public Law 490 77th Cong.) as amended, upon direction and delegation by The Secretary of War, The Chief, Casualty Branch, The Adjutant General's Office, finds Lieutenant Colonel Norman F. Baessell, Army Serial Number 0905387, Air Corps,

to be dead. He was officially reported as missing ~~in action~~ as of the 15th *day of* December 1944. *For the purposes stated in said Act, death is presumed to have occurred on the* 16th *day of* December , 1945.

BY ORDER OF THE SECRETARY OF WAR

George F. Herbert

ADJUTANT GENERAL
CHIEF, CASUALTY BRANCH

SUMMARY OF INFORMATION

AREA	FLYING STATUS	JUMP STATUS	LINE OF DUTY	OWN MIS-CONDUCT	ON DUTY STATUS	ABSENCE AUTH'D
European	No	No	Yes	No	Yes	

PREVIOUS REVIEWS
None

DATE OF BIRTH	HOME ADDRESS	DATE OF ENTRY ON CURRENT ACTIVE SERVICE	LENGTH OF SERVICE (AS OF PRESUMED DATE OF DEATH)		
			YEARS	MONTH	DAYS
2 Aug 1900	Washington, D. C.	18 May 1942			

EMERGENCY ADDRESSEE

NAME	RELATIONSHIP	ADDRESS
Mrs. Amanda L. Baessell	Wife	

BENEFICIARIES

NAME	RELATIONSHIP	ADDRESS
Amanda L. Baessell	Wife	
Karl B. Baessell	Brother	

REMARKS

Distribution __56__

Circumstances of Disappearance: The aircraft in which he was a passenger failed to arrive at its destination, Bordeaux, France, on a transport mission from England.

(handwritten notations) Comp, No rec,
N-25 30 35 8 No record of service as an enlisted man.
no = K-H-T-U-J-P,
12 - 2 7 - 45/55.

WD AGO FORM 0353
1 FEB 1945

THIS FORM SUPERSEDES WD AGO FORM 0353, 1 NOVEMBER 1944,
WHICH MAY BE USED UNTIL EXISTING STOCKS ARE EXHAUSTED.

Fig. 30
Finding of Death Document - Lt.Col. Baessell

REPORT OF DEATH   no 1B 719   DATE   25 March 1948

FULL NAME Baessell, Norman F.	**ARMY SERIAL NUMBER** 0905387	**GRADE** Lt. Col.
HOME ADDRESS Washington, D. C.	**ARM OR SERVICE** AC	**DATE OF BIRTH** 2 Aug 1900
PLACE OF DEATH European Area	**CAUSE OF DEATH** Incident to disappearance of airplane	**DATE OF DEATH** 15 Dec 1944
STATION OF DECEASED European Area	**DATE OF ENTRY ON CURRENT ACTIVE SERVICE** 18 May 1942	**LENGTH OF SERVICE FOR PAY PURPOSES** YEARS MONTHS DAYS

EMERGENCY ADDRESSEE (Name, relationship, and address)

   Mrs. Amanda L. Baessell, wife,

BENEFICIARY (Name, relationship, and address)

   Amanda L. Baessell, wife, same as above
   Karl B. Baessell, brother,

INVESTIGATION MADE	IN LINE OF DUTY	OWN MISCONDUCT	WAS DECEASED ON DUTY STATUS	AUTHORIZED ABSENCE	IN FLYING PAY STATUS	OTHER PAY STATUS (Specify below)
YES NO X	YES X NO	YES NO X	YES X , NO	YES NO	YES NO X	YES NO

ADDITIONAL DATA AND/OR STATEMENT   [ ] BATTLE   [X] NON-BATTLE

     Finding of death has been issued previously under Sec 5, Public Law 490
7 Mar 42, as amended, showing presumed date of death as 16 Dec 45. This
Report of death, based on information received since that date is issued in
accordance with Sec 9, of said Act, and its effect on prior payments and
settlements is as prescribed in Sec 9.

     In accordance with the provisions of Section 2 and 7 of the Act of
7 Mar 42 (56 Stat. 145) as amended, the records show that this officer
completed 2 years 6 months and 28 days of active service at the time of
his death.

                                    BY ORDER OF THE SECRETARY OF THE ARMY

                                                  ADJUTANT GENERAL

Fig. 31
Report of Death Document - Lt.Col. Baessell

6 February 1946

Mrs. Glenn MILLER
Cotswold Apartments
TENAFLY, NEW JERSEY

Dear Mrs. MILLER:

Your recent letters to Lt. Col. E.H. Koreman, AGD, were referred to this Headquarters on 23 January 1946, in keeping with the policy of obtaining all available data connected with missing persons.

Further investigation by this Headquarters, and a search of the records, do not reveal any substantiation of the various occurrences embraced in your letters.

The official records indicate the C-64 Eighth Air Force Service Command airplane, No. 44-70285, on which Major MILLER was a passenger, departed Twinwood Field at 13.55 hours (1:55 P.M.), 15 December 1944. The plane was unreported after take-off and failed to arrive at its destination, consequently the aircraft, passengers and pilot were reported and have since been carried in a missing status, presumed deceased.

It has been established that the aircraft was a C-64 model, and it is believed any reference to a C-46 model was due to a clerical error which resulted in transposition of figures.

Major MILLER has never been reported as a prisoner-of-war, nor has information from sources, other than your letter, indicating his presence in different localities, been reported to this Headquarters.

The matter of proper clearances by the pilot appears clarified by the fact that he had clearance from Abbotts Ripton Field, under operations orders for Bordeaux, France, via Twinwood Field. The plane was not a passenger-type aircraft conforming to a fixed schedule, and it is not apparent that the procedure followed by the pilot varied from that normally followed in the combat zone. As stated in your letter, the missing aircraft was not one of the ATC planes on which Major MILLER was booked as a passenger, but a service plane, on which it is presumed he became a passenger upon the invitation of Lt. Col. Baessell, also carried missing and presumed deceased.

It is regretted that no additional information is available, and that further investigation failed to substantiate as fact the reports included in your letters. You may be assured that the Theater Commander and his staff have the fullest realisation of the mental and physical strain you are undergoing and no effort or individual will be spared in bringing to light any reports that can be substantiated as fact by further investigation of Major MILLER's or any other missing case, in this theater. All such cases are kept open under constant survey and any additional information will be furnished you immediately upon availability.

Sincerely,

J.N. DONNELL
Colonel, AGD
Asst. Adjutant General

Fig. 32
Adjutant-General's Letter to Helen Miller

(Gironde FF-13)

2nd Ind

HEADQUARTERS, 3046 QM Graves Reg Company, APO 809, US ARMY
21 June 1946

TO : Commanding Officer, 551 QM Group, APO 809, US ARMY
(Attn. Operations)

1. During the investigation of the area of Bordeaux, a search was made for the mentioned deceased, and it was found that there is no trace of them in the area of Bordeaux.

2. In order to locate the bodies, more detailed information as to the area of crash must be had by this organization.

FOR THE COMMANDING OFFICER:

Tel : Limoges 7201

Incls: n/c

DONALD K. BRINKMANN
2nd Lt.   Inf
GRS Officer

Fig. 33
The Bordeaux Search Letter

AG 201-AGT-Willer, Alton Glenn (Off)

SUBJECT: Report of Missing Personnel.

TO   :   Commanding General, European Theater of Operations, U. S. Army, APO 887.

1. It is reported that on 15 December 1944 Major Alton Glenn Miller, O-505273, AC, Army Air Force Band (Special), Headquarters Command, Supreme Headquarters AEF, departed from an airport in England enroute to Paris, France, in an Eighth Air Force Service Command airplane (C-64) piloted by a Flight Officer Morgan. There was one (1) additional passenger on this plane - a Lieutenant Colonel Baessel of the Eighth Air Force. Major Miller was taken to the air field by an officer of the Army Air Force Band who witnessed the take-off. No trace of this plane can be found and this headquarters has been advised by the Eighth Air Force Service Command that this airplane is considered missing. Likewise, Major Miller is considered to be missing.

2. It is requested that an immediate radio casualty report be rendered to the War Department on Major Miller, and the War Department be advised that in view of the circumstances set forth in paragraph 4 below, it is considered highly desirable that this information be released to the press here at 1800A hours, 24 December, and that the War Department should confirm to your headquarters the next of kin has been notified prior to that time.

3. The next of kin of Major Miller is Mrs. Helen D. Miller (wife), Cotswold Apartments, Byrne Lane, Tenafly, New Jersey, telephone, Englewood 3-7311.

4. A Christmas Day broadcast has been scheduled which will be released to the United States. Major Miller was to have participated in this program. It is thought considerable publicity has been given to this broadcast in the United States.

For the Supreme Commander:

T. J. DAVIS,
Brigadier General,
Adjutant General.

8.--1163

DECLASSIFIED
DOD Dir. 5200.9 Sept. 27, 1958
NMW by____ date 8/28/70

~~CONFIDENTIAL~~

DECLASSIFIED
NND760210
By____

Fig. 34
General Davis's Letter to General Eisenhower

State of New Jersey

DEPARTMENT OF HEALTH

CN 360, TRENTON, N.J. 08625-0360

MOLLY JOEL COYE, M.D., M.P.H.
COMMISSIONER

April 10, 1987

Name: Alton G. Miller
Dod: 12/44
Pod: Ohio

Wilbur Wright
The Shrubs Allington Lane
Southampton S03 3HP
England

Dear Mr. Wright:

The death of Alton G. Miller occurred in the State of Ohio. You should write to:

Division of Vital Statistics
Ohio Department of Health
G-20 Ohio Departments Building
65 South Front St.
Columbus, OH 43215

Enclosed is a refund statement for $4.00.

Very truly yours,

Charles A. Karkut
State Registrar

SK:bp

Fig. 35
Letter from New Jersey State Registrar

AG 704 (11 Mar 48)   WIN/mrsh/18735/9049

MEMORANDUM TO: Officer in Charge,Casualty Section
               Personnel Actions Branch, AGO

SUBJECT :   Report of Death

    1. The following named officers of the Air Corps were reported miss-
ing, non battle, in flight from England to Paris, France on 15 December
1944,by Casualty Branch Message Numbers 006037 and 358007 :

                Baessell, Norman F.   Lt.Col.   09053387
                Miller, Alton Glenn   Major   0505273
                Morgan, John R.S.   F/O   7190776

Flight Officer Morgan, only, was in a flying pay status.

    2. Under the provisions of Section 5,Public Law 490, as amended, a
Finding of Death was made in the case of the above-named men (Sh&B No.4902)
showing the presumed date of death as 16 December 1945.

    3. Missing Aircrew Report No.10770,dated 15 December 1944, reveals
that subject persons constituted the crew and passengers aboard a UC-64A
(Noorduyn transport plane), Aircraft No. 44-70285,nicknamed Norseman,
which departed Abbots Ripton, England for Bordeaux, France, via A-42.The
aircraft was last sighted at 1355 hours on 15 December 1944 at Twinwood
Field,England.

    4. The Casualty Section File of Major Miller shows that Flight Officer
Morgan took off from Abbots Ripton at 1325 hours on 15 December 1944 for
Twinwood, with operation orders for A-42,Bordeaux. He departed Twinwood
Field at 1355 hours on 15 December 1944, after having picked up two passengers,Lt.Col.Baessell and Major Miller, for Bordeaux, France via A-42
(Villacoublay, France on the outskirts of Paris, France). General weather
conditions over the English Channel on 15 December 1944,obtained by telephone from Forecast Weather Division,Assistant Chief of Air Staff, were
"intermittent rains,stratus clouds,ceiling 1,000 - 2,000 feet, southerly
wind at 2 miles per hour,warm front"

    5. The Quartermaster General, Washington,N.C.,forwarded to this
office a copy of a letter to the Commanding General,American Graves Registration Command, European Area,APO 58,dated 18 December 1947,"Subject
- Non-recoverability of Remains" reporting the proceedings of a Board of
Officers,Case No.B,convened at that Headquarters on 7 October 1947. The
findings of the Board are as follows :

Fig. 36
Letter with Norseman True Take-Off Time

National Archives

August 5, 1986

Reply to: L86-2005-rlb

Mr. Wilbur Wright
The Shrubs
Allington Lane
Southampton SO3 3HP
ENGLAND

Dear Mr. Wright:

We double checked the Missing Aircrew Report 10770 microfiche
against the original copies in that file. The fiche is complete.
We are unaware of any additional information pertaining to that
report, or of a flight plan for the flight in question.

We contacted the Department of the Army, Casualty and Memorial
Affairs Division, and inquired about the burial file for Major
Alton G. Miller (files are created even if a body is never
recovered). They are unable to locate the file.

We contacted Air Force History and inquired about documentation
pertaining to the loss of this plane. They were unable to supply
the information you requested. Additionally, they were unable to
provide any information pertaining to the 35th Air Depot Group
that may have been of value to your research.

Finally, we contacted the Military Reference Branch of the
National Archives. Although they have several files relating to
the loss of the Miller plane, none of these contain the engine
serial number.

We regret that we cannot be of more assistance in this matter.

Sincerely,

RICHARD L. BOYLAN
Assistant Chief
Military Field Branch
Military Archives Division

Fig. 37
National Archives Letter August 5 1986

DEPARTMENT OF THE ARMY
U.S. ARMY MILITARY PERSONNEL CENTER
2461 EISENHOWER AVENUE
ALEXANDRIA, VA 22331

REPLY TO
ATTENTION OF

November 6, 1986

Mortuary Affairs and Casualty
Support Division

Dear Mr. Wright:

This responds to your corresponence pertaining to Major Alton G.
(Glenn) Miller.

We have made repeated attempts to retrieve his individual deceased
personnel file from the Washington National Records Center. Requests for
his file have been ongoing for years. These attempts, and our current
attempts have met with negative results.

This agency is merely the custodian of the individual deceased
personnel files which are stored at the Washington National Records Center.
The files document individual deceased service members from date of death
or missing status through final disposition or determination of
nonrecoverability. The data in the files was compiled by the various
agencies who were involved in actions pertaining to the decedent. We are
unable to opine on the alleged discrepancies you present. We have
exhausted our resources in an attempt to determine the significance of the
shipment number entry on Major Miller's Battle Casualty Report.

I am sorry we are unable to provide a more favorable reply.

Sincerely,

John F. Manning
Assistant Chief
Mortuary Affairs and Casualty
Support Division

Fig. 38
Alexandria Letter November 6 1987

METEOROLOGICAL OFFICE Met O 7a
London Road Bracknell Berkshire RG12 2SZ

Telex 84160   Telephone 0344 (Bracknell) 20242 ext 2349

Our reference
AF/M1074/69/Met O 7a

Date
2 October 1972

Dear Mr Edwards

As promised in my letter dated 22 September, I am now able to supply an appraisal of the likely weather conditions over the route from Twinwoods, Bedford to Orly, Paris during the late afternoon of 15 December 1944.

Considering each of the main elements in turn, to the best of our knowledge the position was as follows. Please note that all heights quoted are above mean sea level.

<u>Cloud amounts and types.</u> For take-off there was probably only small amounts of thin layered cloud base between 2000 and 4000 feet but cloud would have soon increased to become ½ to ¾ cover over Essex, and probably remained so over the Thames Estuary and Kent. Along the south coast and over the English Channel, cloud probably was full cover of stratus base 1500 feet top 2000 feet, possibly with further broken layers of stratocumulus above, with tops up to 3500 feet. Over France itself ¼ to full cover of layered cloud would be expected, base 800 to 1500 feet tops 2000 to 3000 feet. In addition, over the Channel and France ¾ to full cover of medium layered cloud base 8000 feet top 11000 to 14000 feet was reported.

<u>Visibility.</u> To the north of the North Downs, a good deal of fog and mist were reported on the day in question, with visibilities varying between 500 and 2000 yards. Over Kent and the English Channel visibility was of the order 1½ to 2½ nautical miles. However, over France visibility was probably curtailed to 1500-2500 yards, and perhaps with some fog patches in the vicinity of Paris itself with visibility around 500-1000 yards.

<u>Winds and temperatures.</u>

	Bedford - south coast	South coast - Paris
At 3000 feet	180 degrees 12 knots - 1°C	160 degrees 15 knots - 1°C
At 5000 feet	190 degrees 10 knots - 1°C	190 degrees 15 knots - 1°C
At 10000 feet	230 degrees 10 knots - 9°C	240 degrees 15 knots - 7°C

<u>Icing.</u> The height of the zero Celsius isotherm over the route was generally 2000 feet except over France where it was probably somewhat lower at 1500 feet. Temperatures were close to zero Celsius between 2000 feet and 6000 feet over much of the route. No reports of aircraft icing during the period in question can be traced. However, medium opaque icing had been reported over Kent at about 0800 am, in the layer of medium cloud which had moved to France by the late afternoon.

Yours sincerely

C F NEAVE

Fig. 39
Weather Data December 15 1944

Fig. 40
Synoptic Weather Chart December 15 1944

PUBLIC RELATIONS DIVISION

S H A E F

_____

24 Dec.   1944

Memo to: Capt Wade
          Information Room

Here is the release on Glenn Miller, with the
embargo of 1800 hours tonight.

Colonel Dupuy merely wants a factual announcement
that he is missing. However, he also wants a statment
added to the effect that"no members of his band
were with him." Or something very much like that.

Capt. Cosgrove.

THIS CORRESPONDENCE MUST BE RETURNED. COLONEL DUPUY
DOES NOT HAVE TO SEE THE RELEASE BEFORE IT GOES OUT.

Done.

Signature 1150
           24 Dec 44
           P.V.W.

8   1159

Fig. 41
SHAEF Press Release Memo

Supreme Headquarters
ALLIED EXPEDITIONARY FORCE
Public Relations Division

REF NO. 605

FOR RELEASE AT
1800 HOURS

24 December 1944

Major Alton Glenn Miller, director of the famous
United States Army Air Force band which has been playing in Paris
is reported missing while on a flight from England to Paris. The
plane in which he was a passenger left England on December 15
and no trace of it has been found since its take-off.

Major Miller, one of the outstanding orchestra
leaders in the United States, lived at Tenafly, New Jersey, where
his wife presently resides.

No members of Major Miller's band were with him on
the missing plane.

* * * * * * * * * *

8   1158

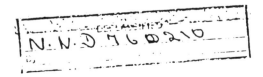

Fig. 42
SHAEF Press Release 18.00 hours December 24 1944

Fig. 43
Mr. Alex Sleap with Morgan's Norseman
Bovingdon November 8 1944

Fig. 44
John Edwards - Glenn Miller Researcher

THE LOSS OF GLENN MILLER

AEROPLANE

Noorduyn C-64 Norseman. (Contemporary USAAF designation UC-64A).

1 Pratt & Whitney 600hp R-1340-AN-1 Wasp radial engine.

USAAF serial 44-70285[1].   (Engine number unknown).

On charge to 35th Depot Repair Squadron (2nd Strategic Air Depot detachment), 35th Air Depot Group, 8th Air Force.

Based at Abbots Ripton, Cambridgeshire.

PERSONNEL

Crew (1) – Pilot : Flight Officer John R.S. Morgan (personal pilot to General Goodrich), personal serial T-190776.

Passengers (2):   Lieutenant Colonel Normal F. Baessell, personal serial O-905387.
Major Alton G. Miller, personal serial O-505273.

FLIGHT

Type "A" mission (non-operational flight).

RAF Station Twinwood Farm to Bordeaux, via Villacoublay [2].

Take-off 13.55 hours, 15 December 1944.

Cause of loss – unknown; fate of aircraft – unknown; fate of crew/passengers – unknown; whether or not aircraft was sighted en route – unknown; whether or not aircraft was contacted by radio en route – unknown; witness(es) to airborne incident, forced landing or crash – unknown.

No search was carried out following confirmation that aircraft was missing; official acknowledgement of loss not provided until 1947 (retrospective "inventory" entry in Cumulative Loss Listing).

NOTES

(1)   44-70285 has sometimes been confused with Norseman 43-5367.   The latter was on charge to the 314th Transport Squadron, 31st Transport Group, 9th Air Force based at Grove, Berkshire, and was lost on 26 December 1944. Confusion has arisen in part becuase 44-70285 was the subject of a Missing Air Crew Report, but did not appear in the official Cumulative Loss Listing.   43-5367 did, however, appear in the Cumulative Loss Listing but was not quoted in a Missing Air Crew Report.

(2)   Villacoublay, 40 kilometres west-southwest of the Eifel Tower, Paris, was designated AAF Station A-42, being used in December 1944 as an advanced air depot by the 9th Air Force Service Command.

Fig. 45
MOD Air Historical Branch Report *circa* 1973

C O P Y

SUBJ: MISSING AIRPLANE

HQ VIII AFSC

AAF Sta 506, APO 636

G-1 SECTION, SHAEF (MAIN)
  Attn GEN BARKER

thru: Eighth AF, AAF Sta 101, APO 634

20 Dec 44

Info copy: SHAEF (REAR)
          CG, US Strategic AF in Europe

VIII AFSC-D-832-G-27-A

CONFIRMING VERBAL INFORMATION TO G-1 SHAEF REAR C-64 AIRPLANE

NUMBER 44-70285 MISSING AND UNREPORTED SINCE DEPARTURE

TWINWOOD FIELD 1355 HOURS 15 DECEMBER FOR FRANCE PILOT FLIGHT

OFFICER MORGAN TWO PASSENGERS INCLUDING MAJOR GLENN MILLER.

EARLY

OFFICIAL:

ALBERT G. BUELOW
Major, AGD
Adjutant General

C O P Y

Fig. 46
Confirmatory Signal, 8th AFSC to General Barker

day. The others went to the usual addressees on the Distribution List - 8th AFSC, 8th Air Force in London, SHAEF REAR at Bushey Park, attention of the AG Department, and SHAEF MAIN at Versailles for Gen. Barker.

We can visualise the consternation in all these offices when the unsigned MACR arrived - and we believe that Cramer may have attached to it a deposition outlining his reasons for refusing to sign the document. He had to cover himself against the investigation he knew would follow. He succeeded better than he ever knew. Any investigating Board would discover the facts, read his deposition. They would learn that the Haynes story was false, that Gen. Barker and Major May almost certainly knew it, but went along with it. They would discover that Report 10770 was a fabrication, and that Colonel Donnell of the AG Department had concealed important information from Helen Miller in his letter. In the circumstances, there could be no investigation, at least officially, and the fact was entered on the Reports of Death documents - but no official US agency ever explained why. When USFET reported back to Washington in February of 1946 in those terms, we feel this was part of the exercise in misinformation - the AG Department knew already. This was the conclusion at which we arrived after long and heated discussions on the missing signature - because we could see no other explanation.

4. **THE CONFIRMATORY SIGNAL (Fig.46)**

Lt. Don Haynes, it will be recalled, was in General Barker's office on Tuesday evening, December 19 1944, when the call to Gen. Goodrich took place (Pp.17,36). Haynes, as he records in his diary, `put Goodrich in the picture' and Barker told Goodrich to include the information in his MACR at the time Barker authorised it. In order to get Haynes' story into the record, Barker asked Goodrich to signal back confirmation, and this was done the following day.

From that point, we can only speculate on events at 8th AFSC. Goodrich, a sick man, would delegate the task to Colonel Early, but how far would the Executive Officer go in checking the story out ? There were problems : Baessell was dead and he had not called in on Gen. Goodrich as Haynes related; that incident occurred on another occasion. Morgan was dead too, and the man from whom the information had come was in Paris, out of reach.

Further, General Barker had telephoned Goodrich some time on the evening of Tuesday December 19, probably about 19.00 hours. On one copy of the Signal in Baessell's Burial File we found a scrawled annotation, indicating that the Signal was originated at 8th AFSC at 09.35 next day, Wednesday December 20. This suggests that Colonel Early spent little time in checking out the information given by Haynes : rather, he appears to have simply relayed it back to Versailles. What he *should* have done is easily established :

(a) Checked Morgan's route/passenger details with Alconbury Ops.
(b) Checked Haynes' story with Milton Ernest personnel.
(c) Confirmed the Dymchurch sighting.
(b) Checked with Twinwood Farm Air Traffic Control.
(e) Confirmed that Baessell did not board at Abbotts Ripton.
(f) Confirmed Haynes' stated take-off time with Alconbury Tower.
(g) Checked on Haynes' movements that particular week-end.

But if this information had come directly from G-1 at SHAEF via Gen. Goodrich, would anyone doubt its veracity ? What did happen at Milton Ernest ? Reason suggests that Col.Early probably learned that Don Haynes had driven Col.Baessell to Abbotts Ripton soon after noon on December 15. If it was true that Morgan made an unauthorised landing at Twinwood to pick up Glenn Miller, he had done so in total contravention of Air Regulations, landing at a closed field with no radio contact or emergency vehicles, and would have to answer some questions if and when he returned.

Colonel Early would surmise that Haynes had probably driven Miller to Twinwood Farm after returning from Abbotts Ripton. Morgan's take-off had been delayed until 13.25 by poor visibility, but the departure time from Twinwood advised by Major May at SHAEF - 13.55 - seemed logical and provided adequate time for the flight from Abbotts Ripton to Twinwood Farm. We believe that Colonel Early sent off his signal to Barker, and despatched a Memo to Capt. Cramer at Abbotts Ripton, to outline the information to be included - and excluded. This leaves only one outstanding problem - the engine number.

We could evolve no viable explanation for this, other than that it may have been a direct order to Cramer from General Goodrich (which is doubtful) or from SHAEF itself (which seems more logical). Very probably,all the aircraft documents had been impounded by 8th AFSC. Curiously, while the signal names both John Morgan and Glenn Miller, it omits Col.Baessell's name, and we found that peculiar.

5. **THE SPECIAL SERVICES LETTERS**

Two letters in the Miller Burial File were written by a Major Johnny Hayes, Deputy Director of Troop Broadcasting at SHAEF REAR, Bushey Park, to Special Services Division, SHAEF MAIN at Versailles in November 1944. They are of particular interest because they provide substantive proof that Glenn Miller travelled to Paris Orly by USAAF C47 shuttle flight on Thursday December 14 1944, the day before the Norseman was reported missing. They refer to a Mr. Wood and Mr. Teddy Gower, who were BBC engineers working for the USAAF Band in 1944. Edward Gower was still alive in 1973, and he gave an interview to researcher John Edwards : in it, he claimed that he had flown to Paris in a Dakota from Bovingdon at the time Glenn disappeared and sat in the seat behind him. Miller,he said,could not have been lost aboard the Norseman. The story that unfolds is convoluted but of supreme importance in the mystery, and it begins with an audio-taped interview by Mr.Woods in 1968, shortly before he died, plus a letter he wrote to the Radio Times on September 19 of that year. He said that in November 1944, he was sent by the BBC to Paris to survey and improve the landline link between London and Paris so that Band concerts could be relayed and rebroadcast from London.

He flew to Paris on November 8 with Glenn Miller, whom he met at R.A.F.Bovingdon, and returned with him November 18. Glenn, Wood related,said *'Why don't we travel over together next time ?'* and Woods agreed. But there was not to be a next time. From the Major Hayes letters,it is clear that Mr.Woods, who was not attached full time to the AAF Band, was replaced by Mr.Gower, who was. Hayes writes that Glenn was insistent on Teddy Gower travelling in full Army uniform minus badges.

Now, Mr.Wood's account of the November 8 flight is very relevant to the inquiry. He was unsure of the date, but he went several times to Bovingdon before getting away, due to inclement weather. The weather was bitterly cold and snowy. He and Miller were given reservations on Flight 2 to Orly, and on the day they flew out, they arrived at Bovingdon just as Flight 1 was taking off. To his dismay, Wood learned that all his equipment, plus a sizeable package of black market goodies for friends in Paris, had inadvertently been loaded on Flight 1 ! The Customs people were most interested and detained him for questioning; Glenn, meanwhile,was allocated a seat on Flight 2 which duly took off,and Wood got away on Flight 3 some time later. The trip was hazardous, with heavy icing, and they were lucky to land at Orly during a temporary break in the cloud - but after landing, Wood learned that Flight 2 was reported missing after ditching in the Channel, following heavy icing en route. Glenn Miller, Wood maintained, went down with the C47 and could not have been lost in a Norseman weeks later. Wood,in fact, thought the date had been November 26, but on that day, Glenn appeared with the AAF Band at the Granada Theatre in Bedford !

For the next part of the story, we turn to Lt.Col. George W. Ferguson, USAF Ret. of Ohio, who was one of Lt. Col. Baessell's pilots in 1944, flying Norseman 44-70285. The then Lt.Ferguson was detached to Brussels Everes in September with one of the new UC64A aircraft from Wattisham, and in late October John Morgan flew into Brussels with General Goodrich and Baessell. The Colonel told Ferguson that Glenn Miller was going to Paris soon to entertain the troops, and Baessell wanted to take him over there *'a week early to show him the town'*. The plan was for Ferguson to bring his own Norseman over to Twinwood Farm, pick up Baessell and Miller and drop them in Paris. George agreed, provided he could clear the flight with his local Commander in Brussels. But on the day,permission was refused. Col. Baessell called Ferguson early from England to check he had clearance, and when the pilot said he had been refused permission by his Commander, Baessell was furious.

"Get the hell back up there," he said, *"and try it again !* Call me back at The Castle." George's Commander was obdurate and later in the day, George telephoned Milton Ernest and was advised that Baessell and Miller had already taken off - their pilot was John Morgan. For many years George believed that these events took place on December 15,but this was impossible for several reasons. The AAF Band tour was authorised only after a conference at SHAEF on November 15, chaired by Lt.Col. David Niven, and was to begin December 16. It was manifestly impossible for Col.Baessell to know about the tour in late October !

What actually happened was this : in order to make sure he would be on time for the conference Glenn decided to travel over early, taking advantage of Baessell's offer to show him the town (Baessell was notorious in Paris for spending his money like water, buying drinks all round in restaurants and bars; this may have given rise to the many rumours that he was involved in Black Market dealings.) On Tuesday November 7, Glenn and the AAF Band broadcast from their Bedford studio at 18.30, and he was booked on a flight from Bovingdon to Orly next day for the conference. It was a tiring 50 mile drive from Bedford,and Col.Baessell (who was flying to Orly next morning) had earlier introduced Ferguson to Miller as `the guy who's flying us to Paris'. Don Haynes was standing by to drive Baessell and Glenn to Twinwood Farm, a mile away, to meet Ferguson's plane.

But in Brussels, George had run into trouble. The morning wore on, and Baessell realised he would have to write off Ferguson and fall back on the Abbotts Ripton Norseman and Johnny Morgan. The pilot's flight records reveal that he made several local flights in UK on November 6, one of which was to the 8th AFSC Air Depot at Troston, Honington, Suffolk. After Baessell had called Ferguson in Brussels and learned that he could not get clearance for the flight,he contacted Morgan at Honington (Station 595) and instructed him to fly down to Twinwood Farm to collect himself and Major Miller. But it was a cold foggy frosty morning, and Morgan did not obtain flight clearance until noon : while waiting, Haynes, Col.Baessell and Miller lunched at Milton Ernest. During the meal, Morgan called again to say he had clearance and would be at Twinwood `within the hour', i.e.before 13.00 hours.

In fact, when the three officers arrived at Twinwood, the Norseman had arrived and was waiting beside the Tower. Here we digress momentarily to a recorded interview by a wartime ATC assistant, the late Dixie Clerke, stationed at Twinwood Farm at the time. She said that on the day Glenn Miller vanished she arrived on duty at the Tower, where a USAAF Norseman was parked. From the Tower balcony she saw three men arrive in a staff car, one of whom she recognised as the `tall entertainments officer' she had seen before with Glenn Miller - Lt. Haynes.

The pilot, she said, was a Warrant Officer and she watched three of the men go aboard the Norseman, which took off shortly afterwards for Bovingdon, where it was to drop a passenger. On the radio she heard it land, call for take-off clearance and take off again : shortly afterwards she heard Bovingdon calling the pilot without success, and she assumed the plane had crashed. (Morgan had probably changed frequencies).

Now, Dixie (like many others) had confused dates. She said the airfield was open for flying, that a large four-engined aircraft had taken on board most of the AAF Band and others were being picked up at Bovingdon by another aircraft. The weather,she said, was cold but reasonably good. Morgan, we learned from his flight records, was bound for Paris Orly that day, and the date was November 8 1944. But Glenn Miller was going over on duty and had to check in at Special Services SHAEF, Versailles. He accepted Baessell's offer of a lift, but only as far as Bovingdon, where he was booked on a shuttle to Villacoublay.

The story is taken up by a Mr. Alex Sleap who contacted researcher John Edwards in 1973. In November 1944, he said, he was a civilian ground engineer employed at Bovingdon to receive visiting aircraft. A Glenn Miller fan, he remembered seeing the bandleader arrive in a Norseman; shortly after that, Glenn boarded a C47 for Paris. Mr.Sleap sent Edwards a photograph of himself standing beside the Norseman; he was asked to check a possible fuel leak, but it turned out to be an over-flow from the filler cap which is clearly visible in the photograph (Fig.43). This, we felt, was unassailable evidence that Miller had flown to Paris in November, and a fellow-passenger was Mr. Wood. But could we identify the date ? The solution lay in the snow on the ground in the photograph : we checked past weather records for R.A.F. Bovingdon and found that it had not snowed on December 15 1944. *But there had been light snowfalls on November 8 !*

The story was now taking shape : after dropping Glenn, John Morgan flew on to Orly, and Baessell and Miller spent a pleasant ten days in Paris; after the SHAEF conference on November 15, Glenn and Mr.Wood returned to the UK on another shuttle on November 18. Back now to Mr.Wood. We had assumed earlier that the BBC engineer who flew to Paris with Glenn in December was Wood, but the Special Services letters make it clear that he was only employed temporarily,and Teddy Gower was appointed the full-time Band engineer on November 24 1944. He travelled to Paris only once with Glenn, sitting behind him - and that flight must have been *after* November 24 !

We began at once to trace Glenn's movements after that date, looking for any other flight he made to Paris. We accounted for every moment of his time, up to 02.30 on Thursday December 14 1944. The Band played their last UK concert in the Queensberry Club Tuesday December 12; Don Haynes walked back to the Mount Royal Hotel with Glenn, and the following day he booked Glenn onto a Thursday shuttle flight to Orly. On that Wednesday evening, Haynes took Glenn's several bags round to the Old Quebec Street Air Terminal; in the evening, with John Morgan (who had come down from Alconbury to see the final concert) they visited the Milroy Club in Stratton Street, Mayfair, with a girl singer. There, they met Sqdn.Ldr. Tony Bartley, DFC and Bar, and Lt.Tony Pulitzer, and the party went on until the early hours. But before midnight, Haynes and Morgan left to drive back to Bedford in thick fog; soon after 02.30 am, Glenn said goodbye to the others and walked away in the fog early Thursday morning towards Marble Arch. He was never seen alive again, and the only viable conclusion is that he caught an Orly shuttle flight that same day, Thursday December 14 1944 - the day before Morgan and the Norseman were lost.

All these conclusions were based on the Special Services letters in the Miller Burial File. But there is a still more important development. We think that discerning readers will have noted the extraordinary similarity between the events on November 8 1944, and those described by Don Haynes as happening on December 15 1944. We were able to identify no less than 19 direct correspondences and many more remarkable coincidences. At this point we put it to the reader that while the December 15 flight as Haynes described it 24 years later never occurred, *he used many of the details of the November 8 flight to give his story a modicum of authenticity.* We will analyse his diaries in the next chapter, listing these discrepancies, making only one point at this time - that the Special Services letters and the 'ORIGINAL' MACR were crucial in establishing the real truth of the events in 1944.

5. **THE AG LETTER TO HELEN MILLER (Fig.32)**

We have already described on P.20 the sequence of events which followed the release of the Finding of Death document in December 1945, which forced the Washington Adjutant General's Department to order the fabrication of a fraudulent MACR. The letter written by Col.Donnell confirms clearly the AG Department's policy of concealment and containment. Col.Donnell had full access to the personal files of Miller, Morgan and Baessell in addition to documents such as Miller's Casualty Report and the Confirmatory Signal to SHAEF (Fig.46).

Now, at that time early in 1946, there were two conflicting versions of the events on December 15 1944 : on the one hand, the Don Haynes story related verbally to Gen. Barker and Major May, a story which migrated via the Confirmatory Signal into the Miller Casualty Report, Finding and Reports of Death documents and numerous other official files. The story had been officially endorsed, supported and circulated by top echelon personnel at SHAEF to the War Department, the next of kin and the general public. For reasons of its own, SHAEF had decided that an investigation was not only unnecessary but potentially dangerous, and hoped the affair would fade into obscurity.

On the other hand, there was the indisputable evidence in the National

Archives, specifically the unsigned but undoubtedly genuine `ORIGI-NAL' MACR, Morgan's Service Record Card and Form 5,Record of Flight Times. There was possibly a copy of his flight plan from Alconbury ATC, and a copy of his operation orders issued by 2 SAD, Abbotts Ripton. From these sources,it is certain that Donnell was aware that huge inconsistencies existed between this evidence and that of Lt.Haynes. He knew that Morgan's destination was B42 Beauvais, not A42 Villacoublay. He knew Morgan had not landed at Twinwood Farm,but had cleared Abbotts Ripton direct for Beauvais. He knew that Col. Baessell had boarded the Norseman at Abbotts Ripton, and there was some doubt if any third person had been on board. Col.Donnell knew that Twinwood Farm had been closed for flying on Friday December 15, and that Miller had left his London hotel on Thursday December 14 to catch his booked flight to Paris. Almost certainly, Donnell knew that all Glenn's effects were missing, since the AG Department was responsible for the disposal of such effects.

The second paragraph of the letter hints at a number of previous letters from Helen, referring to various rumours and theories, but it does not refer to any answers to her queries. The paragraph itself commences with an untruth - there had been`*no further investigation'* at all, either in Europe or the United States ! But Helen's letter provided an impetus for the cursory European inquiry which followed. Paragraph 3 clearly cites information from the Confirmatory Signal (Fig.46) but not from the unsigned `ORIGINAL' MACR in the Burial Files, and this is logical : Donnell could hardly quote from that Report. And the data in the Signal had come directly from Haynes in his telephone call to Gen.Goodrich.

The sixth paragraph is a cause for deep concern. In it, Donnell tells Helen Miller that Morgan was cleared direct from Abbotts Ripton under operations orders for Bordeaux, France (which was perfectly true). He then adds `*via Twinwood Farm'*(which was not true). But incredibly, *Donnell omits all mention of a proposed stop at Villacoublay !* And in Para. 3 he carefully avoids specifying Morgan's destination. There is no mention of Paris at all, to justify Miller's presence on the Norseman - the only document mentioning Villacoublay at that time was the suppressed `ORIGINAL' MACR. And in the final paragraph, Col.Donnell regrets that `*no further information is available....* Well,of course there was a great deal more information available. So why did Donnell conceal important details from Helen Miller ?

Taken in the context of the numerous other minor and major deceits which resulted in the fabrication of an official document, we have to take the view that once SHAEF took the decision to endorse Haynes' account,the deception would have to continue into the foreseeable future : in this, SHAEF sought and obtained the co-operation and support of the AG Departments in Paris and in Washington. This required a strict control on releasing any vital information, including a moratorium on official statements by Don Haynes or any US Government or Archival departments, and a firm ban on circulation of the Burial Files. Such decisions are made at top level; we have no reason to doubt that Col. Donnell was given firm guidelines on the information to be released. All we know for certain is that within 6 weeks of Helen writing to the AG's Department, the falsified MACR 10770 was produced at Maxwell AFB, certified by the National Archives as the genuine sole article, and circulated for the next 44 years - while the real `ORIGINAL' MACR N-19 lay hidden in the Burial Files.

6. THE SHAEF PR MEMO AND PRESS RELEASE (Figs.40/41)

Let us go back in time to Christmas Eve 1944 in Paris, where the streets were covered in snow and slush, and rail depots were crowded with reinforcements for the Ardennes. In SHAEF Public Relations Division on Friday morning December 24, a Capt. Wade received a Memo from Capt.Cosgrove about the Press Release on Glenn Miller. The previous day Cosgrove had been briefed by his PR Chief Colonel Dupuy,who had received careful instructions from General Davis, Adjutant General in Europe. The Memo laid a strict embargo on any premature news release before 18.00 hours that day. Further, Colonel Dupuy required only a factual announcement that Glenn was missing and that no Band members were with him on the aircraft. There was an unusual post-scriptum. The Memo itself must be returned, and Col.Dupuy did not have to see the Release beforehand.

The 18.00 hours embargo itself was a consequence of Gen.Davis' letter to Eisenhower (Fig.34) and Gen. Barker's decision to delay all reporting procedures until the very last moment, hoping Glenn Miller would turn up in time for a broadcast to America on Christmas Eve. The BBC had been informed, and at SHAEF's request delayed publication until the same time. Why did Colonel Dupuy want 'only' a factual announcement that Miller was missing ? Why did he want the Memo returned to him ? Col.Dupuy, seemingly, knew a good deal more about the case - but how much more ?

We can only speculate, but there is some indication that he moved within the small circle who knew that Major Miller had arrived safely and vanished. In his diary, Haynes asked Major May to ensure that a Press Release would state clearly that no Band members were on the Norseman, to avoid distress to the musicians' families. As Chief of PR Division Dupuy would have to be consulted at an early stage. This conclusion is reinforced by the Memo : `Col. Dupuy does not have to see the Release...'. Why not ? We think he was trying in an oblique way to dissociate himself from the Release. There were bound to be serious repercussions, even perhaps an inquiry; he could always say that he had not seen the Release beforehand ! And what of the admonition that the Memo must be returned to its originator ? All memoranda are ephemeral documents that may be stored for brief periods, but normally they are destroyed at a convenient time. Why, then, was this apparently innocuous document preserved for some 44 years in the Washington files ?

7. **FINDINGS OF DEATH DOCUMENTS (Figs.22,25,30)**

The Findings were released one year and a day after the disappearance of the Norseman - December 16 1945 - and were official documents released in lieu of a death certificate, enabling such matters as wills and probate to be decided. In all the documents the destination is recorded as Bordeaux, which must have perplexed Helen Miller : until she received a copy, the only documents she had been given were the telegram from the AG Department on December 23 1944,and Glenn's Casualty Report. As far as we know, she did not receive a copy of the fabricated MACR 10770 until November 1948. The letter from Col.Donnell dated February 6 1946 had specified Bordeaux as Glenn's destination, with no mention of a proposed stop at A42 Villacoublay. Helen, we believe, was given the whole Haynes story in a telephone call from General 'Hap' Arnold on December 24, prior to the AAF Band broadcast from Paris.If we are to believe Don Haynes'diaries, she was told Morgan was heading for Paris Orly to drop Glenn Miller ! No wonder Helen wrote at once to the AG Department, demanding to know what was going on !

Replying to that letter was no easy task, but the compiler of the Findings documents had no such problems : it was a stereotyped form including a signature of Assistant Chief of Casualty Branch,George F.Herbert. A compiler had only to insert appropriate details. The format of `Circumstances of Disappearance' is identical - the destination was Bordeaux. How are we to explain that statement ? Only by suggesting that certain documents had already been abstracted from the Archives before a year had elapsed,i.e. those confirming that Morgan's destination was B42 Beauvais, plus the `ORIGINAL' MACR N-19 quoting the primary destination as A42 Villacoublay - but this was unsigned and therefore unviable.

A further complication arose from the USFET investigation (Fig.47) which reported Morgan as being en route Bordeaux via A42 Villacoublay - with no reference at all to Twinwood Farm ! Such inconsistencies are endemic throughout the Miller mystery.

8. **REPORTS OF DEATH DOCUMENTS (Figs.22,27,31)**

All three documents confirm no investigation occurred in 1944. They are dated on consecutive days, Morgan on March 23, Glenn Miller on March 24 and Baessell on March 25 1948. All three were completed on a stereotyped pre-signed form, but while the status of Glenn Miller and Baessell was given as `Non-Battle Casualty', John Morgan was a `Battle Casualty' ! Was this, we wondered, the source of persistent rumours that

Morgan's aircraft was shot down by enemy fire ? In November 1952 a corrective ROD was issued, showing Morgan as a `Non-Battle Casualty'. It confirmed again that no investigation had taken place.

9. **MILLER'S PERSONAL EFFECTS**

The Burial Files contain a letter from Mssrs. William M. Mortimer, a firm of attorneys in John Street, New York acting for the Miller family, to the Army Effects Bureau in Kansas City Mo. asking if any personal effects of the bandleader were returned to his widow. The reply, dated March 28 1946, was signed by Lt.Garnhardt and it states: `*To date the Army Effects Bureau has not received any property belonging to Major Miller'*.

The AAF Band returned to the UK in August 1945, prior to leaving for America to be disbanded, after an extended tour of Allied bases on the Continent. Members of the Band took all their personal effects to Paris with them and Glenn was no exception. We know normal procedures required personnel travelling overseas by air to deposit their main baggage at the Old Quebec Street Terminal at least 24 hours prior to departure time. Before he returned to Bedford on Wednesday December 13 1944, Haynes booked Glenn on a Thursday shuttle flight from Bovingdon and it seems reasonable to assume he used the Band staff car to take Glenn's effects from the Mount Royal Hotel to Old Quebec Street Air Terminal, only a few hundred yards away off Seymour Street. Glenn, a VIP of the day, would take at least 3 suitcases to accommodate the dress uniforms and accessories he would need for a 6-week tour in France, with a possibility of entertaining the troops further east as the advance went on. He would retain a 'small kit', hand baggage with shaving and washing materials which he would carry round to Old Quebec Street Terminal on Thursday morning.

All writers on the case agree that none of Glenn's personal effects were ever traced. Haynes makes no mention of them in his diary,although he does describe the variety of equipment loaded onto the aircraft when the Band flew to Paris on Monday December 18 1944, including music, arrangements,music stands and instruments. It is true that in his diaries he described loading Glenn's single D-bag (a folding uniform case) into the Norseman, but this would accommodate only a single change of uniform for a week's stay. And since we know that the the flight described by Haynes took place on Friday November 8, not December 15, and Glenn Miller was going to Paris only for the conference on November 15, a single bag made good sense.

We located a taped interview by the late Alan Stilwell, a batman/valet assigned to look after Glenn Miller on the rare occasions he stayed at 8th AFSC. Mr. Stilwell was old and senile when he was interviewed. He said that the day after Miller disappeared, some Provost Marshal officers came to `The Castle', packed Glenn's effects and took them away,

away, but this is clearly unviable evidence. For one thing, Glenn's disappearance was realised only on Tuesday December 19, some four days after he was last seen in London on Thursday December 14. Again, he was not associated with the Norseman loss (known at Milton Ernest on Saturday December 16) until the same day, December 19. Further, he would clearly take all his effects with him, and if there were items he wanted to leave behind, he would deposit them in the storerooms provided. Accommodation was always in short supply at `The Castle'; a Billeting Officer would hardly reserve for months a room occupied briefly by a visiting bandleader. Miller, in fact, rarely stayed at 8th AFSC, although he and Don Haynes were frequent and welcome visitors to the Officers Club.

The only possible scenario we could devise to explain the removal of Glenn's effects from 8th AFSC on Saturday December 16 was that of foul play of some sort, causing his death in London after leaving the Milroy Club at 02.30 am on Thursday December 14. But a check of New Scotland Yard records proved negative, and there were no reports of V1 or V2 bombs in the area. We concluded that Stilwell, like many others, confused his dates. Finally, if any of Glenn's effects had been left behind, we believe they would have been in his permanent accommodation in the Mount Royal Hotel. The fact that none were returned to his wife suggests strongly that they vanished in France with him. In comparison, we found in the Morgan File no less than 14 pages of personal effects inventoried, with details of their return to his family: they included a final statement from the National Provincial Bank Stowmarket, showing his closing balance as £1.18.10d (about $9 at the 1944 rate of exchange).

Few soldiers become rich men in wartime...

9. **THE BORDEAUX SEARCH LETTER (Fig.33).**

Of all documents found in the Burial Files, this letter was perhaps the most puzzling. Dated June 21 1946 (only a few weeks after the MACR 10770 was fabricated at Maxwell AFB as a result of Helen Miller's letters to the AG Department) it was written by Lt.Brinkmann of 3046 QM Graves Registration Company near Limoges to the Commanding Officer, 551 QM Group at APO 809 in Europe. The letter was manifestly in response to an instruction to carry out a search of the Bordeaux area for a crashed aircraft, near which bodies had been seen. But there were a number of anomalies in the text. First, it was a single and isolated letter in the File with no follow-up material, which had been carefully preserved for 44 years. If nothing had been found as a result of the search, there was no logical reason for retaining the letter - but if some important evidence had been discovered, why was it not in the Files ?

Reading between the lines, it seems certain that this aircraft had been observed from the air. Whether this was an accidental discovery or the result of an organised search, we do not know. The area was heavily-forested in 1944, but there seems no doubt that bodies were seen. Further, 3046 QM Company knew the remains they sought were those of Norseman occupants, since the letter was in Miller's File. We tried to trace Lt. Brinkmann without success. We concluded that the search was part of a European investigation ordered by USFET following their signal to the AG Department in Washington in February 1946, but indirectly we are reminded of the terrible dilemma faced by Gen.Barker at SHAEF in December 1944. He delayed all reporting procedures as we know until the penultimate moment; no official report was ever issued by SHAEF or the AG Department and only the Miller Casualty Report and the Confirmatory Signal were released to the public before March 1948.

But the real nightmare that haunted SHAEF at the time was this : suppose Glenn Miller turned up unharmed *after* SHAEF released the Norseman story ? Suppose the wreckage of the Norseman was found - without Miller's remains ? Suppose Baessell and John Morgan had been picked up by some neutral ship and surfaced alive in Sweden or Spain, without Glenn Miller ? Certain steps could be taken. Don Haynes could be sworn to silence. The Confirmatory Signal, while on file to prove the Norseman story was a matter of record, could be quietly destroyed if Miller returned - and released long after the war if he did not. The Adjutant at Abbotts Ripton had refused to sign an MACR, but it could be worked out. And if the fabric-covered Norseman was eventually found, identification would hinge upon the engine number (which had quietly been removed from the records). If there were incriminating documents in Morgan's File, they could be removed, or the File suppressed. Most of all, the thing would probably die a natural death in a year or two and the boat would cease rocking.

They hoped...

But what of the `Bordeaux Crash' ? There were several possible scenarios.Even if it was not located quickly,it would be found in the years to come : if not, it could be conveniently forgotten. If it was found, and Miller was not aboard, the news would have to be suppressed. One can see the banner headlines :

GLENN MILLER AIRCRAFT FOUND !
BANDLEADER NOT ABOARD !
MYSTERY DEEPENS !

If he was found in the wreck, it would vindicate Haynes and SHAEF, and they would hasten to release the news. On balance, we believe the wreck was found, but was not Morgan's Norseman - see Chapter 4.

10. MILLER'S ORDERS FOR PARIS (Fig.19).

We were the first researchers to note that an incorrect serial number was included in the Orders - 0606271, instead of 0505273. We wrote to National Personnel Records Center at St.Louis Mo. for the name of the person allotted 0606271, and after some delay they advised that it was Cpl. Elsie Wright, a WAC typist stationed at SHAEF REAR, Bushey Park, London in 1944. This at first sight appeared to be a reasonable explanation; Elsie was almost certainly the clerk who typed out Glenn Miller's Paris orders on December 12, inadvertently inserting her own number instead of his.

But on reflection, we were not sure : the prefix `0' was used for officers, and her own serial number was `606271'. It did not seem possible that she would add an `0' to her own serial number, even in error. We wrote several times more to St.Louis, but each time they said that while 0606271 was an officer's number, they were unable to trace the owner ! This seemed strange, because they had had no difficulty in tracing Cpl. Elsie Wright. There were two disturbing factors here : first, if as rumour had it, Glenn had received cranial injuries in an accident of some kind and was unidentifiable visually, the incorrect serial number in his orders could lead to misidentification. Second, even if very far-fetched, it was remotely possible that the orders had been cut for some other officer and Glenn Miller's name was subsequently inserted.

We had two other factors in mind when we considered this possibility. First, other documents in the case had been fabricated. And second, the orders were not in the Miller Burial File when we received it. We were given a copy by his brother Herb in London.

We knew, too, that certain documents had been abstracted from John Morgan's File, and the `ORIGINAL' MACR N-19 had been suppressed, while Report 10770 was circulated as genuine. If Miller's orders had been deliberately abstracted, it was in no way unusual, and there must have been a very good reason. Reading the orders, that reason is immediately apparent : Glenn was ordered to proceed to Paris `on or about' December 16 1944, and this flexibility in his orders made total nonsense of Haynes' assertion that he had Glenn's own orders changed, thereby laying the foundation of the Norseman story. Indeed, the number of missing documents is such that we began to wonder if a separate and MOST SECRET file had been opened for them...

There is, however, a postscript to this strange incident involving the serial number, and a possible solution was provided by Mrs.Dorothy Wiltshire of Herne Hill, London, who was herself a wartime typist. She pointed out the similarity of the two numbers :

0 5 0 5 2 7 3   (Miller's number)
0 6 0 6 2 7 1   (Incorrect number)

Four of the seven vertical pairs are identical, while two other pairs (5 and 6) vary by only one number. In touch typing, Dorothy suggested, are two sets of `home' keys, one for the four fingers of the left hand as follows : **A  S  D  F**, and four for the right hand : **J  K  L  ;**. When the typist wishes to press the `5' key, she would lift her left forefinger from the `F' to the `5'. But if she inadvertently placed her left hand on the `home' keys but one key to the right, i.e. **S  D  F  G**, she would strike the `6' key instead of the `5'. Further, on wartime typewriters there was no number `0' key (the upper case `O' was  used instead) and the letter `1' key was used for the figure `1'. The net result would be that the typist would strike  the `0' with the right little finger and erroneously strike the `6' key instead of the `5' with the left forefinger, producing `**0606**' instead of `**0505**'. But what of the `271' ? It seems reasonable to assume that seeing part of her own serial number appear in print (606) Elsie might finish by adding `271` instead of 273.

Whatever the explanation, the incorrect serial number has important connotations in the Miller mystery.

11. **THE MOD AIR HISTORICAL BRANCH REPORT (Fig.45).**

This report was released *circa* 1973, based on information received from USAF Historical Center, Maxwell AFB Alabama. It states that Morgan's Norseman was not included in the Cumulative Loss Listing until 1947, and we can offer no reason for that delayed retrospective insertion. The Report states also that 44-70285 was sometimes confused with another C64, number 43-5367, reported missing December 26 1944 from Grove Field, Wantage, Berks. This prompted us to check just how many Norseman aircraft had been lost in December 1944 : the first thing we learned was that while 5367 was on the Cumulative Loss Listing, there was no Missing Aircrew Report ! And this is quite unprec-edented.

We obtained a detailed list of the units based at Grove, which included the 43rd and 45th Air Depot Repair Squadrons performing the same task as 35th ADRS at Abbotts Ripton. But neither unit had a C64 on strength. Also based at Grove was the 314th Air Transport Squadron operating 13 C47 aircraft; six additional aircraft were attached during December 1944, and returned subsequently to their own units. The 314th had no Norseman aircraft on strength, and no aircraft were reported missing in December 1944. The 313th Air Transport Squadron arrived at Grove Field on December 7/8 with 12 C47 aircaft; they operated no C64s and reported no losses in December. However, one Norseman recorded as having been serviced at Grove AFB was 43-5367. But it was on charge to 1st Transport Group,France, not to the 31st Transport Group at Grove.

We wrote once again to Maxwell AFB and Norton AFB, and were astounded to learn that no less than eight more C64s were reported missing, or were allocated elsewhere, in December 1944 ! This, from Norton AFB which had previously denied holding any record of a Norseman incident !

Ignoring 5367 in the MOD Report, we identified the aircraft involved :

43-5313   302 Transport Wing Grove,missing 16 December
43-36329 2nd Base Air Depot   28 December
43-35340 302 Transport Wing Grove   10 December
43-39366 On Allocation   18 December
43-35394 10 Air Depot Group   19 December
44-70244 5 Strategic Air Depot   28 December
44-70280 4 Mobile Repair/Recovery Sqdn   19 December
44-70348 2nd Air Depot Group   6 December

Discounting 39366 on allocation, but including 44-70285 and 43-5367 nine C64s were lost in Europe in December 1944. A Canadian research- er Henry Whiston traced a Grove Executive Officer Frank Kelly, who said that 314th Transport Squadron, 31st Transport Group, was trans- ferred in late November from Base A40 Chartres in France,to Base 519 Grove. We traced the record card of 5367 in America. It was completed in February 1944, flown to Fort Dix on February 24, sent to Newark Field, New Jersey on March 31 and delivered to the UK April 1.

The Operating Unit of 43-5367 at the time of loss was `1st Transport Group'. *It was reported missing on December 15...*

So now we had a mystery C64A Norseman, recorded in the CLL as `Missing in Action', for which no MACR had been originated,which Maxwell AFB suggested in 1973 was often confused with Morgan's aircraft 44-70285, yet was neither of the machines missing from Grove ! Further, no C64s were missing from Grove on December 26.

We found that 1st Transport Group and 326th Ferry Sqdn. were based at A81 Creil, France. Some elements were deployed at A40 Chartres (326th Ferry Squadron `A' Detachment) and A42 Villacoublay (`B' Detachment). Using C64s, they ferried delivery crews taking bombers and fighters to forward units near the combat zones. In December 1944 a special operation was mounted from A81 Creil and Verdun, France, covering the Ardennes counter-offensive. They also used A93D Liege and A97C south of the `Bulge'. To summarise, in December 1944 :

(a) 43-5367 was based at Creil, France with 1st Transport Group.
(b) Part of the group was at A40, Chartres.
(c) 313 and 314 Squadrons moved to Grove December 6.
(d) Neither unit reported losses that month.
(e) 302 Transport Wing at Grove AFB lost 2 C64s in December -
43-35340 on the 19th and 43-5313 on the 16th. None on the 26th
or the 15th !
(f) 43-5367 was reported missing on December 15, and according to
Maxwell AFB was at Grove at that time.

We know a visiting C64 was serviced/ repaired at Grove in December

1944 (which was 43-5367). The picture is now beginning to take shape : on December 15, Norseman 43-5367 visiting Grove from France had been repaired and set out to return to its base A80 Creil, or possibly to A42 Villacoublay. It was not on the Grove aircraft strength and predict- ably it was not reported missing by Grove AFB. That would be the responsibility of the operating unit, 1st Transport Group. But here the story takes on an ominous slant : as stated in the MOD Report, 43-5367 was entered in the Cumulative Loss Listing - but no MACR has ever been traced !

The implications of this cannot be understated. On December 15, two Norseman aircraft left the UK : 43-5367 was heading from Grove AFB to Creil or Villacoublay, probably via Bovingdon, but quite possibly direct via Beachy Head. We have no take-off time,but almost all other flights that day were delayed until noon or later,waiting for visibility to improve. In that category was Col.Corrigan's C47 from Tempsford to Orly,Tony Bartley's Anson from Northolt to Brussels, the force of 137 Lancasters from East Anglia - and John Morgan's Norseman. It is very probable that the take-off times of the two Norseman aircraft were very close, but they were far apart in space. For 43-5367 was west of London, heading out from Beachy Head, whilst Morgan in 44-70285 was flying east of the City, heading for Dymchurch and Cap Gris Nez. The track followed by 43-5367 to Creil would take it directly through the Channel Bomb Jettison Area (Fig.51) while the route from Beachy Head-Dieppe- Paris would run some 10 miles east of that Danger Area.

But why is this important ?

On December 15, 137 Lancaster bombers from East Anglia flew south to Tunbridge Wells and Beachy Head, en route to bomb a rail junction at Siegen near Cologne. The mission was abandoned soon after the force left Amiens, and a number of aircraft dumped heavy bombs in the Channel Jettison Area. One Lancaster carried navigator Fred Shaw, who reported seeing from 6000 feet bombs bursting all round a low-flying Norseman. He believed that this was Morgan's plane carrying Glenn Miller.

Listening to Fred Shaw's taped interview, he comes over as a genuine and forthright individual, who is totally convinced that he saw from their safe jettison altitude a low-flying Norseman surrounded by exploding heavy bombs. He was standing in the cockpit staring down through the `bubble' side window, which would permit almost a vertical view.

The criteria which would be involved in assessing the Fred Shaw story comprise :

(a) Were the weather conditions at the time conducive to the correct id- entification of a small (50 feet wingspan) aircraft at a distance of more than a mile ?

(b) Would the C64's camouflage make identification difficult ?

(c) What evidence can we present on the routes taken by the two C64 aircraft, including take-off times ?

(d) What was the danger period during which the force of Lancasters passed through the Jettison Area ?

The Lancaster-Norseman interception is assessed at length in Appendix C, but much more interesting is the implications inherent in the MOD Report. The information on 43-5367 was provided by Maxwell AFB Alabama (already familiar to us as the birth-place of the falsified MACR 10770), and on the basis of the information we obtained, there are many disquieting aspects. No C64 was reported missing from Grove AFB on December 26, but two were reported on December 16 and 10. Norseman 43-5367 was repaired at Grove and departed December 15 for Creil or Villacoublay. Since SHAEF were aware of the impending Ardennes offensive, the latter seems more probable.

Norseman 43-5367 was entered in the Cumulative Loss Listing, but there was no MACR on file. It departed some time after noon in common with Morgan's aircraft, and its route would take it close to the Channel Bomb Jettison Area.

On the other hand, the inclusion of Morgan's aircraft in the Cumulative Loss Listing was delayed until 1947; the `ORIGINAL' MACR N-19 was suppressed in the Burial Files and a falsified MACR was fabricated at Maxwell AFB in March 1946, and was subsequently certified, guaranteed and promoted by National Archives as the genuine and original document.

Maxwell AFB, we feel, have a great many questions to answer...

12. **SUMMARY**

We submit that the documents found in the Burial Files constitute unassailable evidence in support of our belief that Glenn Miller reached France safely and disappeared, and that SHAEF and Don Haynes had no clues as to his fate; they confirm our contention that a widespread but covert search of Paris for Glenn Miller went on from Monday December 18 to 18.00 hours on December 24, although the records state that no investigation took place.

The documents further confirm that reporting procedures were deliberately delayed, the `ORIGINAL' MACR was not compiled until December 23 and was sent to Washington unsigned. There, it was suppressed for 44 years in the Burial Files, while a fabricated MACR was circulated as genuine by the National Archives. Most important, they prove that Glenn Miller flew to Paris on Thursday December 14 with Mr. Teddy Gower, a BBC engineer, and that the AG Department Washington deliberately withheld vital information from Helen Miller.

Certain documents, of which we were able to obtain copies elsewhere, were abstracted from the Files. No official explanation or statement was ever issued by the US Government or Haynes, and the latter was never officially questioned or interrogated.

Further, our efforts to obtain the Burial Files from National Archives from June 1986 to March 1987, as evinced by the correspondence from various Archival departments, demonstrates clearly an ongoing official policy of delay, diversion and obfuscation with the aim of denying access to the Burial Files for Major Alton Glenn Miller, Lt.Col. Norman F. Baessell and Flight Officer John R.S. Morgan. That we succeeded at all was due solely to the personal intervention of President Ronald Reagan. We received only a curt acknowledgement to our letter, but action resulted quickly.

Our next task was to establish definitive proof of the unviability of Lt. Don Haynes' account of events in December 1944 : once that was accomplished, we could devote all our attention to the paramount question :

`If Glenn Miller was not lost aboard the Norseman en route to France, what in fact did happen to him ?

+   +   +

THREE

THE HAYNES DIARIES

1. BACKGROUND

Don Haynes (see Fig.2) was a long-standing friend and employee of Glenn Miller before the latter achieved his breakthrough into the big time. In the Thirties, Haynes was a band booking agent well respected in the business and became a fulltime manager of the Glenn Miller Band during their residency at the Cafe Rouge in the Hotel Pennsylvania, New York City. Don Haynes married Glenn's office manager Polly Davis, and when Miller formed the new AAF Band in New Haven Conn., Don was inducted into the US Air Force as a Lieutenant, serial number 0583260. He travelled to England with the Band as Executive Officer in July 1944, remaining with them until their return in August 1945 for demobilisation.

Following Miller's disappearance, Don Haynes was promoted to Captain, and with the possible exception of Sergeant (later Warrant Officer) Paul Dudley, he spent more time with Miller than anyone else. He died in June 1971, after service in the US Mail, and Polly died in 1988. Don Haynes published nothing relating to his experiences with the Miller Band in Europe, but after a while copies of a `Haynes Diary' began to circulate, and we traced this back to the 1953 movie made by Universal Studios entitled *THE GLENN MILLER STORY*, starring James Stewart and June Allyson. During research the studio scriptwriters received a package of papers from the Miller family containing a diary roughly typed on onion-skin paper by Don Haynes, and a promise to provide additional material. This failed to materialise and after the movie was completed, the diary was presented by Universal Studios to the Library of Congress in Washington DC. It has become known as the `LOC' version; while copies are available from the Library, the account has been in general circulation since the early Sixties.John Edwards obtained a copy in Bahrein in 1960,and the late Jack Taylor was sent a copy by a friend in America in 1979.

Around that time, a second diary appeared, and we traced copies circulating between researchers in the United States and South Africa, as well as UK and Australia. But while the LOC version appears to be a genuine and factual account of Don Haynes'experiences, the second seems to be a fictional variant clearly intended for eventual publication, and it is entitled `MINUS ONE', seen as a reference to Miller's loss.

In 1974 Mr. George T. Simon published his excellent book *GLENN MILLER AND HIS ORCHESTRA (Bigbee Promotions)* which deals largely with the musical aspects of the European tour. He was an old friend of the Haynes family and in 1971 Polly presented him with a copy of what she assured him was a definitive and factual version of Don's diaries, with her full permission to quote from it. In 1988, Mr. Geoffrey Butcher published *NEXT TO A LETTER FROM HOME (Mainstream)*, but both these fine works deal almost exclusively with the AAF Band. The disappearance of Glenn Miller forms only a minor part of the narrative. Now curiously, when we began to compare these accounts with the copies of the two diaries we had obtained, we found that both writers had used as a reference the `MINUS ONE' version, which is generally recognised to be fictional and based largely upon the LOC version in an expanded format. We found vital clues in both versions, and in this book we quote from the diary copies, not from the Simon or Butcher books. We are, however, deeply grateful to these authors for permitting us to quote generally information on Glenn's life and other matters relating to the AAF band.

Needless to say, these diaries created a furore among the world's researchers, including John Flowers and Henry Whiston in Canada and John Edwards in Britain. They contain the first comprehensive account of the events between November 8 and December 24 1944, the critical period of the Miller mystery, and the initial reaction was unanimous : the Haynes account was totally flawed and unviable. It is plain to see why he had not been asked to make a statement in the MACR. There could be no doubt about that verdict : there were too many anomalies, errors and inconsistencies to be accounted for by coincidence, bad memory or faulty recording of events in 1944.

Glenn Miller could not have been aboard the Norseman at all.

+ + +

Analysis of the diaries reveals some 27 major discrepancies with each other and with official records and papers now available, from which we were able to draw the following conclusions :

(a) Haynes' account of the December 15 flight was blatantly based upon his recollections of the November 8 flight.

(b) He last saw Major Glenn Miller on leaving the party in the Milroy Club, Stratton Street in Mayfair, just before midnight on Wednesday December 14 1944, in company with pilot John Morgan,to return to Bedford.

(c) Miller stayed in the Club with Tony Bartley and Tony Pulitzer until 02.30, when he set off to walk to the Mount Royal Hotel, Marble Arch.

(d) That Wednesday morning, Don Haynes had booked Glenn onto a Bovingdon shuttle to Orly next day, and had taken Glenn's baggage round to the Old Quebec Street Air Terminal.

(e) Haynes did not have Glenn's orders changed as he related : the orders permitted Glenn to travel `on or about' Saturday December 16. Haynes always believed that Glenn caught his booked Paris shuttle flight on Thursday December 14 to Orly.

(f) At Milton Ernest, Don Haynes spent Thursday supervising preparations for the Band flight to Paris on Saturday. He knew that Morgan was flying Baessell to Paris on Friday; although Baessell had offered Haynes a lift, the Executive Officer said he had to fly with the Band on Saturday.

(g) Don Haynes spent Thursday night at `The Castle', because he had a dental appointment on Friday afternoon. It is possible he drove Colonel Baessell to Abbotts Ripton on Friday morning, where Morgan's take-off was delayed until 13.25 because of poor visibility.

(h) It is possible also that he may have driven Baessell to Twinwood Farm, but reason suggests otherwise : the field was closed for flying and no eyewitnesses saw a Norseman land on December 15. This, we suggest, is why Baessell boarded the aircraft at Abbotts Ripton.

(j) After two days delay due to bad weather, the AAF Band flew to Paris Orly on Monday December 18, landing at 13.45 hours. Glenn Miller was not there to meet them.

We can check these conclusions against the evidence in the diaries, but this is an opportune moment to talk about the Band itself and the men who controlled it.

2. AAF BAND ORGANISATION

In 1944, there was no `United States Army Air Force' as such. There were 16 Army Air Forces controlled by a Washington HQ. Originally, the Band was part of AAF Training Command, and by spring 1944, it acquired and retained the name of the Army Air Forces Band (Special). From July 1944, the Band and its small speciality groups performed at many venues, including US AAF bases, hospitals and Service clubs. They made live and recorded broadcasts on AEFN and BBC networks, arranged by the Director of Troop Broadcasting, Special Services Division, SHAEF MAIN, located at Bushey Park London until Paris was liberated in August 1944. Thereafter Bushey Park became SHAEF REAR, while SHAEF MAIN moved to Versailles.

Until October 1, the Director of Troop Broadcasting was Colonel Ed.Kirby and the Associate Director was Lt.Col.David Niven of the Rifle Brigade, seconded to Special Services because of his showbiz connections. After Kirby went home on October 1, Niven became Director, and his Associate Director at SHAEF REAR was Major Johnny Hayes. The Paris tour was approved subject to a major Band prerecording programme which was completed on December 10). A Band Movement Order was completed and distributed on Tuesday December 12.

Next day, the Band gave its final UK performance in the Queensberry Club London, after which Lord Queensberry gave them a farewell party in Kettner's Restaurant. Miller and Haynes spent Tuesday night in the Mount Royal Hotel, and we know the events which followed.

3. **THE DIARIES ASSESSED.**

For the sake of clarity and brevity, the following extracts from the LOC and MINUS ONE versions are not verbatim, but have been carefully edited without distorting the main gist of the narrative. We will append brief notes to each extract, but it must be born in mind that while Don Haynes probably maintained a wartime diary to help in keeping track of Band bookings, these later documents were written largely from memory over two and a half decades. We have made due allowance for that, and we have selected the daily entries for the critical period from December 13 - 24 1944.

Wed.Dec.13   Got Glenn's orders cut to fly to Paris tomorrow. Drove back to Bedford in fog so thick that the bus conductors walked ahead carrying torches.

NOTE : The Milroy Club party is not mentioned, nor the time Haynes left for Bedford, or if he was alone.

Thu.Dec.14   Had lunch with Col.B. He is flying to Paris tomorrow - would I like to go ? I said I was flying out with Band on Saturday, but Glenn was grounded in London waiting for a flight.B.said nothing was flying out of UK (weather too bad). Called Glenn as B. advised; he said to come down to collect him.

NOTE : If everything in the UK was grounded, including well-equipped Air Transports, how did Col.Baessell expect to make it in a UC64A with sub-standard radio and no navigational aids, flown by a rookie pilot ? Totally illogical. But we note this as the point at which Don Haynes began fabricating his story.

Thu.Cont.   Picked up Glenn at 16.00, drove to Officers Club at Bedford. Dinner and poker with Col.B, Major Koch, WO Earlywine at 'The Castle', back to Bedford early for good night's sleep as B. would be calling us early next morning after getting clearance. But stayed up talking with Glenn until 03.30 about post-war plans. He promised to deed part of his Tuxedo Junction Ranch to me and Polly, as well as putting a big financial nest-egg away for us.

NOTE : some anomalies here. Why go back to Bedford in thick fog when they were returning early next day to fly out ? Transient quarters were available at Milton Ernest. The `poker game' is in MINUS ONE, not in LOC. The mention of a `nest-egg' is surprising : it could have formed the subject of a claim against Miller's estate post-war, but there is no record of this. The important item refers to Baessell getting `clearance' but this was the responsibility of the pilot, not a passenger. If our theory is right and this narrative originated in the November 8 flight (see P.47) then Baessell was waiting for George Ferguson to obtain `clearance' for the flight from his local commander.

Fri.Dec.15   Awakened by a call from Col. B. Weather still bad. Pilot couldn't get clearance but it should clear early afternoon. He suggested we came out to Milton Ernest Club with Glenn's baggage. He had spoken to Morgan at Station 595 - 100 miles north. Pilot said weather was improving, he'd know by lunch if he had clearance.

NOTE : As we know from Ferguson's taped interview, Baessell telephoned him in Brussels early on `the day of the flight' and was disappointed to learn that George's CO had vetoed the trip. Col.Baessell told him to try one more time, call him back at 8th AFSC. But Baessell had clearly written off Ferguson, contacting Morgan at Honington (Station 595). But George, of course, confused dates; all these events occurred on November 8, not December 15. Further, Morgan's flight records tell us he made no positioning flight to Honington prior to December 15. He flew only once, on December 2. He did, however, fly several local missions on November 6, including one to Troston (Honington). Haynes used all this data in his account of the flight on December 15. There is one interesting corroboration in his flight times; the flight to Orly on November 8 took 3 hours 30 minutes, instead of the usual 2 hours 45 minutes. The extra 45 minutes represents the Honington-Twinwood leg.

Fri.Cont.   Visited Band quarters, drove to Milton Ernest, lunch with Col.B. Morgan called during lunch, said he'd pick us up within the hour. Seen off by WO Earlywine and Major Koch, stopped briefly at Goodrich's house `The Bury' for Col.B.to get final orders. It was raining heavy now : Glenn said `Even the ----- birds are grounded today !'.

NOTE : If Baessell stopped to see Gen. Goodrich to discuss the mission, why did Goodrich tell Gen.Barker on the telephone he did not know that Morgan was using a Norseman, or that Glenn Miller was a passenger ? One interesting note : Glenn Miller's remark about the `birds being grounded' is found  three times in Don Haynes' story - outside `The

Bury' waiting for Baessell; waiting for Morgan outside Twinwood Farm Control Tower, and on the runway boarding the plane !

+   +   +

At this point, we digress from a single diary account to extracts from both diaries as noted.

MINUS ONE
Fri.Cont   **Drove to Twinwood, waited in car for Morgan. Rain, cloud now down to 200 feet. After half an hour, B. entered the Tower, came back in 10 mins. He had spoken to Station 595. Morgan took off 55 minutes ago, was due any minute. We heard a motor in the overcast going south. `What  did I say ?' Glenn said. `He can't even find the field !' `Don't bet on it,' Col.B. said. `He's a helluva pilot, flew 32 missions on B24s. He's used to weather like this.'**

NOTE : Haynes is totally at variance with the MACR. Morgan came 30 miles from Abbotts Ripton and should have taken 25 minutes, not 55. Also, in the LOC version, Baessell enters the Tower at once, calls `Station 525' Heston and says `Morgan took off 10 minutes ago'. It was a 20-minute trip to Twinwood. In LOC, he says the plane approached from the north - but Heston lies south of Twinwood ! Note the vast difference between the weather Haynes describes, and the true observations in Fig.39. As for Morgan, he had flown under 600 hours total, and no operational missions. In the LOC version, Haynes said Morgan had completed a tour of operations on Flying Fortresses ! There are 6 major discrepancies in this single entry.
We now have 3 different departure airfields :

Abbotts Ripton (cited in the MACRs)
Honington (in MINUS ONE) and
Heston (LOC Version).

We will also have 3 destination airfields !

B42 Beauvais (Morgan's Record Card).
A42 Villacoublay (the MACRs) and
Orly (the Haynes diaries).

From where did Haynes obtain `Heston' ? We learned that Morgan was stationed there on 87 Ferry Command Sqdn. before he was assigned to Wattisham and Abbotts Ripton. Don Haynes probably heard Morgan mention it.

We will suspend the diary analysis temporarily, because we believe it is essential to examine the `Honington' story in detail. Haynes' whole story hangs upon it. If we can prove it false, then his whole account is false. We begin with John Morgan's Form 5, Record of Flight Times : his November 1944 missions, with number of landings, were as follows :

6th : 1hr.45m. 4 Various UK bases incl. Troston (Honington).
8th : 3hr.30m. 3 Twinwood/Bovingdon (drop Miller) Orly.
10th : 1hr 10m 1 Local flight around Orly.
18th : 2hr 40m 2 Twinwood (drop Baessell) Abbotts Ripton.
28th : 2hr 50m 2 Twinwood/Orly with Baessell.
29th : 2hr 15m 2 Twinwood (drop Baessell) Abbotts Ripton.
30th : 2hr 10m 2 Twinwood/Orly with Baessell.

And in December :

2nd : 2hr 40m 2 Twinwood (drop Baessell) Abbotts Ripton.
15th : Unknown. 1 Abbotts Ripton/ditched in Channel.

The penultimate landing on December 2 positioned Morgan at Abbotts Ripton, and he did not fly again for two weeks, until his fatal mission on December 15. He was not in good flying practice at that time. Now, let us assume for the sake of argument that the flight from Honington (which actually occurred on November 8) took place as Haynes said, on December 15. From his diaries we can construct a timetable :

08.20 Baessell calls Morgan at Honington, fog too thick.
08.30 Baessell calls Haynes in Bedford, to come to 8th AFSC.
11.00 Haynes/Miller visit Band, reach Milton Ernest 11.30.
11.25 Baessell again rings Morgan. He `will know by noon'.
11.30 Haynes/Miller arrive and Baessell briefs them.
12.00 They eat lunch in the Officers Club.
12.15 Morgan rings.`With them within the hour'(before 13.00).
12.30 Morgan departs Honington, ETA Twinwood 12.50.
13.00 Haynes/Baessell/Miller arrive at Twinwood. No Morgan !
13.50 Morgan arrives - one hour overdue !
13.55 Norseman takes off, never seen again.

So where was Morgan during the hour he was adrift ? Perhaps, as John Edwards joked, he was `hanging from the local skyhook' ! Haynes, of course, was no pilot, and when a layman starts writing about professional matters, he will come to grief, every time. But there is a logical explanation here. On P.46 we related how ATC assistant Dixie Clerke came on duty at Twinwood at 13.00 (not on December 15, as she believed, but on November 8) to find the Norseman parked outside the Tower; as she watches, a staff car arrives with Haynes, Glenn Miller and Col. Baessell.

Now, this fits in exactly with the arrival of the three men at 13.00, as per timetable, and if we allow about 20 minutes for boarding and taxying out, the take-off time is 13.25 - and that was the time originally quoted by Haynes in his diary for the December 15 flight !

It all fits, far beyond the bounds of coincidence...

+   +   +

MINUS ONE

Fri.Cont. **The plane came down through the overcast and landed. Morgan taxied back down the runway, kept the motor going.`Hi,'he said. `Ran into some heavy squalls but the weather's clearing.' I put Glenn's bag on board; Morgan showed me a Luger he'd traded for 200 cigarettes. I loaded on Col. B's box of empty champagne bottles, said `Good luck !' Glenn & Col B. were the only passengers. John Morgan was an able pilot having finished his required B17 missions. `Thanks Haynsie,' Glenn said. We may need it !' Then Morgan revved the motor, took off and disappeared into the overcast at 01.45. I drove back to the Officers Club.**

NOTE : Haynes knew little or nothing of meteorology. In the synoptic anti-cyclonic situation on December 15 (Fig.40) there were only light southerly winds and it was a cold calm damp day with visibility about 1 mile, a 3000-foot cloudbase and no rain.`*Heavy squalls'* were quite impossible in this weather system. The remark on empty champagne bottles requires an explanation : immediately after liberation in August 1944, the French transportation systems were in a shambles. An empty champagne bottle had to be proffered in order to buy a full one. By December, the problem had been solved; Haynes perhaps recalled this from an earlier flight. We discussed the modification of the take-off time on P.19/20.

Fri.Cont. **Back to Bedford ARC Club.They took off at 01.45 - they should arrive at Orly in 2 1/2 hours.Kept a dental appointment at 8th AFSC, went back to the Band billet, back to the Club, showered, hit the sack.**

NOTE : This was our first intimation that Don Haynes always believed Morgan was going to Orly on December 15 1944,and we were astonished. There is a further interesting diary entry for Friday December 15, which we have mentioned previously : Haynes said that while saying goodbye to Morgan, he said `*See you in Paris tomorrow'*. But had the flight gone according to Morgan's operation orders, he would not have been in Paris ! He planned to night-stop at Beauvais before heading on

68

to Bordeaux on Saturday morning,and Haynes would not have seen him. But had Haynes' story been true,Morgan would have replied : `No way ! We're not bound for Paris today !' Writing his diary many years later, Haynes probably recalled that Orly was Baessell's customary destination,and it was a good bet he was going there on December 15.From this we can safely assume that Haynes never saw an MACR. The Band flight was postponed on Saturday December 16, and again on Sunday the 16th. Some of the Band opted to sleep at Bovingdon on Sunday night, to avoid a third tiring bus journey.

Mon.Dec.18 Bovingdon called, said that 3 C47s would pick us up at Twinwood Farm 10.45. As we arrived, the 3 planes were circling to land ! We loaded equipment and men,took off 11.25, passed White Cliffs of Dover 12.15, crossed 90-mile Channel corridor (Germans held coastal positions preventing a shorter crossing). Crossed French coast 12.55, landed at Orly 13.45.

NOTE : Haynes' memory was faulty here. Three C47s were allocated to fly the Band to Paris, two by stand-by crews of 315th Troop Carrier Group. A C47 from 34 Sqdn was flown by Capt.Wm.M.Perkins; another from 310 Sqdn was flown by Capt.Tappen and co-pilot 2nd.Lt.Richard J. Kucklik from 34 Squadron. These aircraft landed at Twinwood as Haynes related. The third, a C47 from Air Transport Command, collected the Bovingdon group.(ATC assistant Dixie Clerke refers to this in her taped narrative). All the Band equipment including instruments, music sheets, music stands and personal effects, was carried by the Twinwood aircraft but a party of nine musicians under Lt. Paul Morden remained in Bedford.

There are other inconsistencies in Haynes' account : the standard route was via Bovingdon - Beachy Head - Dieppe - Paris. Further, the flight time he quotes (50 minutes) from Twinwood Farm-Dover is quite impossible in a C47. Probably, he assumed the cliffs at Beachy Head were those at Dover. (See Chapter 4). A more serious error involved the `90-mile crossing'. After the Canadians liberated Dieppe on September 1 1944, the remaining German enclave was Dunkirk, far to the east of Channel crossing routes and the Straits of Dover. From Beachy Head to Dieppe is 65 miles.

LOC Version :
Mon.Dec.18 No transportation, despite code message via Bovingdon.Glenn was to alert Seine Base. Checked in Operations - Glenn's plane had not landed Orly.Called Major May, hadn't seen Glenn since November trip but had been expecting me since Friday (he knew bad weather had grounded all flights from UK for the past

week). Called Billeting Officer - neither Glenn nor B. had checked in. Now I began to worry ! Glenn had left UK in a single-engined ship with cruising speed 100- 125 mph. They should have made Orly by 16.00. They took off at 13.45. Checked with Orly Ops.- they were socked in from 15.00 Friday until late the next day. I called Le Bourget,Villacoublay,same deal.

NOTE : A revealing entry, compared with the following MINUS ONE version. Haynes insists Morgan was bound for Orly - and we found that significant. He had booked Glenn on a Thursday flight, but the Band would not arrive for two days. Glenn would not have to report to SHAEF until Monday at the earliest and the obvious destintion was Orly, for the city of Paris. This agrees with the evidence given to John Edwards by BBC engineer Teddy Gower, who described flying to Orly in the seat behind Glenn Miller. Second, Haynes beats the weather drum again:`*All flights from UK were grounded for the past week* and `*Paris Orly was open until 15.00 on Friday afternoon,December 15'* ! We traced several UK-Continental flights on that day : Lt.Col.Tom Corrigan flew a C47 into Paris from Tempsford, Gloucester, and Sqn.Ldr.Tony Bartley,DFC and Bar, took an Anson into Brussels from Northolt. Third, Haynes says `*Now I began to worry !'*
Why had he not worried when Operations at Orly told him about the missing Norseman...?

MINUS ONE version :
Mon.Dec.18 **Told May Glenn and Col.B. left Twinwood in a UC64 at 13.45. General Barker's voice said `Where did they get clearance ?'so I said *Station 595* (Honington.Auth.) Morgan picked up Glenn and Col.Baessell at Twinwood. Gen. Barker said to fix up the Band, get out to SHAEF quickly. Meanwhile, he and May would start checking. Said I'd be with him about 18.00 (it was now 15.00).**

NOTE : There is an important conflict of detail here. Haynes in the fictional MINUS ONE reports to General Barker on Monday, telling May the Norseman story. In the factual LOC account he reports to Barker on Tuesday, after spending two days searching Paris for Glenn Miller ! Significantly, he fails to enquire at Operations or Air Traffic Control about a search for the Norseman. Further, he sticks stubbornly to his `Honington' tale which indicates that he never learned about Morgan's Service Records.

LOC Version :
Mon.Dec.18 **Buses arrived.I took Band to billet,reported to Billeting Officer.No word yet from Glenn.Called Hotel des Etats**

Unis, also Major May at SHAEF.He suggested waiting until tomorrow - `Glenn will no doubt be here then.' Went to Ritz, saw concierge Max (Col.B's buddy). Hadn't seen him since November. Dined Hotel Crillon (Officers Club.Auth.) **went to bed, couldn't sleep.**

NOTE : Haynes clearly assumed that Glenn had arrived safely in Paris and was out of touch. Why would May say that `*Glenn will be here tomorrow*', if Don Haynes told him Morgan was probably down in the Channel ?

MINUS ONE Version :
Mon.Dec.18   Tried to locate Baessell, called Max, concierge at Ritz. Hadn't seen Glenn since November.Maitre D' at Raphael said same thing. Billeting Officer at Seine Base said neither Glenn nor B. had checked in.Called Lt.Jerowski,Special Services : he had not heard from Glenn.*I was sure he hadn't arrived in Paris.* Checked Band into billet, got to SHAEF at 18.00.May & Barker had been checking bases in UK and Continent.They found a rather startling fact - *a single-motor ship had been charted out froma southerly point heading in the general direction of Paris, unreported crossing the French Coast.*

NOTE : Some remarkable entries. The Norseman had been missing 5 days but Haynes does not connect it with the `overdue single-motor ship'. From Dymchurch, Morgan would be on a south-easterly course for Cap Gris Nez and not due south for Paris. And Haynes checks with Lt.Jerowski, Special Services - but not with his boss Lt. Col. David Niven...

MINUS ONE Version :
Mon.Cont.   Suggested Barker called Goodrich; I was listening on the extension. Barker asked Goodrich if Col.Baessell was there : the General blasted, saying Baessell flew to Paris Friday, was due back Sunday. Barker told him the situation, that I was on the extension. I augmented the information. Goodrich was furious, learning they had taken a Norseman which had no de-icing gear. Icing conditions were prevalent,temperature at Twinwood on Friday was 34 deg F, even colder over the Channel. Morgan should not have taken a C64 in such weather. General Goodrich said he'd organise a search at daybreak, but he thought they'd iced up, gone into the Channel. Barker hung up, said "It

looks bad. I am afraid Major Miller has had it."

NOTE : An absorbing entry. Goodrich was a dying man,unlikely to `blast' at anyone. How could he quote correctly, during an unexpected call from Paris, the ground temperature at Twinwood (one of scores of bases in the area) - and know icing conditions were prevalent,when confined permanently to bed with less than two weeks to live ? (The quoted temperature figure of 34 degrees F was true - on November 8,and also on December 15 ! See Fig.39). Clearly, Haynes was setting the scene for a possible explanation: in the LOC version, he describes Miller getting out of the car at Twinwood Tower,reading the temperature on the external thermometer - 34 F ! He was using Goodrich as a ventriloquist's dummy....Further,according to Haynes himself, Baessell stopped for a last-minute briefing from Goodrich, saying he was returning on Sunday. This was true for the November 8 flight, when Goodrich was still well enough to handle his duties, but not on December 15, when Colonel Early had taken over the day to day running of the Headquarters. But even had Baessell visited Goodrich on December 15, it it possible he would not tell the General that they were using Morgan's Norseman and carrying Glenn Miller as a passenger ? He was, after all, a VIP.
The more probable explanation is that when 8th AFSC was advised Saturday morning the Norseman was overdue, probably down in the Channel, Goodrich ordered Col.Early to initiate his own local inquiry, as did Captain Ralph S.Cramer at Abbotts Ripton.

LOC Version :
Tue.Dec 19 Up early,called Major May. No word of Glenn. Went to SHAEF at 18.00, told Barker the whole story and suggested we called Gen.Goodrich. I spoke to him - very weak,a bad connection or his weak voice. Said he hadn't heard from B., due back Sunday. He would have Air Ministry check all UK fields, and we should do the same. Dudley and I searched all Col. B's old haunts, no results.

NOTE : Here is the real truth. It is Tuesday evening before Haynes tells Barker the Norseman story. Goodrich, predictably, is weak, a sick man. There is no blasting, or talk of icing conditions or ground temperatures, or that he did not know Morgan and Baessell were in a Norseman. We begin to get an inkling of what happened at SHAEF. Haynes told General Barker that Miller came over to Paris on Thursday December 14 and was out of touch. Haynes had been searching for 2 days. Barker brought in the CID and Provost Marshals and a covert search began.While Haynes was at SHAEF, they learned that a Norseman was listed as missing on Friday, and had been seen crossing the coast at Dymchurch. And at that point, the penny dropped. If Glenn Miller never turned up, an explanation was vital - and the Norseman story was born. General Barker called Goodrich at 8th AFSC. But now see how Haynes develops the story in MINUS ONE...

MINUS ONE Version :
Tue.Dec 19 Up at dawn, called May, nothing new. Got car, went to SHAEF,lunch with Major May. He had talked to UK three times and would have reports soon. He asked me to stay to verify the take-off time. Four full days have passed since I saw them off at Twinwood. No trace of that plane since it went over the coast heading for France. In the narrow England-France corridor which was 90 miles, all over water, the German-held positions prevented Morgan from going short route.

NOTE : Subterfuge upon subterfuge. Haynes gives Morgan's time of take-off in both diaries as 13.45 - yet ATC would advise May that he left Abbotts Ripton at 13.25, as confirmed by documents in the Burial Files. So Haynes, we suspect, added an arbitrary 20 minutes to include the Twinwood landing. But with the overcast he said existed, Morgan could not have taken off,flown the 30 miles to Twinwood, come down through cloud without a radio contact, landed, taken on passengers and taken off again, all in 20 minutes ! The experienced Major May knew this was unrealistic and had to be amended. So he added a further 10 minutes, making the take-off time 13.55, telephoning 8th AFSC to insert that time in the MACR at Abbotts Ripton. Early next morning, Colonel Early telephoned Capt. Cramer at 2 SAD, Abbotts Ripton, and gave him the corrected time for the MACR. This,of course,was not to be compiled until so advised by SHAEF through 8th AFSC.
This sequence of events tells us something of vital importance : first, there is no other way that Capt.Cramer could have obtained the take-off time from Twinwood Farm - the base had been closed to all flying, and no Norseman had landed or taken off. Second, it confirms indisputably that Major May knew the Norseman story was false - and we cannot avoid the conclusion that General Barker must also have known. Note Haynes' reticence to connect `that plane' with Morgan's Norseman,even at that stage. Mention of the a 90-mile crossing and non-existent German enclaves was intended to add authenticity to the tale, but the ploy back-fired. There is no reference to these things at all in the corresponding factual LOC version.

LOC Version :
Wed Dec 20 Up at dawn, too early for May - called later. They had heard nothing. Lacking any clues by this time tomorr-ow Glenn would have to go on the Casualty Report. General Barker will wait one more day. This means

> **Helen will receive a telegram `Glenn missing in flight'.
> No way to get news back home except by letter - too
> slow.**

NOTE : `Glenn would have to go on Casualty List' - but why not
Baessell and Morgan ? They were 8th AF personnel but Miller was
Special Services, SHAEF. Also, Haynes confirms that General Barker
deliberately delayed the reporting procedures.

MINUS ONE Version :
Wed.Cont. **Called May.Barker has given up all hope of finding
Glenn, Morgan and Col.B. Only hope newspapers will
carry complete story - that Band personnel landed
safely. First concert in Palais de Glace tomorrow.Build-
ing v.cold. Jerry Gray will conduct first 2/3rds of
program,Ray McKinley the rest. One more call to May,
talked him into deferring the Casualty Report one
more day.**

NOTE : Here is the link with the PR Division Memo (Fig.41). What else
did Haynes tell Col. Dupuy ? Note how he assumes credit for delaying
the Casualty Report.

4. **CONCLUSIONS.**

Reading these entries, one cannot avoid the conclusion that SHAEF
and Haynes knew Glenn Miller had arrived safely in Paris before the
Norseman was reported missing. The slant of the narrative is to substantiate the story that he was a passenger, that the aircraft had iced up and
ditched in the English Channel because it had no de-icing equipment. It
is never specifically identified with the `missing single-engined aircraft'
but the inference is there. Haynes explains the two-day delay in calling
Goodrich by stating that he reported to Gen.Barker on Monday
(MINUS ONE) and not Tuesday (LOC). He seeks to authenticate his
phoney `Honington' story by advising Barker that Flight Officer Morgan
cleared from there. There is an intransigent problem with the Twinwood
Farm take-off time Haynes quotes, but Major May solves it neatly.
But the basic problem was that Glenn, by Tuesday evening, had been
missing five full days. In all probability, it would take Don Haynes no
more than an hour on Monday afternoon to confirm that Glenn had not
booked into any known hotel or Club. It is difficult to believe that
Haynes had not telephoned or sent a teleprinter message to Miller
during the weekend advising of the Band flight delay : he would know
precisely where Miller was planning to stay that weekend. Glenn, he
said, had a `social engagement' in Paris on Friday (December 15), and
had decided to fly over on Thursday.It would be natural,indeed obligato-

ry, for Miller to advise his second in command where he could be reached that weekend. And of course the fact that Haynes never mentions this `engagement' again, and does not divulge any details of Glenn's hosts or location suggests that the whole thing was a figment of Haynes' imagination, introduced to support his fictitious story.

Further, Haynes would establish perhaps as early as Saturday noon, that the Major was out of touch. In retrospect, we believe that Haynes made contact with General Barker immediately on landing at Orly after finding that Glenn was not there, and the covert search probably began that same day. Why, therefore, the two-day delay in calling Barker ?

We return inevitably to the conclusion previously outlined : for SHAEF, the situation was fraught with risk. The covert search for Miller had found nothing, and there were now only a few options. One, Miller was simply out of touch, enjoying a break after six months of hard work. He would rely on Haynes taking care of administrative matters; he need not appear in person until the first concert in the *Palais de Glace* on Thursday December 21. Two - he may have been involved in an accident and was physically incapable of making contact. But this option geneated more questions than it answered. Three, he may have been the victim of foul play - but where ? And why ?

+   +   +

The plan Barker evolved on Tuesday was simple. They would wait until Thursday night, suspending standard reporting procedures. If Glenn turned up, there was no problem. If he didn't, they could still extend the delay period, by making no official announcement at the Thursday concert, other than that `*Major Miller cannot be present this evening*' Two concerts were planned for Friday and Saturday, December 22 and 23 - and they could not continue to gloss over Major Miller's continued absence. The obvious solution was to cancel both performances, and Barker announced the reason : the black-out, and the danger that Colonel Otto Skorzeny's cloak-and-dagger American-speaking saboteurs might ambush and kill Band members !

But on Sunday December 24, a radio broadcast to America was scheduled, setting an effective deadline on releasing the news. Even so, Generals Barker and Davis kept their options open by delaying the Release until 1 hour before the radio broadcast from the Olympia Theatre. All this could be (and probably was) pre-planned on Tuesday.

How do we know this ?

By Tuesday evening, they all knew the Norseman was missing, probably down in the Channel. Indeed,Haynes introduced the proposition himself. During Tuesday, the Twinwood Farm story developed,using the conveniently-timed Norseman loss.SHAEF dared not release that story just yet - not as long as there was a chance that Miller might return. If he did so after the story was released, SHAEF would lose all credibility and would face many searching questions.

But it was essential that something should be on record, to confirm that SHAEF had been informed at an early stage that Miller was on board the missing plane. Yet that record, for obvious reasons, could not be revealed ! Suppose the C64 was found, *after* the Norseman story was released, but with no evidence that Miller was aboard ? The repercussions would be colossal.

It was a situation that required exquisite timing, with a need to keep everything under wraps : hence the covert but extensive search of Paris for Miller,and the apparent failure to initiate an immediate official investigation which mystified researchers for almost half a century. Hence the telephone calls to General Goodrich outlining the Haynes story, the instruction to signal back written confirmation to General Barker (Fig.46) and the suppression of the Confirmatory Signal until 1948.

The really puzzling factor is the omission in the Haynes diaries of any reference to Lt.Col.David Niven,Director of Troop Broadcasting at Special Services, SHAEF - the man who had chaired the November 15 conference approving the Band concert tour in Paris, who had arranged the concert program and laid on suitable transmitters. Haynes contacted Lt.Jerowski at Special Services - why not Niven ? More important, why did David Niven omit from his books all references to his close association with the AAF Band, from the day it arrived in UK ?

This aspect of the case merited further investigation, the results of which are described in a later chapter. But the evidence thus far accumulated from the Miller File, the diaries and other documents in circulation appears to confirm that the Don Haynes story was fabricated from start to finish, that the coincident loss of the Norseman was used as a cover-up to conceal the fact that no one in Paris in 1944 what had happened to Miller after he stepped down from the shuttle Dakota at Orly on Thursday December 14.

But why had Haynes lied ? Certainly not for any reasons of personal gain : unsure what had happened to his boss and friend, but fearing the worst, he either invented the story and made Barker believe him, or collaborated with Barker in formulating it, or cooperated when Barker proposed the plan. We cannot be sure which was the case, but Haynes kept his part of the agreement scrupulously.He was never interviewed or interrogated, and published nothing in writing while he was alive.There is no doubt he could have become a rich man by revealing the truth, but he kept the faith. Indeed, the patent loyalty of the man shines through his narrative like the glare of a Shuttle booster rocket.He did what had to be done at the time, loyally and uncomplainingly, and if we all had friends of such calibre, we would count ourselves lucky. Haynes did nothing with which he could reproach himself : he obeyed orders like a good soldier to the very end.

+ + +

FOUR

THE UC64A NOORDUYN NORSEMAN

1. HISTORY AND DESCRIPTION (Fig.1,App.'B')

The UC64 Norseman was a high-wing single-engined monoplane passenger/cargo aircraft manufactured by Noorduyn Aviation Company Inc.,Montreal, Canada. Its Pratt and Whitney Wasp R-1340-AN1 radial aircooled engine powered by a 2 or 3-blade Hamilton-Standard Constant Speed Propeller directly from the crankshaft without a reduction gear. (The Constant-Speed device maintained engine RPM at a level set by a cockpit lever,avoiding an increase in the RPM in a descent and vice versa). The engine produced 550hp at 5,000 feet, with 600hp available for take-off. The gravity-fed wingroot fuel tanks held 240 US gallons, while extra under-floor tanks provided a further 150 gallons,giving the aircraft a still-air range of 1150 miles on full tanks. The enclosed cockpit contained side-by-side seats for a pilot and copilot, with dual controls. Behind the seats was a full-width bulkhead with access to a cabin accommodating eight passengers in bench-type seats along each side. Aft of the cabin,another bulkhead formed a rear baggage compartment in which the lifejackets and life-raft were stored. The metal tubular structure and wood formers were covered by doped fabric; wing leading edges were metal-covered. The standard de-icing equipment included a heated Pitot Head (airspeed sensor) and carburettor heating by means of engine hot oil circulating round a jacket. It was possible to fit wing de-icers, inflatable rubber bags on leading edges to dislodge ice as it formed,but 44-70285 was not so equipped. No standard navigational equipment other than radio was fitted to 70285, but directional beam loop equipment could be installed, working on ground beacons. The C64A carried an SCR-274N radio with 3 receivers and 2 transmitters working on pre-set frequencies, and was not equipped with an SCR 595 (Identification Friend or Foe) used by combat aircraft. The radio had poor range except at altitude, with a maximum 25 miles at 1,000 feet. At maximum load the C64A cruised slowly, between 100/110 IAS, but could carry a useful load of 2,692 pounds. It had a low stall speed of 55 mph.

2. PILOTS AND PASSENGERS

George Ferguson related that 4 UC64As were delivered to 44 Strategic Air Depot Wattisham in June 1944. When he was detached to Brussels, George took one with him; two of the others remained at Wattisham while the fourth was assigned in September to 35 ADRS, Abbotts Ripton with the pilot who would fly the last fatal mission, Flight Officer John R.S. Morgan. The aircraft were general workhorses, carrying spare parts, personnel and ferry crews; the prefix '44' indicated the year of manufacture, and the new aircraft had virtually zero flight time when delivered.

Norseman pilot Ferguson had already met Col.Baessell. He completed his flight training at Turner Field,Albany Ga. in April 1943 and was assigned to the 22nd Air Base Group, New Orleans; Baessell was his Commanding Officer. The Colonel, George recalls, was a braggadocio, a very loud individual. `*You could hear him blocks away'*. Very career-conscious, he was impatient, often irrational - an aggressive pugnacious officer who disliked to be proven wrong. He was a `ground- hog' staff officer, not a pilot, and he gave Ferguson and his fellow-pilots plenty of trouble. George was unsure of his background but thought he came from a plantation-owning or managing family. He was a racial bigot with a loud voice, who carried a big stick and never hesitated to use it on black workers. Something of a snob,too : when negro trumpeter Louis Armstrong played at Baessell's home, he was treated like a white man, but outside he was just one more of the blacks. Ferguson described Col. Baessell as a stocky individual, 69 or 70 inches in height and in good physical condition. He was what we know today as a male chauvinist: at 8th AFSC he was placed in charge of a unit of female WAACs and tried in all ways to evade the duty.*"Who the hell,"*he said to Ferguson, *"wants a unit that goes on sick call every month ?"*

George was assigned to 44 Air Depot Group,Mobile Ala.in July 1943, and went overseas with them to R.A.F. Wattisham in Suffolk (Fig.10).He was a rated pilot responsible for testing newly repaired aircraft,mostly fighters such as the P38 Lightning and P51 Mustang. Wattisham was an 8th AFSC base depot under General Goodrich. Lt.Col. Norman F.Baessell, the General's Special Assistant at Milton Ernest, was responsible for the location and setting up of Advanced Repair Depots on the Continent which would service damaged aircraft, instead of returning them to UK bases. Ferguson was in charge of the Mobile Repair Teams which serviced aircraft in the field, and ferried Baessell to the Continent several times before going to Brussels in September 1944. Their relationship was impersonal : the Colonel never asked to take over the controls, or interfered with the flying. Yet Ferguson had constant problems arising from Baessell's foolhardiness : on one occasion they spent the day at a rear USAAF base and Baessell ignored all pleas to leave because the weather was closing in.Ferguson had to fly back under a 100 foot cloudbase, following rail lines and finally a tramcar to get into his base at Everes. On another occasion they were flying north from Brussels to Antwerp and ran into the huge Arnhem air invasion fleet. But rather than order George to retreat, Baes-sell had him follow them up into the combat zone ! They narrowly escaped being shot down. No professional pilot could tolerate such interference; George requested the Wattisham Base Commander Col. Howard A. Moody to relieve him of the Baessell duty.

His application was approved, he was detached to Brussels and Lt.Jean Pace was assigned to the mission.

Meanwhile, Col.Baessell had been attached to 44 SAD Wattisham as `Deputy Dog' (Deputy Base Commander) and Moody was not amused. Baessell, he confided to Ferguson, was `something of a horse's ass...'. But Pace fared no better : en route to Paris with Col.Baessell, 70285 developed a severe propeller hydraulic leak and the flight was aborted. Baessell, predictably, was furious and back at Wattisham Pace too requested to be relieved. The Norseman and its new pilot John Morgan were sent to Abbotts Ripton.

These events all have a curious connection with the last tragic flight of 70285. Morgan, George Ferguson says, was a quiet and unassertive non-commissioned pilot with limited flying experience, five ranks junior to Baessell, and while Ferguson and Pace as officers could and did protest about Col.Baessell's recklessness,Morgan could only grin, bear it and obey. It seems extremely possible that, faced with a bad situation in marginal weather where the Colonel demanded that they pressed on regardless of risk, Morgan would almost certainly acquiesce and obey orders.

3. **BAESSELL AND THE BLACK MARKET.**

Controversy has always raged on this point. Numerous reliable witnesses confirm that Col. Baessell spent money in London and Paris as if it was going out of fashion, thinking nothing of buying drinks for the house in restaurants and nightclubs. He may, of course, have been a wealthy man in his own right, and he earned generous pay and allowances, some of which he sent home to his wife Amanda in St.Asaph St,Alexandria,Va. His brother Karl lived in the same town. Baessell was born August 2 1900, and was almost the same age as Glenn Miller. He entered the Army on May 18 1942, and his rank and status as a Lt.Colonel and Unit Commander at New Orleans, as well as his serial number, indicate that he was a reserve regular career officer.

When asked about Col.Baessell's black market connections, George W. Ferguson was not prepared to commit himself, and there is no sound evidence to support the rumours. George related that when he flew Baessell to Paris, the latter invariably took along several large plain crates of what he said were cigarettes `for some units with supply problems'. Curiously, they were always the same brand in sealed cases; they were loaded into the jeep which somehow was always waiting for them, and Col.Baessell would drive off happily alone, after arranging a rendezvous for the return flight.

We could find no concrete evidence of black market activities, but we did stumble on one curious fact. In France in 1944,there had been an endemic shortage of drugs for four long years, but because of a lack of consumer goods, money was plentiful.A set of bicycle tyres and tubes,for example, would attract the present-day value of £400. There was, not surprisingly, a huge demand for morphine ampoules at any price the vendor liked to name. We learned that the Troston 8th AFSC depot at R.A.F.Honington, among others, stored vast quantities of ampoules for the first aid kits fitted in all aircraft. Honington, of course,was the `Station 595' quoted by Haynes in his diaries, and we know that Morgan was there on November 8 when he received Baessell's orders to come to Twinwood Farm and pick up the Colonel and Glenn Miller.

If,as a matter of speculation, Baessell's `crates of cigarettes' contained morphine ampoules, there would be very big money involved : one crate could carry drugs with a wartime street value of at least 250,000 dollars. It may have been sheer coincidence that Morgan was at Troston, of all depots in 8th AFSC, but we found the connection disturbing.

4. **FLIGHT OFFICER JOHN R.S.MORGAN (Fig.3).**

Until we commenced this investigation, the pilot John Morgan was a shadowy figure in the background, of whom little was known; when John Edwards tried to obtain his personal file from National Personnel Records Center, St.Louis Mo. in 1973, he was advised that `*the files... may have been lost in the fire...*' But we began to accumulate details of his history, and the pattern which emerged was fascinating. John Robert Stuart Morgan was born in Hamilton, Scotland,on June 14 1922 and shortly afterwards his family emigrated to America and settled in Detroit,Michigan. In 1942,at the age of 20, Morgan travelled north to enlist in the Royal Canadian Air Force as a trainee pilot. We know little of his family life : we traced his sister, who regretted she could not help us, since she was already assisting another researcher in America. But in the three years which have elapsed,no book has appeared.

But certain documents came to our attention, including two specimens which had been apparently abstracted from Morgan's Burial File, since they were not included in the copy sent to us. They were his Service Record Card from Abbotts Ripton (Fig.27) and two pages from his Form 5 (Record of Flight Times) for the two vital months, November and December 1944. The last items were sent by a National Archives employee who wished to remain anonymous.

Morgan's Service record shows :

1942
Apr - Jul No. 3 E.F.T.S. London, Ontario, Canada.
Jul - Nov No.16 S.F.T.S. Haggersville, Canada.

1943
Feb - Mar No. 9 E.F.T.S. Anstey, Leicestershire, England.
Mar - May No.14 A.F.U. Ossington, Yorkshire,England.

MILLERGATE

Morgan transferred to the US Army Air Force on May 23 1943.

1943
May - Jun Beam Approach Training Course.
Jun - Aug 27 Group, 87 Ferry Command Sqdn. Heston, Middlesex.

1944
Aug - Sep 44 Strategic Air Depot, Wattisham, Suffolk.
Sep - Dec 35 ADRS Abbotts Ripton, Alconbury, Huntingdon .

At the time of his death on December 15, Morgan had flown rather less than 600 hours *in toto* : by April 1944 his total time in the air was 481 hours. During ferrying and similar duties, he flew the Airspeed Oxford, D.H. Tiger Moth, Cessna, P38 Lightning and the Percival Proctor. Ferguson suggests that he may also have flown B17s on test occasionally at Wattisham. Morgan was non-commissioned, a Flight Officer who was permitted to use the Officers Club; on the operational squadrons Flight Officers were usually commissioned as 2nd Lieutenants after completing 8 or 9 operations, but in his non-combat status Morgan could not hope for that. He never flew on operations.

Ferguson describes him :

`Sort of a dapper little guy, five feet six or seven. He wore lifts in his boots. About 135 pounds, black hair. A quiet type who got boisterous at times singing raucous songs in the Club, but he had to be cajoled into it. We had already checked him out in the Oxford and Proctor... He was a good VFR (clear weather) pilot, but a lousy instrument pilot. I flew with him in the Oxford to a base in Wales, mostly in thick cloud; he got into a steep spiral dive, recovering with great difficulty close to a dangerous barrage-balloon concentration'.*

When Morgan came to Abbotts Ripton in September 1944, his Primary T/O (Table of Organisation) mission was Assistant Engineer Officer, working as Assistant Flight Test and Flight Line Officer, but his principal duties involved flying spare parts and personnel in any available aircraft, and he was not (as some writers state) General Goodrich's personal pilot. He was the appointed pilot of Norseman 70285 but flew other aircraft too. His Forms 5 confirm he flew it seven times in November and twice in December 1944 (see P.67). He was clearly not in good flying practice on December 15 - two weeks had passed since he last flew on December 2, returning from Paris with Baessell. But the December 15 weather was reasonable, once the early morning fog had cleared; there was a 3000 foot cloudbase, visibility about 1.5 miles, light southerly winds and there was no rain. The forecast weather to the south was not too good, with cloudbase reducing to 800 feet over the Channel with 100% overcast and poor visibility. Researchers pondered on how the inexperienced Morgan obtained clearance to fly in such marginal conditions : either he did not wait for clearance, or Baessell cleared the flight direct to France on the telephone to R.A.F.Bovingdon.

5. **THE NORSEMAN ROUTE**

Controversy has raged for four decades around the route taken by Morgan in the Norseman, but we submit respectfully that the evidence we discovered in the Burial Files in 1988 settles the issue beyond doubt. Before the Canadians freed Dieppe on September 1 1944, the mandatory route for scheduled flights was via Bovingdon (for clearance) Guildford to Beachy Head and St.Valery (see Fig.51), avoiding Dieppe. But after the town was liberated, all scheduled flights could go directly from Beachy Head to Paris, overflying Dieppe. That track was some 10 miles west of the Emergency Bomb Jettison Area due south of Eastbourne, involving a 65-mile crossing.

After September 1 1944, the remaining German enclave was at Dunkirk, well clear of the main cross-Channel routes. This made nonsense of Don Haynes' diary account of a `90-mile' crossing. Operations involving non-scheduled flights such as the Norseman were not subject to route controls like scheduled flights. George Ferguson and Jean Pace affirm that the 65-mile crossing was considered unsafe for the single-engined C64, especially in wintertime when survival in an icy sea was measured in minutes, not hours. When filing a flight plan and obtaining clearance, they would insert their route from Abbots Ripton - Bovingdon - Paris, but the specific route to be followed between those points was left to their own discretion. If they had to land at Bovingdon to submit a flight plan and obtain clearance, they would follow a route south to Guildford, along the rail lines to Ashford and Hythe and crossing the coast at Dymchurch, en route to Cap Gris Nez (Fig.50).

This reduced the sea crossing to about 35 miles. If cloud was low on the Cap Gris Nez headland, they would fly south a few miles offshore towards Boulogne/Le Touquet, looking for a good spot to penetrate inland under cloud. Remarkably, almost every researcher in the past has assumed that Morgan went from Abbotts Ripton (or Twinwood Farm if he believes Haynes' story) overflying Bovingdon and south to Beachy Head-Dieppe-Paris. Mr.Roy Nesbitt, in an excellent article in `*THE AEROPLANE'* magazine about the Fred Shaw story of seeing a Norseman destroyed by jettisoned bombs, assumed that Morgan took the westerly route around London. He did not have, of course, the benefit of evidence found in the Burial Files. But reason suggests otherwise : there was no sign of wreckage along that route, and we have shown that the ATC assistant Dixie Clerke, like George Ferguson, confused dates. Morgan landed at Bovingdon to drop Miller on November 8, not December 15.

There have been some unsubstantiated rumours of debris located in the

Chiltern Hills, but no concrete evidence.

The primary reason most researchers opted for the westerly route was a Danger Area in the Thames Estuary (Fig.51) called the `Diver Gun Box', a prohibited area in which very concentrated AA batteries were deployed against the V1 flying bombs. This would have been an effective barrier against Continent-bound flights from north of London, but research produced some relevant facts. With the Allied advance overrunning the V1 sites along the French coast,the AA guns along the South Coast were redeployed around the Thames Estuary after September 1944, to handle buzz-bombs launched from Northern Holland or Heinkel 111 bombers over the North Sea. `Diver' was a code name for the V1s, and the Gun Box had two operational modes : active and inactive.The current state of the Gun Box was displayed in all Crew Rooms,Operations Rooms and ATC towers in NOTAMS (Notices to Airmen); a pilot planning his route to France would avoid the easterly route around London if the Box was `active'. There was nothing, however, to stop him flying through the area if it was inactive, and official records confirm that the Gun Box was indeed inactive throughout December 15 1944 : no V1 activity was reported.

Indeed, the force of 137 Lancasters from East Anglia flew through the Gun Box about noon the same day, bound for Tunbridge Wells,Beachy Head and Siegen. Here is the evidence confirming Morgan took the easterly route direct, Abbotts Ripton-Dymchurch-Cap Gris Nez (Fig.54) :

* He was cleared directly from Alconbury (Abbotts Ripton) to B42 Beauvais. Evidence : his Service Record Card, and Col.Donnell's letter to Helen Miller (Fig.32).

* The weather was fair initially, cloudbase 3000 feet,visibility 1.5 miles,no rain or icing conditions. He could fly `contact' (in sight of the ground).

* He did not land at Twinwood Farm.Evidence : three serving R.A.F. personnel confirm no Norseman landed that day. The Twinwood Form 540 Daily History states the airfield was closed. Haynes' evidence is flawed in relation to weather, take-off time, departure and destination airfields, flight times etc. and was based on the November 8 flight. The `original' MACR (with a single reference to **`Twinwood'** was not signed by the Adjutant Ralph Cramer, and MACR 10770 has been proven to be a fraudulent document.

* He could have departed from no other base but Abbotts Ripton. Evidence : Firstly, his Form 5 (Record of Flight Times) which show no positioning flight to Honington or Heston,and secondly his Service Record Card, which does not mention a landing at Twinwood Farm.

83

*   Flight time from Abbotts Ripton to Beauvais, overflying Bovingdon and depending on the route selected, was as follows :

Bovingdon/Guildford/Beachy Head/Beauvais	2hr.30m.
Same route + 1 hr flight plan/clearance Bovingdon	3hr.30m.
Bovingdon/Guildford/Cap Gris Nez/Beauvais	3hr.30m.

and

Abbotts Ripton/Dymchurch/Beauvais direct	2hr.10m.

Dusk at Paris and at Beauvais was 16.22 hours. With the known Norseman take-off time from Abbotts Ripton of 13.25, John Morgan could not have reached Beauvais before darkness fell taking any route west of London which would involve landing at Bovingdon for clearance, or over-flying Bovingdon along the `iron compass' railway. Further, if he had landed at Bovingdon as stated, no Operations Officer would have cleared an inexperienced pilot on a night flight in marginal weather over water. There was only one feasible route to reach Beauvais before dusk : direct from Abbotts Ripton, given telephone clearance from Bovingdon.

*   A single-engined aircraft was reported heading out to sea from Dymchurch at a time consistent with a take-off time of 13.25 from Abbotts Ripton. It was at such low altitude that it was reported to the local Observer Corps. The sighting reached General Barker at SHAEF on Monday December 18 1944.

*   The `Diver' Gun Box was inactive. Other aircraft, including the 137 Lancasters, flew through the Box at noon December 15.

*   At approximately 14.40,using the direct route east of London from Abbotts Ripton to Dymchurch, Morgan would have been several miles out to sea off Le Touquet (the 800 ft cloudbase would lie low on the Cap Gris Nez headland). In 1980 survey-vessel owner Clive Ward located a C64 Norseman, almost complete, 6 miles west of Le Touquet.

*   We identified 8 additional Norseman aircraft notified as `missing' in the ETO in 1944. By a process of elimination, the Clive Ward aircraft can only be 44-70285.

*   George W. Ferguson and Jean Pace, surviving pilots of the same aircraft on similar missions, confirm they never flew the Beachy

Head-Dieppe-Paris route. George (a rated pilot) checked out John Morgan in the C64, and advised him on the best route to follow.

The map below illustrates three routes relevant to the inquiry.

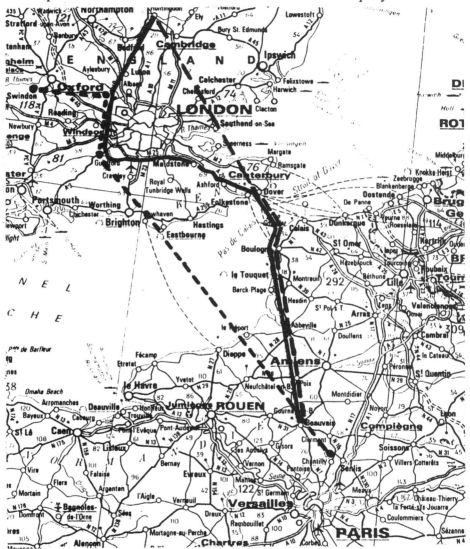

▪ ▪ ▪ Route of 43-5367 on December 15 (Grove/Bovingdon/Creil).

▬▬▬ Morgan's westerly route overflying Bovingdon.

▬ ▬ Morgan's true easterly route direct to B42 Beauvais.

6. **THE `BORDEAUX SEARCH' LETTER (Fig.33,P.57)**

This extraordinary document was found in the Miller File in 1988, and the date June 21 1946 is significant.It will be recalled that Helen Miller's letters to the AG Department in January 1946 (following the issue of a `Finding of Death' document on December 16 1945) triggered off an investigation by USFET (US Forces,European Theater) and USAFE (US Air Forces Europe). Col.Donnell replied on February 6 1946,suppressing some vital information, and fabrication of MACR 10770 was implemented at Maxwell AFB, Alabama, using the `ORIGINAL' MACR N-19 as a template. The falsified Report was declassified on March 26 1946 and released in 1948. The `Bordeaux Search' letter was written 3 weeks later, in response to previous correspondence, and it seems certain that this search was a part of the USAFE/USFET investigation. The text is intriguing. Seemingly, a crashed aircraft had been spotted in the Bordeaux area. Bodies too had been seen and we can assume it was a sighting from another aircraft. It was clearly linked with the missing Norseman, since the letter was in the Miller File. We were unable to trace the foregoing ccorrespondence, but this letter raises some pertinent questions.

First, if this was the Norseman, had Morgan flown directly from Abbotts Ripton towards Bordeaux ? Or had he landed at Beauvais long enough to drop a passenger before pressing on to Bordeaux, risking a night landing ? Would the Bordeaux- Merignac airfield have been open for night landings ? How did this theory fit in with his official operation orders in his Record Card (Fig.27) ? The Card is somewhat ambiguous : `*TD (Temporary Duty) Bordeaux France B42...'* It is a fact that some researchers believed `B42' was Bordeaux, but we identified Beauvais. Bordeaux, in fact, was Y37, signifying a non-operational airfield unused by combat units. In the following Card entry,doubt is removed : `*...ferrying flight over English Channel en Bordeaux'.* A flight time of 5hr.15m would involve a night landing about 7pm.An anticyclonic trough covered all of France (Fig.40) with a high risk of fog after dark; deteriorating cloudbase would force Morgan to fly ever lower, or to enter cloud and fly on his instruments. The possibility of a direct flight seems remote in the extreme - the critical factor was the facilities at Bordeaux, by way of rescue vehicles, a flare path, radio and direction-finding equipment.

But why was Baessell going to Bordeaux anyway ? His main duty was the establishment of Advance Repair bases; before June 1944, all 8th AF replacement aircraft were flown via a northerly route through Labrador, Greenland, Iceland to bases like Prestwick in Scotland. Winter weather made that route hazardous, and the possibility of a southern route was quite attractive.

What do we know about Bordeaux in December 1944 ?

Fortunately we located R.A.F. Sqd.Ldr. Tony Bartley, DFC and Bar, a

Battle of Britain ace who was ordered to fly a C47 Dakota into Bordeaux-Merignac with Lt. Tony Pulitzer on December 10 to assess the field's potential as a Staging Post for Allied aircraft. It was occupied by Free French troops, and after a day of tight negotiation and a payment of $2000 for essential equipment, the pilots left for London on Tuesday December 11.

On Wednesday afternoon, they met Glenn Miller, Haynes and Morgan in the Milroy Club in Mayfair. But at Bordeaux,the Free French had only 3 days to bring the field up to operational standard, assuming that they could buy the necessary equipment. We believe that Baessell's mission was to inspect Bordeaux, check the equipment needed to make the field available as an 8th Air Force Staging Post on the United States-Azores-France-UK delivery route. There was no time to equip the airfield to an acceptable standard : if he was heading direct for the west coast airfield, Morgan faced a night landing in bad weather on an airfield lacking basic aids like radio and landing lights.

Returning to the `Search' Letter, the writer of the letter is asking not `if' an aircraft had crashed, but for additional information on the location. The search, clearly, had been in progress for some time; the Bordeaux area was heavily wooded and underpopulated at the time. Bodies had been seen : the writer does not say : `In order to locate "any" bodies'.. he says `the' *bodies'*.

Strangely, there is a letter in the Miller File referring to the Bordeaux Search Letter. It is from HQ American Graves Registration Command in Europe, written to the Non-Recoverability Board of Officers convened in America in June 1947, written by a Major W.B.Morrow in charge of Isolated Burials,Europe. He gives a short synopsis of the circumstances of Miller's disappearance - yet oddly omits any reference to Bordeaux ! The text of his letter is startling :

> `*The C64... departed England en route to Paris, France. The pilot took off from Abbotts Ripton, England and stopped at Twinwood Farm where he picked up the other two men as passengers...Reference is made to the 2nd Indorsement from 3046 GRS,* (the Bordeaux Search Letter) *and the letter to Mrs.Miller dated 6 February 1946'.*

The Bordeaux letter is the only document we ever located which contained the statement that Colonel Baessell was picked up at Twinwood, and we found that quite extraordinary. Further, the writer was a middle-rank officer, a Major in charge of Isolated Burials in Europe,two full years after Glenn Miller vanished, reporting to an investigatory Board in the USA.

Yet he is in possession of information not found in any other document (Baessell's boarding) and some items found only in MACRs - one of which was suppressed, unsigned, and the other was falsified and under lock and key in the National Archives in Washington ! Major Morrow

87

also knew about the Bordeaux Search Letter, and the AG letter to Helen Miller - but that information was in America !

How did Major Morrow acquire this information which he included in a letter to the Investigating Board in America ? There is but one possible conclusion : it had been provided covertly by the Adjutant General's Department in Washington DC. No official document stated that Miller and Baessell boarded the Norseman at Twinwood Farm. The Confirmatory Signal simply states carefully that there were `two passengers including Major Glenn Miller' - but does not specify where they boarded the plane.

But this `priming mechanism' infers that the AG's Department was conspiring to deceive its own Board of Officers ! We would need firm corroboration of that scenario.

7. **THE SEARCH FOR THE NORSEMAN.**

Enigmas like the disappearance of Major Glenn Miller tend to attract the dedicated type of researcher who is prepared to spend weeks and years without reward patiently sifting through existing evidence and tracking down new information. People like Mrs.Connie Richards in Oakley village on the Twinwood Farm perimeter, whose father worked at the airfield; Connie, as a girl, often danced at the Milton Ernest Officers Club to the music of Glenn Miller and the AAF Band, and she knew several of the central characters in the mystery. People like Ken Perfect of the Glenn Miller Society, who interviewed, with John Edwards,the ex-WAAF Air Traffic Controller - the late Dixie Clerke. People like Dale Titler, American author and long-time investigator of aviation mysteries, and the father of them all, Canadian Henry Whiston who spent countless days and months delving into the Public Records Office Kew, and who reputedly took with him to the grave some incredible earth-shaking secret. And that other Canadian John Flowers, and the aviation historian Royal Frey - who interviewed Don Haynes and forgot to take along his tape recorder... Frey was one-time curator at the Wright-Paterson Air Force Museum, Ohio, and a personal friend of the Miller family in California. It was Frey who interviewed George Ferguson in Columbus Ohio in 1983. Mr. Roy Nesbitt, who has investigated many aviation mysteries including the disappearance of Amy Johnson during the war, wrote of the Fred Shaw story of Lancasters bombing a low-flying Norseman.

Michael Harrison in `VANISHINGS' (The New English Library 1981) comes up with a curious account in which `Basselle' is the pilot of the Norseman in which `Glen' Miller was a passenger; Miller had been `excused military service because of his age', and by `Friday December 13' (which was a Wednesday) he had completed enough recordings to give him `a sort of ubiquity amongst the troops'. Convinced he could make Orly despite the fog if he could take off at once, `Basselle' manages to convince Miller, takes off at once and is never seen again'. `*Certain oddities'*,Mr.Harrison goes on, `*began to creep into the Miller story'*. The distance to be covered was `*a mere 250 miles, little more than an hour's flying in the Norseman'*. (It cruised at 100 mph.) Miller's band arrived two days later on 17 December'(three days,in fact - the 18th).

Was the aircraft swallowed up by no ordinary fog - rather, by a more sinister `Cloud' described by Mr.Harrison ? We shall never know...

We obtained many audio tapes in the course of research. A narrative by bomb-jettisoning Lancaster navigator Mr.Fred Shaw, and another by the Milton Ernest valet, the late Alan Stilwell. We were given the Ferguson tape by Connie Richards, and there was a recording of Haynes being interviewed on a 1950s Andy Williams show in America. We have a hilarious recorded interview with musician Bernie Privin by the late Kenneth More. Privin claimed that he was at Twinwood Farm when the Norseman took off. We obtained a recording of the late General Dwight D.Eisenhower talking about Miller (but not about the time and date he heard that the Major was missing). We were fortunate to tape several interviews with the late Herb Miller in London, and we were among the few to attend his funeral in 1988. Ken Perfect's interview with Dixie Clerke reveals that she too confused her dates, like other witnesses.

The most fascinating tape is by Dennis Cottam, who found in Paris in 1954 a prostitute whose 1944 boyfriend, a Provost Marshal captain, claimed to have seen and identified Glenn Miller's body. The Cottam account is vague. One wonders why he failed to ask the woman her boyfriend's name and where he had seen the body, what was the cause of death and whether a doctor was present. Yet there is an odd ring of authenticity; Cottam had travelled to Paris in 1954 with a friend to pick up a car. Miller had stayed in the Hotel Scribe and used the Hotel Crillon Officers Club during his November conference visit; further, during his own November 30 visit, Don Haynes arranged for the Hotel des Olympiades in Montmartre to be used as the Band billet, and Miller knew this : the Hotel was not far from Fred's Bar.

In 1954, the barman said to Cottam : *"Isn't it odd ? You English have always believed Miller was lost in the Channel on December 15 1944. Yet he was in here drinking, that very same night !"* This was remarkable - but there was more. *"If,"* the barman continued, *"You walk up the other side of the street towards Sacre Coeur, you will see a house with a blue-painted door with brass studs. Speak to the lady there and she will tell you more."*

Dennis Cottam obeyed but the lady, in fact, was a madame. The house was a brothel; she had worked there as a whore in 1944. Her boyfriend, she told Cottam, was a Provost Marshal Captain and he told her he had seen and identified the body of Glenn Miller.

Cottam said : "But why was he killed ?"

"He knew too much, m'sieu. Too much about the Black Market - and they killed him to keep him quiet."

And that was the whole story. No names, dates, times, places to back it up. Yet Dennis Cottam was a dedicated researcher : why had he not squeezed the last shred of information from the madame and the barman ? In our view, they were possibly pulling his leg, which is not unusual in France. On a research visit to Paris, we too experienced concealed mirth and giggling whenever we mentioned Glenn Miller. To the French he is as much of a tourist attraction as is the Loch Ness Monster to Scotland. But one name stands out among Miller researchers - that of John Edwards, the ex-R.A.F.electronics engineer who worked for Plessey Communications and provided us with the vital leads to Teddy Gower, the BBC engineer who flew with Glenn Miller to Paris on Thursday December 14 1944; to Alex Sleap the ground engineer at Bovingdon who saw Miller transship to a Paris-bound C47 on November 8, and finally to American Jack Donnelly, who went to college in the Fifties with Edward Pecora, whose cousin US Army doctor Capt.David Pecora had always been linked in some way with the Miller mystery.

John Edwards was stationed at R.A.F. Bahrein in the Fifties as a radio engineer, and ran a local Forces radio programme in which he played Glenn Miller records constantly. Becoming absorbed by the mystery, he devoted most of his time after 1964 to research, corresponding with the Canadians John Flowers and Henry Whiston. He attracted the interest of the media and as described on P.39, he flew along the `route' of the Norseman with TV presenter Angela Rippon. Soon, letters arrived from all over the world, including one from a WW2 veteran with a strange tale to tell (See P.1). He had been in the same military hospital ward near Columbus, Ohio as Major Glenn Miller when the bandleader died from severe head injuries. Edwards regarded this as just one more hoax letter and put it in the trash can - something he would later regret. Another letter from a F/Sgt Fox, coxswain of an R.A.F.Air Sea Rescue launch, described a search of the Dover Straits on Saturday December 16 1944 for Morgan's plane - but all available records disprove this.

There were no official reports of any search that day; further, there had been no `Mayday' call giving the plane's position, and it was Monday December 18 before Morgan was officially listed as missing after news of the Dymchurch sighting reached SHAEF. Edwards relates that in 1973, he became convinced that a personal file existed somewhere for each of the three men supposedly lost in the Norseman. He wrote to the National Personnel Records Center.St.Louis,Mo. but they replied :

`We have probed our computer regarding Col. Norman F.Baessell and John R.S. Morgan, and have not located any records.It is possible they were destroyed by the fire...'.

But NPRC omitted to mention that the Files were located in Washington in custody of Casualty and Memorial Division, Eisenhower Avenue,

Alexandria,Va., with access via the Washington National Personnel Records Center. Edwards was not deterred; in 1976 an article about him appeared in the now-defunct newspaper`*REVEILLE'* (Fig.48). He maintained that Glenn Miller was murdered in Paris three days after the Norseman was lost (i.e., on Monday December 18, the same day the AAF Band arrived in Paris). The Major, Edwards said, had died of a fractured skull after a brawl in Pigalle, the red light district.The Norseman crash provided a convenient cover story. But Edwards's story was built on fragile foundations. He believed that Alex Sleap met the Norseman at Bovingdon on Friday December 15, and saw Miller catch a shuttle flight while the C64 went on to crash in the Channel. We know that flight took place on November 8 1944. During an interview John told us that Lt.Col.Tom Corrigan, USAF, had seen Glenn Miller's death certificate, but we traced Corrigan : he had seen a Finding of Death document, which functions as a death certificate in the case of missing military personnel.

John Edwards' problem, as he now cheerfully admits, was a total lack of objectivity, analytical shrewdness and native caution. He believed absolutely the information which came to him, and wasted no time informing the media, instead of checking out the material thoroughly. In the late Seventies he enjoyed an ephemeral notoriety as a leading researcher, and gave lectures to the Glenn Miller Society.

From the outset he claimed that a cover-up had occurred, but we could neither confirm nor refute this at an early stage in our own researches. John claimed that he had eye-witness statements from three officers who had seen Morgan crash into the sea, from a point 6 miles west of Dunkirk. It happened, he said, a few miles offshore. "But the visibility," we said,"was only a mile or so at that time of the afternoon in the Channel."

Edwards hesitated. "We found later that it was less than a mile offshore. It was dusk and distances are difficult to judge. But by using a huge computer in Cleveland Ohio, feeding in all the relevant data, we came up with the location of a Norseman - precisely where the computer predicted !"

We wondered where John had obtained details of Morgan's route - no flight plan was ever found. This was the precise problem - no one had any data at all. John showed us what he claimed was a side-scan sonar image of the aircraft sitting on the sea bed (Fig.55).

"Did you ever find a sponsor ? Did you ever dive on the aircraft ?"

"Yes.Several dives were made,the last in November 1985."

Strange, we thought...There had been no Press reports...

"Were you there ?"

"Uh - I had committments elsewhere."

Committments - after researching for 20 years ? We tried again,producing the map in Fig.52.

"Can you mark the position of the Norseman ?"

"Certainly." We looked at the map, stunned. *It was a long way from Dunkirk, round Cap Gris Nez towards Boulogne.* We said so, and Edwards nodded.

"It probably drifted there on the tide and currents."

"Yes. Well - what was the name of the ship ?"

"I think it was the MIDNIGHT LOON." (This may have been correct but we found no ship of that name in Lloyds Register).

"What were the names of the divers you used ?"

"The sponsors, Southern TV, would know. They provided the divers." (The TV Company had no such record - we checked.)

"What information did the dive produce? Was the aircraft identified as a Norseman ?"

"It was...difficult to confirm. We only had the aircraft number."

"But," we pointed out reasonably, "all the fabric and the number would be rotted away after 40 years."

"True,"John agreed. "The real confirmation will come from the engine number."

"You didn't get it during the dive ?" we said, astonished. *That number was a vital target for any researcher...*

"No."

"What condition was the plane in ? Did the divers say ?"

"A highwing monoplane in reasonably good condition," Edwards said easily. "It was quite heavily silted up but protected by the silt to some extent. Miller wasn't aboard."

We blinked. *Ward's aircraft was on a sandy flat seabed, not on silt. And it was only an empty tubular skeleton.*

"Really ?"

"We already knew this, of course."

It all seemed too good to be true, and it was. It is difficult to figure out what makes John Edwards tick - he had followed up every lead, every rumour with dogged determination. In the end he yielded to the pressure of the media : they demanded sensation after sensation, and when he could not produce on time he let his imagination take over. Yet he is a hugely-likeable man and we owe him a debt of gratitude in that he provided us with three vital clues.

First, Mr. Alex Sleap photographed (Fig.43) with Morgan's C64A at R.A.F.Bovingdon on November 8, which enabled us to prove that both Dixie Clerke and George Ferguson confused flight dates, and that Don Haynes used material from the November 8 flight in his December 15 narrative.

Second, he led us to the mysterious American Army doctor mentioned in the *REVEILLE* article, who was based in Rheims US Military hospital during the Ardennes battles.

Third, he showed us the transcript of his interview with Teddy Gower, a BBC engineer who claimed to have flown over to Paris with Glenn at the time the Norseman was reported missing. The Burial File evidence revealed that the flight was on December 14 1944, a day before the Norseman was lost.

But we were primarily interested in the US Army doctor : if John was correct, here was a man who had been present at the time Miller died, who would know the cause of death and the true circumstances of the tragedy. Edwards could not recall the doctor's name at first - Pakula or Pecora, but there was a way of checking it out. In the late Seventies John worked at Plessey Telecommunications Derby, and his departmental head was an American called Jack Donnelly. Jack, aware of John's interest in the Miller case, came up with a curious story. In the Fifties he had gone to University with a young man who said that his father was a US Army doctor based in Europe in 1944. He had signed a death certificate for Glenn Miller.

This, we thought, could be the breakthrough we needed. We called Derby, to learn that Donnelly had returned home seven or eight years previously. They thought he came from a place with the outlandish name of Paradise Valley, Arizona. With a great deal of difficulty we traced Donnelly and called him.

"John Edwards ? Sure, I remember him - a great guy. Glenn Miller ? Sure, I remember something about that. I went to college with this guy - his name was Pecora. He told me his father signed Glenn Miller's death certificate. Which University ? I gotta think about that - I went to quite a few, and it was a long time ago. Somewhere in the south,I guess. I do recall the family came from Newark."

The only Newark we knew was in New Jersey - and that did ring a bell. The Millers were living in Tenafly New Jersey at the time he went overseas : was it possible Pecora had been their family physician ? We contacted the American Medical Association for information on all New Jersey physicians named Pecora, and began to check on universities : there was a large number of them but we concentrated on those in the Southern states. In the end we got lucky. It was Florida Southern College near Baton Rouge - and they still had their old student records, which included Donnelly and an Edward Pecora. They gave us an address in Connnecticut and wished us luck.

Impatiently, we listened to the telephone bell ringing in a house 3000 miles away.

"Edward Pecora here."

We explained how we had traced him through John Edwards, Jack Donnelly and the College.

"Jack Donnelly ? Say, I remember Jack, for sure. Glenn Miller... yes,I remember something about that too. But no,I'm not a doctor."

"Was your father in the Army Medical Corps in 1944 ?"

Edward laughed. "Hell,no ! He was in World War One." Our spirits sagged.*End of story.* Then he said slowly : "Wait a moment. My cousin David was an Army doctor, and he was in Europe in 1944. Maybe it was he that told me about Glenn Miller."

93

That was better ! "Do you have his address ?"

"Uh - no,sir.I don't. But I could dig it out...I'll call you back,okay ?"

He was as good as his word, and four days later we had an address for Dr.David Pecora - in Newark,Delaware ! So much for New Jersey and all that wasted effort...We wrote Pecora a long letter, explaining how we traced him through Edwards, Donnelly and his brother, and asking for his movements on December 15 1944 - but his letter was disturbing.

> `In December of 1944 I was in transit from England to France.I spent Christmas Day at Etretat. Following that, I was located at Rheims during the Battle of the Bulge - we treated many casualties...I have no recollection of encountering anyone identified as Glenn Miller.'*

Disturbing indeed : first, he gave no details of his location at the critical time around December 15. A day would cover his transit time to France - what about the rest of the month ? Second,the Ardennes offensive began Saturday December 16 at 02.00, twelve hours after John Morgan left Abbotts Ripton - not after Christmas ! By Christmas Day the German offensive had petered out,the Allies regrouping for a counter-thrust. The main battle period was between December 16 and Christmas Day. Etretat is on the French coast north of Le Havre. Third, and most intriguing, there was no reference to his remark to his brother Edward about a death certificate for Glenn Miller. Dr.David Pecora evinced no surprise at being traced after 45 years, and specifically he made no denial of his connection with the case.

We wrote again, listing a few vital questions, but we had no reply : we wrote once more in the summer of 1989, with a similar result,and there we left it. An unsatisfactory ending to a promising lead.

8. POSSIBLE DISASTER THEORIES

With the Pecora story on the back burner and awaiting a reply, we turned to the question of the cause of the crash which killed Morgan and Baessell. We can take up the story at the point when Morgan would be flying southwards a few miles offshore below Cap Gris Nez, looking for a place to penetrate inland; they would be flying just under the cloudbase, probably at 600 feet, over a calm oily-looking sea. Their visibility would be limited - no more than a mile and a half,with wisps of thin grey cloud scudding past the Norseman. They would see vague glimpses of the rocky coast running down towards Boulogne, and while they had plenty of fuel, it was less than an hour to dusk and the light was fading.

Morgan was in the left-hand seat, with Colonel Baessell in the right-hand seat; behind them an open doorway gave access to the 8-seat cabin, in which a third and as yet unidentified passenger may have been seated, probably in the front seat behind Col. Baessell's bulkhead. John

Morgan, beyond doubt, would be wearing his Mae West lifejacket,but as George Ferguson tells us, Colonel Baessell was far from punctilious in obeying the rules.

Then, without warning, disaster...What happened to that tiny passenger aircraft ? The possible explanations are limited in number...

* Fuel Shortage

We ruled this out at once. Even with half fuel load,Morgan could fly at least 4 hours, and it was mandatory for all US aircraft in wartime to carry maximum fuel. We calculated his ditching time as follows : it is 123 miles from Abbotts Ripton to a point 6 miles west of Le Touquet. With a southerly 12 mph wind, the groundspeed would be 100 mph,or 1.6 miles per minute with a flight time of 1hr.15m. This, added to the confirmed take-off time of 13.25, means that Morgan came down in the sea at 14.40 on the afternooon of Friday December 15 1944, with enough gas in his tanks for at least 7 more hours.

* Morgan was Lost

This does not seem a feasible solution. We know that he was a below-average instrument pilot, avoiding cloud flying if possible; moreover in poor visibility and lacking navigational equipment, he would stay in contact with the ground and mapread east of London past Maidstone, Ashford and on to Dymchurch, where he was seen heading out to sea. He would have a good pinpoint there, before heading south-east towards cloud-capped Cap Gris Nez, which he would see in plenty of time to turn south and follow the coast. Further, Morgan had flown this route at least 5 times including October, when he flew Goodrich and Baessell into Brussels. We can be sure he was not lost.

* The Norseman Iced Up

Several points are relevant here.First,the actual weather reports (Fig.39) confirm there were no reports of ice affecting aircraft on December 15. Second, Don Haynes promoted the theory in his diaries, putting his own words into Goodrich's mouth. Third, there are two distinct categories : aircraft `impact' icing, in which supercooled water droplets strike the leading edges of wings and tail surfaces, building up a thick layer of ice. This endangers the aircraft in two ways : the sheer weight of ice may force it down, while the ice layer will distort the airflow over the wing causing severe loss of lift - just when additional lift is needed to counter-teract the extra weight of ice. Many American aircraft were fitted with `boot' de-icing gear, inflatable rubber bags on the mainplane leading edges. Norseman 70285 was not so equipped.

The second hazard was `carburettor icing'. Most conventional aircraft carburettors work on a venturi `choke' system, a restriction in the air intake which forms a low pressure zone. This is used to draw up fuel from a float chamber. A butterfly valve in the choke controls the amount of air ingested; when more power is required, the valve opens, deepening the depression in the choke and drawing up the extra fuel demanded. But the low pressure also cools the airflow : if external temperature is close to freezing, ice forms in the intake and the engine may stop. Most carburettors are fitted with an air heating system, either a hot oil jacket around the intake, or an electric heating element. The pilot receives plenty of warning of the on-set of carburettor icing : there is vibration and a loss of power. By switching on the heating system, the symptoms soon disappear, and aircraft drills before take-off required the system to be switched on at all times in winter. We can rest assured that Morgan, even with his limited experience, would not fall for that hazard, especially on a winter day when icing might be expected.

Moreover, he had been airborne for more than an hour before disaster struck, and we must ask why, if icing conditions were prevalent, Morgan had not experienced icing long before 14.40 hours.

We obtained an audio tape featuring an interview with the ground engineer who, with pilot John Morgan, preflighted Norseman 44-70285 at Abbotts Ripton on December 15 1944 : he stated that the aircraft was fitted with de-icing gear, which he checked and found serviceable. But this runs contrary to the evidence of all the surviving pilots who flew the ircraft, and also the documentation in the Burial Files. In addition, none of the existing photographs of 44-70285 show any wing leading-edge de-icing equipment fitted.

It is difficult to assess if this interview was another example of disinformation, but had de-icers been fitted, this would have rendered even more unviable the theory Haynes was seeking to promote - that the Norseman had iced up and gone into the English Channel.

* **Mechanical Failure**

This is probably the worst type of sudden catastrophic failure a pilot could experience, but there are cogent reasons against it in Morgan's case. First, 44-70285 was one of four brand-new UC64As delivered to 44 SAD Wattisham in June 1944, and it would have minimal engine hours. Second, taking Morgan's Form 5 as an indication, it rarely flew more than 50 hours a month and had probably clocked less than 350 hours before the last mission. Pratt & Whitney Wasps are on record with 100,000 hours ! Third, it was based at an Air Depot Repair Squadron, where it would receive the best of maintenance. Fourth, like most aircraft of the day, the engine was fitted with full dual ignition. We could find no reason not to eliminate engine failure as a cause of the disaster.

We do know that 70285 was subject to endemic hydraulic leaks in the propeller system, and we have previously explained the functioning of the Constant Speed Unit and cockpit lever which maintains the engine RPM to a selected value, regardless of whether the aircraft is climbing or descending. This is accomplished by altering the angle at which the blades meet the airflow - the `pitch' angle. This is set low  for take-off to produce maximum RPM in `fine' pitch, and high for the `coarse' pitch setting. The blade angle is varied  by hydraulic pressure, and a leak in that system allows the blades to go to zero pitch; the RPM increase very quickly and exceed the maximum permissible level - an `overspeed'.

The immediate recovery action is to set the cockpit lever to `fine pitch' and close the throttle : given time,the RPM will fall and some degree of control becomes possible.

But the one thing Morgan would not have, cruising at 600 feet over a darkening sea, was time. Further, there was an additional hazard. With engine RPM far above maximum permitted level, the cylinder-head temperatures would go up fast. If no recovery action was taken, the engine would sieze solid - but what of the propeller ? With its huge momentum,it would twist itself clean off the engine crankshaft and plunge into the sea. The final proof of the theory would be found if and when the Norseman was found - *and the propeller was missing.*

9. **THE CLIVE WARD STORY**

In 1987, the late Sqdn.Ldr. Jack Taylor came across a news cutting about the discovery in 1980 of a Norseman six miles off Le Touquet, France by Clive Ward, the skipper-owner of a hydrographic survey vessel, the *GREYHOUND TRACKER* (Fig.54). Ward, an ex-RN captain, lives in Hamble, Hampshire overlooking the yacht basin, and willingly granted us an interview. He is a tall well-built man, operating his ship on contracts ranging from oil wells to Channel-bed surveys. *GREYHOUND TRACKER* is one of the best-equipped hydrographic survey vessels in Britain,with navigational equipment capable of bringing the ship back to within a yard of a pre-determined position.

Ex-submariner Clive Ward has above-average capabilities in aircraft recognition. He specialises in providing sea-bed information for gas and oil companies; much of his work is for the MOD, surveying for Admiralty charts. In 1980 he was engaged in a sea-bed survey for the CEGB in connection with a cross-Channel powerline link, identifying possible cable routes. They were picking up via side-scan sonar indications of numerous wrecked aircraft on the sea bed, and Clive Ward explained that the Channel is literally one vast cemetery of lost aircraft,largely wartime wrecks.

That day, Clive picked up a particularly good image of a solitary aircraft in an otherwise deserted area of flat sea bed. Intrigued,he donned a wet suit and dived on the wreck site. Conditions were `excellent except for the visibility.

"I found this aircraft," he told us, "sitting on the sea bed and intact apart from one wingtip, and the tail was twisted. In my time, I have dived on more than 100 sunken aircraft and had no difficulty in recognising it as a C64 Norseman. It was about 6 miles west of Le Touquet at a depth of 110 feet, about 30 metres, in a large and featureless expanse of flat sandy sea bed."

We showed Clive the map on which John Edwards had marked the location of the aircraft he said he had found. "Can you show us the position of the aircraft, Clive ?"

"Certainly." He marked the position shown in Fig.52 : we were gratified to note it was precisely on the track we had calculated for Morgan. Clive said : "What is this other location on the map ?"

We explained about the `sighting' by three officers on the coast near Dunkirk. Clive stared at the map, puzzled.

"How did Mr.Edwards account for the wreck being in this position round the corner of Cap Gris Nez ?"

"He said it had probably been washed around there by the tides and currents."

"That's not possible. It would have broken up."

We nodded. "He also gave us this side-scan sonar image of the aircraft on the sea bed." (Fig.58).

Clive looked at it very hard.

"Well ?" we said anxiously. "Looks like no side-scan sonar printout I ever saw," Clive said.

We changed tack. "Tell us about your Norseman."

"It was sitting on the sea bed, virtually in the landing position, tail down, pointing roughly south with one landing wheel buried in the sand and the other several feet above it, still inflated ! The starboard wingtip was broken off and and the tail was twisted out of line; all the fabric skin had disappeared, leaving the tubular steel structure visible rather like a skeleton. Apart from that, the machine was almost intact."

"Really ?" we said.

"Except for the propeller."

"Oh ?"

"*It was missing.*"

+   +   +

We felt ridiculously pleased. This appeared to confirm our theory of propeller overspeed. "There were no signs of human remains ?"

"None," Clive said emphatically. "I've had a lot of experience poking around old sunken aircraft. The only visible signs one finds is scraps of organic material inside flying helmets, but there was nothing in that line at all."

"Was there any sign of the propeller nearby ?"

"No. There were no other metallic indications in a large area around the plane. If the propeller was lost in flight,it probably landed miles away, back up the flight path."

He had not noted if the engine crankshaft itself was intact : that would have to wait for the engine to be raised from the sea bed. But the propeller's condition would be a significant factor : the Norseman stalled at about 55 mph; Morgan would have approached the sea in a glide at 65 mph. The impact would have been comparable to a car being driven off the end of a jetty into the sea. The free-falling propeller, not under power,would be almost undamaged.

10.DITCHING THE NORSEMAN

On impact,Morgan and Baessell would be strapped into the pilot seats in the cockpit; at low entry speed, they would escape injury and be able to scramble out of the doors. But according to George Ferguson, the rules about wearing life-jackets were not always followed : on one flight back to UK with Baessell, he remembered that the jackets were in the aft baggage compartment under a heap of cases, along with the rubber life-raft in its packaging. He told Baessell the problem but the Colonel just laughed.

"Whaddya wanna do ? Live forever ?"

+ + +

Was there another passenger ? We believe so, but we know now that it could not have been Glenn Miller. It seems very probable that Morgan was landing at B42 Beauvais to drop a passenger (his Record Card says `ferrying personnel') but it is equally possible that the `personnel' was Col.Baessell heading for Bordeaux, and Morgan may have been dropping some spare parts at Beauvais, where a wing of B26 light bombers of the 9th Air Force was based.

Further, the Ansell Report on MACR 10770 suggests that the Report was made out for the `pilot only' and the names of passengers added subsequently. It would fall to any passenger in the cabin to climb aft into the baggage compartment, haul out the life-raft and tie its lanyard to the structure near the door. This would prevent it drifting away in the wind after ditching. But with the aircraft in a steep descent, together with an inevitable element of fear and probably no prior briefing, the task the passenger faced was enormous. Worse, if the impact came when he was aft wrestling with the life-raft, he would be hurled forward into the bulkhead. His only real chance of survival might be to sit facing aft with his back to the bulkhead.

A possible scenario, therefore, might be of two or more men struggling without lifejackets in seawater barely above freezing level on a darkening winter afternoon with little or no possibility of rescue.We do know Morgan did not get out a Mayday call : we can now suggest an explanation for this. He would have barely 2 minutes before the aircraft reached the sea : if the propeller was gone, the engine siezed, there may have been fire. He may have had control trouble - it is not beyond the bounds of possibility that the propeller took away the starboard wingtip and aileron. Morgan would be too busy to make a Mayday call - and too low for it to be received by a land station, for he was more than 40 miles from Dover. The maximum survival time under these conditions was ten minutes.

We do have some frail clues : Clive Ward described finding both cockpit doors closed (they could be jettisoned in emergency,but we believe Morgan may have kept them shut to reduce the amount of water entering the cockpit). Clive said :

"Both doors were in position but when I tried to open one, it broke away from the structure. Before I left I replaced it in the cockpit."

There were no traces of harness, parachutes or upholstery and the plyboard floor had rotted away : anything in the cockpit or cabin would have fallen through the gaps in the tubular structure into the sand. He had no way of cleaning off the engine number plate, even if he had thought to note the engine number. In fact, Clive did not know its location, screwed to the front crankcase at the 5 o'clock position as seen looking aft. We were far from sanguine that the brass plate was still *in situ* after our contact with Mr. Rodd at Maxwell AFB (see P.37). Meanwhile, we asked Clive Ward about the feasibility of raising the engine to obtain the number.

"Quite feasible," he said. "But because of poor visibility it's essential to use a professional diver with surface air supply and communication with the deck. Diving on the plane would be like stumbling around a football field in thick fog at most times of the year. The wreck would be visible on sonar but a scuba diver could be within six feet without seeing it."

11. **DIVING FOR TREASURE.**

In the weeks which followed, we sought a sponsor for an exploratory dive, and TVS Southampton agreed to finance the venture in return for full documentary rights. We put them in touch with Clive Ward,who agreed to provide his ship and the location of the aircraft. But when he insisted that a fully-equipped deep-sea diver was essential,the sponsor had second thoughts and relied instead upon a group of amateur scuba divers from the British Aqua Association.

In September 1986 *GREYHOUND TRACKER* sailed from Ramsgate at midnight, en route for Boulogne with one of our group aboard. On arrival they found the TV crew, who had travelled by overnight ferry with their heavy gear. Next morning the ship left Boulogne, and exactly on time in the correct location the aircraft came up on side-scan sonar. But the wind was now Force 5 or 6 with heavy seas and the Norseman was 110 feet down. Such conditions were hopeless for skin divers, despite their undoubted courage and skill. Tight-lipped, a furious Clive Ward took his ship home; with a properly-equipped deepsea diver, the expedition would have been successful. The Norseman is still down there. It is still feasible to raise the engine for identification, at a cost of £25,000. To the time of going to press the author had failed to find a sponsor, despite the confirmation that this was indeed John Morgan's aircraft. The way in which we obtained that confirmation is a story in its own right. (See the MOD Air Historical Branch Report, P.56).

12. **CONCLUSIONS.**

On the basis of the evidence we have presented here, we had every confidence that some of the fundamental questions of the Miller mystery have been answered. We know why no Mayday call was received from Morgan. We know he took the easterly route around London, after being cleared direct from Abbotts Ripton to B42 Beauvais. We know that navigator Fred Shaw may have seen a Norseman destroyed by bombs, but it was almost certainly 43-5367, en route back to its base in France. We know that Miller was not a passenger, that Colonel Baessell may have been the only one. Extensive checks of the Monthly Operation Reports from Abbotts Ripton confirm Morgan was the only man listed as missing.

Our impression of Lt.Col. Norman F.Baessell is that of an aggressive and opinionated officer who would not hesitate to pull rank on a young pilot - a man who was foolhardy to the point of recklessness, and who had forced two previous pilots to apply for other duties. Flight Officer John Robert Stuart Morgan appears to have been inexperienced, underconfident, unassertive and unlikely to argue with a senior officer. He was a below-average instrument pilot, and while it is held by some researchers that he may have lost control in cloud and spun into the Channel, we believe he would have taken scrupulous care that day to stay within sight of the ground to navigate.

We have been able to show that while George Ferguson and Dixie Clerke both confused the date of the fatal flight, Don Haynes used data from the November 8 flight in his diary narratives. Further, while our attempt to identify Clive Ward's aircraft by checking the engine number was unsuccessful, we have succeeded in establishing by a process of elimination that it can only be 44-70285.

It is our considered opinion that the cause of the C64A crash was probably a runaway propeller which flew off when the engine siezed up.

We traced through John Edwards Mr. Teddy Gower's evidence of flying to Paris with Miller on December 14, Mr. Alex Sleap who met John Morgan at Bovingdon on November 8 when he dropped Glenn Miller, and Dr. David Pecora, who opted not to elaborate on his movements from December 15 to December 25 1944.

Finally, we have suggested a reasonable explanation for the Colonel's mission to Bordeaux, and we know Morgan's plane was not that mentioned in the `Bordeaux Search Letter'. If, at some time, someone reaches the wreck of 70285, it is interesting to speculate on what they will find deep in the sand below the aircraft.

Empty champagne bottles, perhaps ?

Maybe.

But a brass trombone mouthpiece ?

No way...

+   +   +

FIVE

THEORIES AND SCENARIOS

1. GENERAL ASSUMPTIONS

   During a detailed analysis of the accumulated evidence in 1987, we gave appropriate weight to the documented items, written and verbal statements by living witnesses, extracts from official histories and records in various archives. We strove to make due allowance for second-hand and uncorroborated evidence,and in accounting for the lack of replies to letters addressed to, among others, Mr.Steve Miller,the R.A.F controller Mr. Bowler, Capt. Pecora in Newark, Delaware, the son of Mr.David Mackay, the Miller family attorney etc. We further took due note of the dubious value of documents known to be falsified, such as the MACR. We also debated very carefully the conclusions to be drawn from the lack of signature on the `ORIGINAL' MACR N-19, and the deletion of Capt.Ralph Cramer's typed identification in the fabricated MACR 10770. Here are our findings based on three years of detailed research :

2. POSTULATES

*   Don Haynes' Twinwood Farm story was either true or false.

*   If false,Miller (and probably Baessell too) was not there.

*   The Norseman may have landed, to pick up Baessell alone.

*   Alternatively, he boarded at Abbotts Ripton.

*   There may or may not have been a second passenger.

*   Without Miller,the Norseman's fate is academic.

*   If Miller left the UK, it was probably by air on December 14.

*   If so, he was lost en route or vanished in Paris.

*   If the latter, no trace of him was ever found.

*   If he died, the reason was either accident or foul play.

*   If the latter, a cover-up would probably ensue.

3. CONCLUSIONS DRAWN FROM THE EVIDENCE

* All the evidence points to Haynes' story being untrue.

* It was evolved almost entirely from the November 8 flight.

* Miller's orders were flexible, and not changed.

* His last public appearance was at the Queensberry Club concert on Tuesday December 12 1944.

* On Wednesday December 13, Don Haynes booked Glenn Miller on a C47 flight from Bovingdon to Orly next day.

* Glenn's bags were sent to Old Quebec St.Terminal Wednesday.

* Miller, Haynes and John Morgan visited the Milroy Club, Stratton St. Mayfair with a so-far unidentified girl singer on Wednesday evening. There, they met Sqn.Ldr.Tony Bartley, DFC & Bar, and Lt. Tony Pulitzer,USAAF.

* About 23.00 Haynes and Morgan left to drive back to Bedford in thick fog. The party went on until 02.30 when the Club closed. Miller was last seen alive by Bartley and Pulitzer as he walked away into the fog towards Marble Arch.

* Glenn had been allocated a flight number and proceeded by bus from Old Quebec St. Terminal to Bovingdon. The BBC engineer Teddy Gower caught the same flight. Boarding procedures did not require names of passengers to be called : Miller was able to travel unrecognised.

* The aircraft landed at Orly in the early afternoon. Major Glenn Miller disembarked and was never seen again. He did not have to report for duty until the first concert on Thursday December 21, and effectively had a week's break from all responsibilities.

* He left no personal effects behind, but probably took 3 or 4 bags with him. They vanished with Glenn and were never traced.

* Spending the weekend at 8th AFSC, Haynes learned of the missing Norseman. He was not concerned : Glenn was was not aboard. But he had to plead ignorance until he arrived at Orly on Monday December 18 - otherwise he would have had to alert Milton Ernest that a VIP was missing !

* When Major Glenn Miller failed to greet the AAF Band at Orly, Lt. Don Haynes made no effort to check if a search was in progress

for the missing C64. Instead, he spent two days searching Paris for him. At the time he was reporting to Gen. Barker on Tuesday, the Dymchurch sighting report came in and provided the basis for the Norseman story.

* Gen.Barker may or may not have known it was fabricated, but his subsequent actions in delaying all reporting procedures, prohibiting any announcement at the first concert,cancelling the remaining performances, delaying all publicity until 1 hour before a broadcast to the USA and ordering a covert search indicates that he knew Miller was in Paris and hoped against hope he would turn up. That was impossible if Glenn had ditched in the Norseman 6 days previously; General Barker seemingly believed he was not on board.

* Barker instructed 8th AFSC to insert Haynes' story in the MACR, excluding his name and identity; to omit details of the weather and the engine number and include a route stop at A42 Villacoublay to `drop off Glenn Miller'.

* Adjutant Ralph Cramer compiled and despatched the `ORIGINAL' MACR to Washington but refused to sign it. MACR 10770 was fabricated at Maxwell AFB dated March 26 1946, and guaranteed as the `sole genuine document' by National Archives in Washington for 44 years. The Cramer identification details were erased on all copies and the `ORIGINAL' unsigned MACR was suppressed.

* Certain documents which cast doubts on Haynes' story were abstracted from the Files. They included Glenn's orders for Paris (showing flexible travel date); John Morgan's Service Record Card and Forms 5, showing his true destination as Beauvais and refuting Haynes' `Honington' story completely.

* The SHAEF cover-up was to conceal, not his disappearance, but the fact that they had effectively `lost' a serving officer, a VIP of the day and when he failed to return, a false explanation was considered better than no explanation at all. It was extended to fabrication and manipulation of official documents authorised at the highest level and is ongoing today, via a widely-applied policy of delay, obfuscation, obstruction and denial of access.

4. CONCLUSIONS - THE NORSEMAN

* The departure field was Abbotts Ripton, and the time of take-off was 13.25 on December 15 1944.

* Morgan's orders were to ferry personnel to B42 Beauvais and pro-

ceed to Bordeaux next day, returning Sunday December 17.

*   He was inexperienced, non-commissioned with less than 600 hours total flying - a below-average intrument pilot but competent in clear weather. He had flown no operations of any kind. He flew only 16hr.20m in the month of November and 2hr.20m in December before his last mission, and he was out of flying practice.

*   Baessell and possibly a second passenger boarded at Abbotts Ripton, Twinwood Farm being closed. Morgan did not land there.

*   The weather at take-off was fair, with a 3000 foot cloudbase, 1.5 miles visibility, light southerly winds and no precipitation. Forecast weather for the route was poor further south, cloudbase falling to 800 feet in the Channel. Icing conditions were not prevalent.

*   Because of a need to reach Beauvais before dusk, and delay of take-off waiting for morning fog to clear, Baessell decided to waive landing at Bovingdon and obtained telephonic clearance direct to Beauvais. The Diver Gun Box was inactive and they were able to fly direct to Dymchurch. The Norseman was seen crossing the coast at low level but unreported inbound over the French coast. This report was passed to SHAEF by the evening of Tuesday December 19.

*   No Mayday call was received, and it was impossible to start a search without a known position report.

*   There are unassailable grounds for asserting that Morgan took the easterly route round London, and that he could not have been in or near the Bomb Jettison Area.

*   After some mechanical failure, probably involving the propeller constant speed system, he ditched about six miles west of Le Touquet in 110 feet of water at approximately 14.40 hours. There were no survivors and the aircraft was located in 1980 by Mr.Clive Ward. The propeller was missing.

*   By a process of elimination, of the 8 Norseman planes listed as missing in 1944, the C64 off Le Touquet is definitely 44-70285. Its identity can be confirmed by obtaining the engine number or raising the engine for examination. Because no human remains were found the aircraft is not categorised as a War Grave.

5. THEORY ANALYSIS

STAFF MESSAGE CONTROL

INCOMING CLASSIFIED MESSAGE

– –·–·–·–·–·–·–

A TRUE COPY:

Taken from 201 file: MILLER, Alton G.
DUAA

TOO 021625A FEB

<u>WALTER B. MORROW</u>
<u>Major, Infantry</u>
USFET 110/03
TOR 030421A FEB

CONFIDENTIAL

PRIORITY

FROM	:	USAFE SIGNED CO MCFENUSAFE
TO FOR ACTION	:	CG USFET ATTN AG CASUALTY DIVISION
REF NO	:	UA-60821 2 FEBRUARY 1946

Reference your teletype WB - 1925 dated 30 January 1946, concerning Major ALTON GLEN MILLER, O-595273.

Extensive search of all records available to this Headquarters fails to reveal information desired. Missing air crew report concerning aircraft on which Major MILLER was a passenger does not give any information as to weather conditions at time of take off or on planned route, type of radio equipment, or whether or not aircraft was equiped with de-icing equipment. Missing air crew report states aircraft was enroute to BORDEAUX via A 42 (VILLACOUBLAY). This Headquarters has made every effort to locate initial investigation of this case without results. Aircraft was assigned to 35th Air Depot Group which has been returned to the Zone of Interior.

WB-1925 is not identified in USFET SMC files

ACTION   :   AG

INFORMATION   :   AG RECORDS

SMC IN 1766   3 Feb 46   0700A   DLH/wbm   REF No: UA-60821

COPY NO: 3

CONFIDENTIAL

Fig. 47
USFET Signal to AG Department, Washington 1946

GLENN MILLER 'WAS MURDERED'

Glenn Miller: New facts

by FRANK DURHAM

A MAN who has spent more than £7,000 and devoted 12 years to solving the mystery of American bandleader Glenn Miller's death has come up with a startling new theory.

Thirty - five - year - old John Edwards says that Miller was not aboard the plane in which most people believe he died when it crashed into the Channel.

He claims he has evidence that the bandleader was murdered in Paris three days AFTER the plane plunged into the sea.

Mr. Edwards believes that Miller, who was a bit of a lad with the ladies, died of a fractured skull somewhere in the city's red light district of Pigalle.

Cover-up

And he suggests that the fact that the Norseman plane he was supposed to have been aboard crashed was seized on by the authorities and became a convenient cover-up for Miller's death.

Among the evidence that Mr. Edwards has collected to support the theory that Miller was not aboard the fatal flight in 1944 is the eye-witness account of a man who says he saw Miller board a Dakota plane at RAF Bovingdon, Herts, the day of the crash.

This, claims Mr. Edwards, is the plane that Miller actually flew to France in.

The original journey began when the ill-fated Norseman aircraft

Continued on Page 21

Continued from Page 1

took off from Twinwoods airfield, near Bedford.

According to Mr. Edwards's research the Norseman later landed at Bovingdon where Miller left the plane before it took off again for Paris.

Then Miller joined the Dakota and made the cross-Channel trip.

The new facts came to light because Mr. Edwards actually set out to disprove earlier suggestions that Miller was not aboard the Norseman when it crashed.

"Now I have to admit that I was probably wrong. It looks as if it is true that he was *not* on the plane."

Now Mr. Edwards wants to put an end to speculation by raising the crashed plane from the sea bed.

He believes he has found the spot where the plane plunged into the sea and hopes to raise the £15,000 needed to salvage the wreck.

"I have the military numbers of all three men who took off in the plane —Miller's is one of them. —Their metal identity tags should still be intact. "But the way the evi-

Did he die in Paris?

dence is piling up I don't expect to find Glenn's body in that aircraft," said Mr. Edwards.

Mr. Edwards backs his theory of an official cover-up of the real circumstances of Miller's death with the fact that there was never a proper official inquiry.

The "missing aircrew report" of the incident is vague, says Mr. Edwards.

"Even the weather conditions were listed as unknown. But more than 30 years later I have been able to discover the most detailed meteorological reports for the day in question."

Mr. Edwards added: "I have met with difficulty when trying to solve the mystery. Records have been reported burned and other information — such as the missing aircrew report— is unaccountably vague.

"A firm which had shown interest in backing my project to raise the aircraft from the Channel was advised not

to do so by the Glenn Miller estate."

Why does he believe that Glenn Miller was murdered?

Mr. Edwards, a former RAF officer and now a sales export manager, says: "Pieces of information that I have collected over the years have all suddenly fallen into place.

"I have evidence that an American military doctor in Paris signed Glenn Miller's death certificate.

"And retired U.S. Air Force Lieutenant-Colonel Thomas F. Corrigan, recalls that a member of the Provost Marshal's police office in Paris had told him of Miller's murder.

"I now have in my possession a list, which includes the name of the provost officer who dealt with the case, together with other names of the Provost Marshal's staff. All can confirm this account.

"I also have the name of a man who played in the band with Miller, who states that it was common knowledge that those close to him knew very well he was murdered in Paris."

A Norseman aircraft similar to the one involved in the mystery

---

Fig. 48
'REVEILLE' Press Cutting - John Edwards

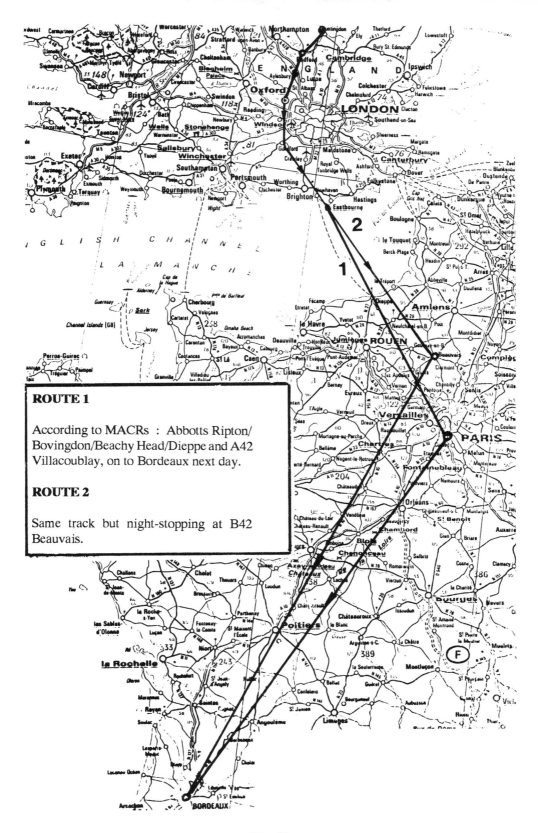

ROUTE 1

According to MACRs : Abbotts Ripton/ Bovingdon/Beachy Head/Dieppe and A42 Villacoublay, on to Bordeaux next day.

ROUTE 2

Same track but night-stopping at B42 Beauvais.

Fig. 49
Morgan Route to Bordeaux as per MACR

Fig. 50
Route - Abbotts Ripton - Dymchurch - Beauvais

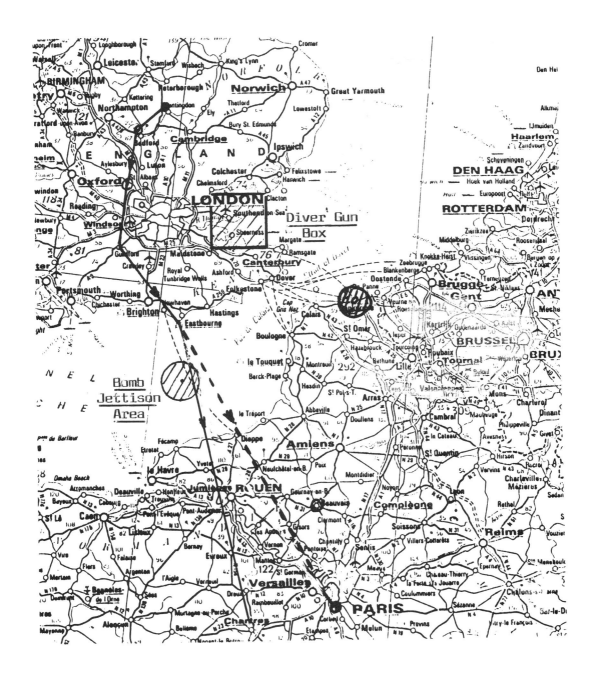

Fig. 51
Assumed Morgan Route to Paris
Overflying Bovingdon - Beachy Head

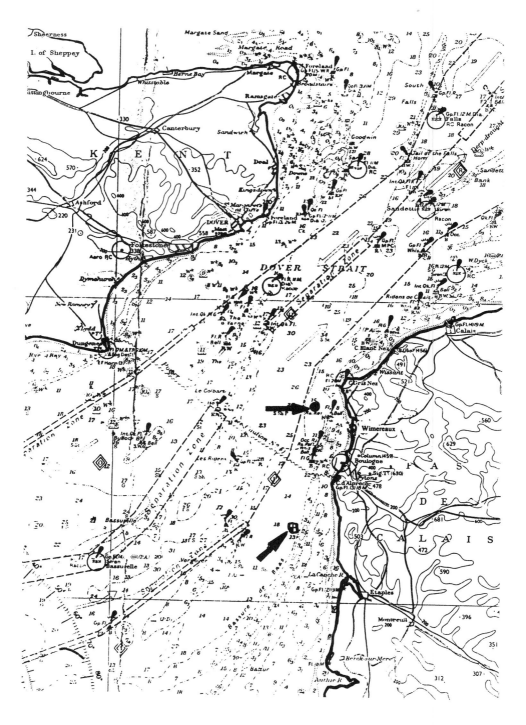

Position of the John Edwards Aircraft ●
Position of Clive Ward Aircraft ▣

Fig. 52
Aircraft Locations - English Channel

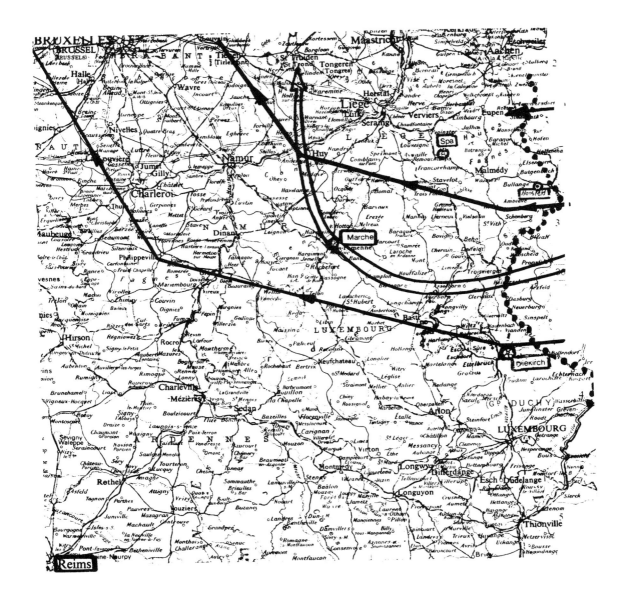

Fig. 53
Ardennes Offensive December 16 1944

Fig. 54
Clive Ward and GREYHOUND TRACKER

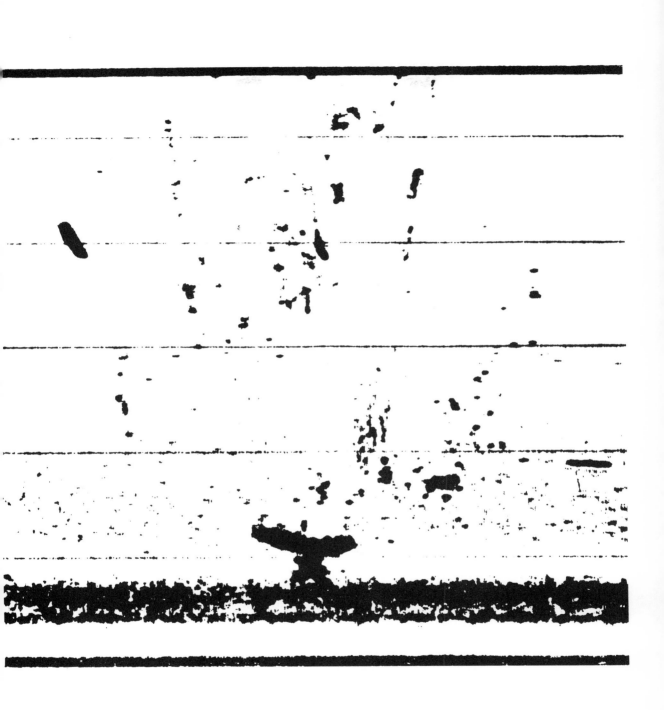

Fig. 55
Side-scan Sonar Image cf John Edwards

NEW CLUE IN GLENN MYSTERY

By ANDREW GOLDEN

THE brother of war-time star Glenn Miller has backed up a claim that the legendary band leader did NOT die in an air-crash.

"My own theory for years was that he never even left England, but died somewhere of cancer," said Herb Miller, 66.

It has always been believed that Miller was on a plane that crashed into the Channel en route to Paris in 1944.

But two weeks ago top British diver Clive Ward claimed exclusively in the Sunday Mirror that he had located Miller's plane . . . and no one was on board when it sank.

Herb, of Dulwich, South London, said: "I have never believed the story that my brother died in the plane crash. I would love to know the truth."

He dismissed Mr. Ward's claim that Glenn died of a heart attack in a Paris brothel.

"He just wouldn't have needed to visit such a place," he said.

Herb, who has a band

Herb—theory

playing Glenn Miller music, said it would help if the plane could be raised from the sea bed.

"Then we can check the serial number and know for sure if it was the plane that Glenn was supposed to have been in." he said.

Fig. 56
Press Cutting - Herb Miller

```
The Adminstrator                          46 Woodwarde Rd
Mountain View Cemetery                    Dulwich Village
Altadena                                     London SE
Cal. U.S.A.                                     England

                                          15 January 1987
```

Dear Sir –

    This letter will introduce Mr.Wilbur Wright from South-ampton in England, who is researching with my permission and approval the resting places of various members of my family.

    I refer particularly to my deceased sister-in-law, Mrs. Helen Miller, who is buried in Grave No. 5, Lot 2584, and her family.

    I would be deeply grateful if you would afford Mr.Wright your full cooperation during his visit to Mountain View Cemetery.

Yours sincerely

John Herbert Miller

JOHN HERBERT MILLER

Fig. 57
Letter of Authorisation - Herb Miller

TELEPHONE OR VERBAL CONVERSATION RECORD	DATE
For use of this form, see AR 340-15; the proponent agency is The Adjutant General's Office.	27 Sep 73

SUBJECT OF CONVERSATION

Col Glen Miller

INCOMING CALL

PERSON CALLING	ADDRESS	PHONE NUMBER AND EXTENSION
Col Halbert	CINFO	76629

PERSON CALLED		AND EXTENSION

PERSON CALLING		AND EXTENSION

PERSON CALLED		AND EXTENSION

Glenn Miller's Plane Said Found

LILLE, France, Sept. 26 —A plane believed to be the one in which band leader Glenn Miller disappeared into the English Channel 29 years ago has been found, it was claimed here today.

The claim was made by a retired degger-fisherman who said he had found the C-64 Norseman aircraft in 32½ feet of water between Boulogne and Calais.

He said the identification of aircraft by sending its engine identification number to the United States, where his correspondent affirmed that the engine came from the plane in which Miller — then head of the Army Air Force Band — disappeared on Christmas Day, 1944, while on a flight from London to Paris.

SUMMARY OF CONVERSATION

CBS news + wire services are running report of a aircraft just found in the English channel. Engine number compares with one for Col Miller's Plane but USAF at Wright-Patt state engines are inter changeable.

needs to verify this with tail number soonest.

GB.

AC-UC-64

SN# 44-70285

Alton G. Miller
Maj 0502273

FILE DISPOSITION DR. 25 JUN 1974

DA FORM 751 APR 66   REPLACES EDITION OF 1 FEB 56 WHICH WILL BE USED.   ☆ GPO: 1970 431-860/1007

Fig. 58
CINFO Memo 1973

It is at this point that we must tread warily the narrow line between unwarranted speculation and assessing the real viability of the many scenarios advanced to explain Miller's disappearance. In discussing each theory and rumour, we are not indulging in wild conjecture. Rather, we are assessing the correspondence, or lack of it, with the available evidence.

* **Glenn Miller never left the UK**

One of the few people who believed this was the late Herb Miller (see Fig.56) but he confessed that he had no evidence to substantiate it. His conviction was based upon his total disbelief in Haynes' story : if Glenn had not been aboard the C64, he must have remained in the UK. Herb had no reason to suspect that his brother had flown out on a scheduled flight unrecognised, until we showed him our evidence. And since no records of Glenn's death or interment in Europe could be found, Herb's thoughts gravitated to the possibility that Glenn had been injured and flown back to America. In later pages we specify the reasons why we thought it deserved investigation, and Herb Miller provided us with written authority to conduct an inquiry in the United States. As Glenn's last surviving blood relative, he felt entitled to do so. (Fig.57)

* **Shot Down by Enemy Fighters**

We were able to discard this theory quickly. The weather on the Continent from December 15 was bad enough to ground Allied recce aircraft, concealing the build-up in the Ardennes forests. No Luftwaffe reports mention a passenger aircraft being shot down on December 15.

* **Died in POW Camp**

This was never regarded as a serious theory. If Glenn had been taken prisoner, the Germans would have announced the news at once as a blow to Allied morale.

* **Shot by Col.Baessell**

This was one of the fanciful rumours in circulation after the war. It was said that Miller became aware that Col.Baessell was engaged in big-time smuggling including drugs. On the fatal mission, Baessell was delivering several large boxes to accomplices at an airstrip in Northern France. Miller objected and was shot after landing; Baessell and Morgan took off at night bound for Bordeaux to board a ship for South America, but crashed somewhere en route.

We found no corroboration of the story at all, but noted some strange connections with the evidence at hand : George Ferguson's account of the plain boxes of `cigarettes' spirited away by Colonel Baessell; the known use of Troston Depot,Honington,as a storage for morphine ampoules; the fact that B42 Beauvais was in Northern France, and the search for a crashed plane in the Bordeaux area. But no concrete evidence of Col.Baessell's involvement in such activities has ever been found. We believe that he may have been a much-maligned character who combined excessive devotion to duty with a macho and aggressive attitude which earned him few friends.

* Murdered in Paris

First broached publicly by John Edwards in 1973 (see Fig.48) we know that this theory was in circulation as far back as 1948. Dennis Cottam encountered it in Paris in 1954 (P.92), when he tracked down the *poule* whose boyfriend, a Provost Marshal Captain, told her he had seen and identified Miller's body. It was also known to many researchers in Canada, America and the Antipodes; we even heard it from a Chinese hovercraft engineer in Southampton in 1986. We believe it originated during the covert search of Paris for Glenn Miller, between December 18 and 24 1944,a search many surviving WW2 veterans remember. It was fuelled by the absence of any explanation of Miller's absence at the Palais de Glace concert on December 21, and the puerile reasons put out by SHAEF (Gen. Barker) for the cancellation of the two following performances. (See P.78 and the account of the `Peter' investigation on P.41). The story is undoubtedly linked with the persistent rumour circulating in the Seventies about a mysterious US Army doctor Capt.Pecora who may have signed a Glenn Miller death certificate. But we found no substance to this story : the Paris Prefecture of Police had no report of a murder of a USAAF officer in Montmartre in December 1944.

* The New Jersey Connection

No outrageous claims are made for this report.Events occurred exactly as we describe below, and it is for the reader to exercise his own judgement. In spring 1987, we were reasonably sure that Glenn Miller had not been aboard the Norseman, that he had arrived in Paris and vanished. We knew there was no trace of any remains buried under his own or similar name and/or serial number. The trail in Europe had petered out but there remained some irritating loose ends. We were still delving into the AMA records of doctors called Pecora in the New Jersey area. If Miller's death had taken place in New Jersey by some odd chain of events, there should be a *bona fide* death certificate held on file at Trenton, New Jersey. Now, we admit this was a very long shot, but such gambles had paid off before, so we wrote a detailed letter to the State Registrar, giving all personal details of Major Alton Glenn Miller including date and place of birth, parents' names and the like. However, inadvertently we stated his place of birth as Clarinda Ohio,instead of Iowa,on March 1 1900. We asked if a death certificate was on file. On April 10 1987, we received the extraordinary communication shown in Fig.35, which declared that `*Alton Glenn Miller died in Ohio in December 1944'*.

+ + +

We were, of course, astounded. Taking our own system of public records as a yardstick, we judged it was quite impossible that Trenton could have made an error in such an important and personal document. Further, we recalled other connections with Ohio, such as the letter John Edwards received from a WW2 veteran, in which the writer described being in an Ohio hospital ward in 1944 with Major Glenn Miller.(P.90). George Ferguson lives in Columbus,Ohio. Royal Frey (who interviewed George in 1983 in a Columbus hotel and also Don Haynes before his death in 1971) was the curator of Wright-Paterson Air Force Museum in Ohio. And some giant computer in Cleveland Ohio had worked out a Norseman location for John Edwards, with what result no one knows ! Coincidence ? Perhaps...

We telephoned the Department of Vital Statistics in Columbus at once, asking if they had a death certificate.*Sorry,* Columbus said...*No information over the telephone.* We called a good friend in Fort Worth, Texas, and he sent off an urgent request enclosing the appropriate fee. *Sorry,* Columbus told him. *Death certificates are available to personal callers only...* We called George W.Ferguson in Columbus, who drove hotfoot into town and found the inquiry desk. *Sorry,sir,* Columbus said. *No certificate without more information on the place and date of death. We have,* they said, *millions on file, including several hundred thousand Millers.* Without allowing the telephone to cool, we called the State Registrar in Trenton N.J., explained the situation and asked for more information.

A lady official us the procedure : if and when a New Jersey resident died out of state, details were sent to Trenton on a small *pro forma* slip, and the death was noted in the records. The slip was then destroyed. We asked her to check the records again. She did so, confirming what their letter had said - that Alton Glenn Miller died in Ohio in December 1944.

At this point, we said carefully : "You realise, of course, that we are

talking about *the* Glenn Miller, who vanished in Europe in 1944 ?"
After a long silence,the official said nervously : "Is that so,sir ?
We'd better call you back on this inquiry."
A second and even more agitated lady called us next day. "We're
terribly sorry,sir. We owe you a big apology. The fact is we made a
bad error here. One of our typists sent you Alton Glenn Miller's
birth statistics, instead of death details."
We said patiently : "But he was born March 1 1900 - not December
1944 as you stated. And he was born in Iowa,not Ohio. It couldn't
have been his birth details."
"I'm sorry,sir," she said. "It was a typing error. And anyway -
Ohio,Iowa - it's the same state."
We blinked. Our geographical knowledge of the United States
might be bad - but not that bad !
"You have to be joking," we said weakly.
"No,sir. The Registrar will be writing to you any day now."
And so he did,repeating the `typing error' story. For a time we almost
believed it. But there was something out of kilter somewhere. We
realised that there was, in fact, an entry at Trenton about Glenn
Miller. Our first girl-friend there had gone back a second time to
check it. It wasn't a slip of paper, but an entry in a ledger or on a
computer disk - and information wasn't entered on the basis of an
inquiry letter, but from a properly-completed advice slip received
from another state.
Further, despite our own error in Glenn Miller's place of birth (Clarinda Ohio) Trenton had not quoted `Clarinda' at all. And they
could hardly confuse Glenn's date of birth(March 1 1900) with the
month of December 1944 ! Finally, no one quotes a date of birth
solely as a month and year, especially State Departments like Trenton. Irritatingly, we'd run into a brick wall in Columbus. It may have
been true that they had many Millers in the death certificate
files, but surely not that many `Alton Glenn Millers'. Further, we
had given them the date and location of his birth (Clarinda,Iowa).
Their statistics are computerised and cross-referenced, and it should
have taken no more than an hour to run down the item. Besides -
we had made it very clear we were dealing with a VIP of world
stature !
 The reader must decide for himself, but we closed that chapter in
the firm belief that there must be record entries in Trenton and the
Statistics Department in Columbus,Ohio.

* The Pasadena Connection

By late 1987, we had established to our satisfaction that Miller was
not lost in the Norseman, had not remained in the UK, and that no
trace of his interment was on record in any European war cemetery.

We knew also that many of the documents released by the end of 1948 were suspect, including the MACR, the `Reports of Death' documents confirming that no investigation had been initiated in 1944,and the Findings of Death documents giving Glenn's destination as Bordeaux. We had exhausted all European lines of inquiry and were no closer to a solution; we had disposed of most if not all of the more outlandish rumours.

Up to that point we had decided against approaching Glenn Miller's adopted son and daughter in America, for various cogent reasons. They were but babies when he disappeared. Further, we believed that Helen Miller had fared no better than countless other researchers in search of the truth : we had documentary proof of the AG Department's perfidy in withholding important details from her, in Col.Donnell's letter. She would not have been able to tell her growing children much about those far-off days, and we saw no possible gain in contacting them.

Further, we were acutely aware of the possibility that we might be intruding into the privacy of the Miller family, despite our authorization from Glenn's sole remaining blood-relative, Herb Miller. Our decision to extend our inquiries to the United States was not taken lightly.

The pertinent question concerned speculation and conjecture, and while many earlier writers had published freely their theories on Glenn's fate including John Edwards, John Flowers, Michael Harrison, Dale Titler and Roy Nesbitt, without being accused of intrusion of privacy (indeed, some writers published their books without offering them for scrutiny) we were determined to follow the rules. But what are the rules ? Collins' English Dictionary defines speculation as `*conjecturing without knowing the full facts'.* No one knows the truth as yet. But the definition of `conjecturing' is `*the formation of conclusions based on what facts are available'.*

`Speculation,'*per se,* is permissible without knowing the full facts,in order to construct an explanation of what may have happened. The viability of any result is a function of the quality of one's evidence. From a literary standpoint, therefore, we were entitled to make speculations, but with reservations : if they were of a wild and defamatory nature with no basis in truth at all, and lacking reasonable evidence, they were unjustifiable. If, however, they were legitimate lines of inquiry signposted by evidence accumulated from various other sources, they were in our view justifiable.

There was a simple criterion : if our researches had unearthed sufficient prior evidence to warrant some investigation of the California connection, so be it. But we would take every possible precaution to avoid any distress or adverse publicity involving Helen Miller and her family.

Finally,there remained the question of Glenn Miller himself, and the extraordinary circumstances of his disappearance. All these events occurred almost half a century ago and have become part of the fabric of history. Miller himself was an innocent party, and we found nothing to diminish his reputation in any way. All the central characters in the drama are now deceased - Glenn Miller, Don Haynes, Col.Baessell, Col.David Niven, John Morgan, Generals Goodrich, Barker, Davis and Eisenhower, Col.Early, Ralph S.Cramer, Col.Donnell, Major May and the rest. And because of the continuing popularity of Glenn's kind of music, many millions of his fans deserve to know the truth behind the mystery. We list here the relevant factors we considered :

* **Herb Miller's belief that Glenn was sent home.**

* **The John Edwards letter from a WW2 veteran.**

* **The persistent references to Dr.Pecora.**

* **Pecora's reluctance to comment further.**

* **Evidence that Glenn was not lost with Morgan.**

* **The letter from the New Jersey State Registrar.**

* **The lack of cooperation in Columbus,Ohio.**

* **The reluctance of National Archives to release Files.**

* **The Haynes diaries,clearly intended to mislead.**

* **Clear evidence of fabrication of documents.**

* **Further evidence of concealment of documents.**

* **The disappearance of Glenn's personal effects.**

* **Helen's disbelief of the Haynes story.**

* **Indisputable evidence of a high-level cover up.**

* **Dennis Cottam's evidence from Paris.**

* **John Edwards' account of the brawl in Pigalle.**

* **The covert search of Paris for Major Glenn Miller.**

* **Burial File evidence confirming that he travelled to Paris on Thursday December 14.**

* **Helen's 1949 purchase of a 6-grave burial lot in Altadena, for her 5-member family.**

* **The incorrect serial number in Glenn's orders, and his reluctance to wear dogtags, with a possibility of mis-identification.**

After a protracted discussion, we decided that these factors constituted adequate grounds for an investigation of a theory that Glenn, after reaching Paris, became involved in an accident or circumstances in which he received severe head injuries, but was not immediately identified as Glenn Miller. We further speculated that he was flown back to Ohio where he died in a military hospital, being interred as `MAJOR ALTON G. MILLER Serial Number 0606271', as per his Paris orders (Fig.19) in the lack of any identity tags.

Could this be possible ? Next of kin of war casualties who died in America were usually notified and the remains sent home for burial, or were interred locally if no next of kin could be traced. This might occur in the case of Major Alton G.Miller if checks were made under the wrong serial number.

But how might such an error have been discovered subsequently ? We knew that Helen, in the three years following the tragedy, ran down every rumour and theory before she moved to California to join her parents at the end of 1948.

It may have been coincidental that certain documents were released at that time, such as the MACR 10770, the Report of Death documents stating that no investigation was made, the Confirmatory Signal which encapsulated the Haynes' story, and specifically Glenn's Paris orders. There was little doubt that the last item was released - John Edwards obtained a copy as far back as 1969. But we had no firm evidence to support the theory that Helen saw the significance of the incorrect serial number and began checking on officers air-evacuated during December 1944. Many, we know, were flown into Wright-Paterson AFB, Ohio. Nor could we conclude on the basis of this evidence that Helen Miller discovered Glenn's remains and had them reinterred in Altadena.

However, we considered it imperative to check it out because of the relevancy of some if not all of the 19 factors quoted above. From writer Dale Titler and Royal Frey (a close friend of the Miller family) we learned that Helen died June 2 1966, and was buried on June 6 in Grave 5, Lot 2584, Mountain View Cemetery in Altadena, California. Herb Miller attended the ceremony.

So, in December 1986, we asked the Administrator to confirm Helen's true dates of birth and death, and we requested details of other relatives interred in the Lot. The Pasadena Cemetery Association (PCA) replied that the graves in Lot 2584 were in two groups of three : numbers 4,5 and 6,and 10,11 and 12. Helen was interred in Grave No.5, while her parents Fred W. and Anna Rose Burger were interred `between' graves 10 and 11, and 11 and 12 respectively. We believe they were cremated and their ashes interred, but we were unable to verify this fully. There was no mention of Glenn Miller.It was clear that there were 5 unoccupied graves in the Burial Lot; we wrote to the PCA in January 1987, identifying our interests and requesting that our letter should remain confidential. In it, we asked for a simple denial that Alton Glenn Miller was interred in Lot 2584. Now, at that time in the spring of 1987, the PCA could quite easily have sent us a note saying :

`*Sorry. Alton Glenn Miller is not interred in Mountain View.'*

We would then have abandoned the whole line of inquiry, moving on, perhaps, to other things. It was just an improbable theory we wished to eliminate like all the others. Indeed, we expected no other result. But we were astonished to find that the PCA were not prepared at that time to issue a denial and some 15 months passed before it was provided, enclosing documentary proof. In the circumstances, we feel that we cannot be blamed for assuming that the PCA may have had something to hide ! Even more astonishing, the PCA sent our confidential letter to Mr.Steve Miller, Glenn's adopted son. He made no attempt to contact us : instead, he wrote an angry letter to Herb Miller in London saying, in as many words, `*Get this guy off our backs !'*
There was no further contact, and faced with this somewhat unusual reaction,we asked an ex-R.A.F. friend living in Los Angeles, Bill Mc. to visit the Mountain View Cemetery in Altadena and check out the situation on the ground. His response was illuminating :

`*In the case of the missing musician,I set off with fellow-sleuths Murray Hamilton,well-known flyboy and oilman,Sterling Blakeman of the USAF 100th Bomber Group Association Historical Committee and a PR man from Green Hills Cemetery. We came up with the following information. From our Cemetery PR man, a comment on the wariness of two of the Admin. Staff at Mountain View who may be indicted for alleged mortuary practices. Helen Miller is in Burial Lot 2584 but no one will confirm who is also in the unmarked Lot with Helen. We identified the Lot with the help of groundskeepers,in lack of any help from the Cemetery Administration, who said later they said they had had many enquiries from English people.*
Finally, all my helpers here agree there is a bizarre strangeness

about the Cemetery's attitude ! Good luck with the book.   BILL

Unable to develop a reasonable explanation for the PCA's continued silence, we wrote to Mr. Steve Miller twice via a mutual friend,historian Royal Frey, but received no response - and similarly no denial. We apologised for any distress our inquiries may have caused, pointing out that the PCA's and his own refusal to issue a denial had only served to kindle our suspicions. We offered, in the event our theory was correct,to delete the location of the Lot from this book, avoiding undesirable publicity to the family, but all to no avail. We next heard from the Miller attorneys, threatening a legal suit if we dared to publish. We offered to provide a copy of the MSS for Mr. Miller,and to make any changes he required in the text. Some months later that offer was accepted, and we offered a stand-off period of three months in which to read the 9 pages of text involved.

At the expiry of the deadline, we wrote to the attorneys.It seemed that Mr. Miller had not had enough time to read the 9 pages... But he did so eventually,upon which some changes and deletions were incorporated and a copy of the amended MSS sent for scrutiny.

No other research group or author, as far as we can ascertain, has ever experienced such a reaction, but that may be because we got closer to the core of the mystery than anyone else. The Miller family attorneys maintain that their initial policy of silence was a reaction to our `unprofessional' approach, while saying little or nothing of the conduct of the PCA in passing on our confidential letter to Mr.Miller, thus precipitating the involvement of the Miller family we had been at such pains to avoid. This may have been true of the Millers - but why did the PCA remain silent for 15 months ? And while we can understand their desire to protect the privacy of the Miller family Burial Lot, there seemed to be no logical reason for them to refuse us permission to make an electronic scan of the Burial Lot, which would leave the site undisturbed and intact.

Finally, we received via the attorneys the denial we sought,which could have been provided much earlier, we feel. We received too a denial from the Pasadena Cemetery Association, and we are now able to confirm gladly that there is no record of Alton Glenn Miller having been interred legally in Burial Lot 2584 of Mountain View Cemetery, Altadena, California.

* The David Niven Connection

Lt.Col.David D.G.Niven, serial number P/449959 of the Rifle Brigade, was a prominent figure in the events which followed the AAF Band's arrival in England in July 1944. He is mentioned frequently in the Burial Files in the National Archives. He was a professional soldier prewar, and on the outbreak of hostilities he returned home from a successful career in Hollywood,to rejoin the British Army. He served in the Commandos under Col.Derek Hignett. Shortly before D-Day, he was seconded to SHAEF MAIN at Bushey Park near London, attached to Special Services Division. There, his showbusiness experience and many contacts were invaluable in receiving and caring for visiting personalities. He was appointed Associate Director of Troop Broadcasting under Col.Ed.Kirby, US Army, and when the AAF Band arrived in Sloane Court in the middle of `Bomb Alley', the threat of the V1s brought Glenn Miller, Don Haynes and Paul Dudley to SHAEF in search of a safer billet.

Glenn and David Niven were old friends. They had met when Miller was making the films *ORCHESTRA WIVES* and *SUN VALLEY SERENADE*, and they were close friends of Miss Marlene Dietrich; when she came to sing in Europe for the troops, she and Niven met whenever possible.
The documents in the Miller File suggest that Col. Niven lost no time in making it perfectly clear who was boss. He was, in fact, Glenn Miller's Commanding Officer, responsible for arranging AAF Band concerts and performances. He had chaired the meeting at SHAEF when the tour was approved; Major Hayes describes in his letters how Lt.Col. Niven had scoured France for suitable radio transmitters for the tour.
Like many researchers, we were unaware of the extent of David Niven's involvement with the AAF Band until we gained access to the Burial Files. He worked with them closely from Day 1, taking over administrative responsibility for the Band; he was effectively Glenn Miller's boss until the day the bandleader vanished. It was Niven who drove the Band officers to Bedford on their second day in England, and he arranged their domestic accommodation and rehearsal and recording studios in Bedford. He worked directly with Miller on their broadcast and concert programmes, arranging the venues and content. He was in the front row of the Corn Exchange Bedford when the Band made their first UK radio broadcast, in company with some of the other central characters including Don Haynes,Colonel Baessell,General Goodrich and Sgt.Broderick Crawford who went on to carve out a good career in movies.
When SHAEF MAIN moved to Versailles after Paris was liberated on August 24 1944, Niven remained at SHAEF REAR, Bushey Park as the Associate Director of Troop Broadcasting, but on October 1 Col.Ed.Kirby went home and Col. Niven was appointed Director at Versailles, while Major Johnny Hayes replaced him at SHAEF REAR. While there was occasionally some friction between Niven and Glenn Miller on a professional level, they remained good friends.
Thus, at this early stage of the investigation we anticipated finding a

great deal of information in Niven's post-war books about his work at SHAEF, with particular emphasis on his role in chairing the conference on November 15 which approved provisionally a Band concert tour in Paris, commencing on Thursday December 21. Don Haynes was given the task of finding suitable accommodation for the Band, while Miller, who had flown over to Paris a week earlier on November 8 as we have described, spent a pleasant week in the company of David Niven and Col.Baessell, before going back on November 18 in company with Mr.Wood.

But we began in an uneasy mood : we knew that Haynes (from the moment he arrived on Monday December 18 to the start of the Christmas Eve broadcast) had made no attempt to contact his boss, Col.Niven. We found that strange, since it was Niven who had arranged the Band concert programme in Paris; he had arranged venues and coordinated publicity with the help of Col.Dupuy in PR Division. Certainly, David Niven would have to be consulted on the announcement to be made at the first concert, and also on the cancellation of the two following performances. Haynes should have told Col.Niven at once that Glenn was missing,and we can safely assume that the reason he failed to do so was that Niven was not available in Paris.

And finally - if there was one man we might have have expected to meet Glenn Miller when he arrived (at Orly on Thursday December 14 by shuttle Dakota from Bovingdon, or on Friday December 15 by Norseman at A42 Villacoublay, depending on which version one favours) that man was Lt.Col.David Niven.

Yet we found in David's books no references to his long association with the Band between July and December 1944. There was no mention of Glenn Miller, or expressions of regret at the untimely passing of an old friend. Nor any reference to the SHAEF conference,the Band tour, the concerts David Niven himself had arranged, or their cancellation. Indeed, we could find no reference to Col. Niven being in Paris during that critical period after Glenn's disappearance.

However,we learned from Charles Higham's biography `*MAR-LENE' (Pocket Books New York,1977)* that she was performing in Paris USO shows on or about December 14,when a `Col.David' (a veiled reference to Niven) of the Special Services provided her with a Cadillac staff car and a driver/escort Col.Robt.Armstrong.She drove to Diekirch in Luxembourg, performing on Friday December 15, later driving at once north to Honsfeld, some 20 miles east of Spa (US 1st Army Headquarters).

We can be certain, therefore, that Niven was in Paris on Thursday December 14, and he could have met Major Miller at Orly. But what does Col.Niven tell us of his own movements on December 15, the day Miller supposedly went down in the Norseman ?

David Niven wrote in `*THE MOON'S A BALLOON*' (Hamish Hamilton,London) :

> `*In the middle of December I was passing through Spa in the Ardennes. I spent the night with Bob Low and he showed me the Map Room in Intelligence. "You see the trees on top of those hills ? In the forest now they are forming the Sixth Panzer Army and any day now, it's going to come right through this room...across the Meuse... go north to Antwerp." The next day I went down to... Marche. Within hours the last great German offensive of the war erupted. Ahead of it,Skorzeny's Trojan Horse Brigade : American speaking with captured American uniforms and transport, sabotaging as they went.'*

There are some remarkable inconsistencies, which are hardly attributable to poetic licence. The middle of December was the 15th,and the German offensive started at 02.00 next morning,December 16. Further, because of low cloud, Allied reconnaissance planes had been grounded; it is a matter of historical fact that von Runstedt very nearly took the Allied armies by surprise. One or two alert SHAEF intelligence officers were warning of an imminent offensive, and Col.Niven at SHAEF was well placed to learn of this impending threat. Only after 3 days heavy fighting did the German plan to strike for Antwerp become clear (see Fig.53). The 1st Army and Mr.Low at Spa may have been expecting trouble before the battle began, but had no way of identifying *Der Tag*.

Niven goes on :

> `*Next day I went down to Marche...within hours the offensive erupted'*.

But if he spent the night at Spa as he said, he was still in bed at 02.00 ! General Hodges was awoken at 07.30 with the news of the German breakthrough at Losheim, 30 miles east. We also know David Niven was in Paris up to Thursday December 14,arranging transport for Marlene Dietrich - and Spa is more than 200 miles by road from Paris. Col.Niven used a jeep provided by 21st Army Group; on battle-ravaged roads wrapped in fog and ice, such a journey would take at least 8 hours. To be at Spa at a reasonable hour he would have to depart Paris before dawn on Friday December 15, arriving possibly about noon. Niven was probably alerted during the Friday night with news of the coming battle; he knew that Marlene was due to perform on Saturday night at Honsfeld, 20 miles east of Spa,and realised she was in danger.

Now, up to this point we had assumed that Niven made this journey alone. He makes no reference to a companion in his books. But we were able to locate Col.Derek Hignett, his Commando chief, to obtain some good background material on that part of Niven's career. Colonel Hignett had an extraordinary story to tell : he was with his battalion in Richmond Park, Surrey, at the time news of the German thrust arrived during the night. Early next morning, Saturday, David Niven telephoned him from France, and as nearly as Hignett can recall, the conversation went as follows :

"Derek, old chap," Niven said breathlessly, *"we need some help out here. Marlene's in real danger of being over-run, and you know what they'll do to her if they catch her.*
"What do you need ?" Colonel Hignett asked.
"Can you send over half a dozen of your roughnecks to help us get her out ?"
"Sorry, old chap," the Colonel said. *"Can't be done. All hell has broken loose here and we're on standby."*

Disappointed, Col.Niven rang off. But Hignett was positive about one thing : David was not alone. Throughout the conversation it was `we' and `us', not `I' and `me'. It was possible, we thought, that Niven's friend Bob had been roped in, but this seemed improbable. Mr.Low had enough on his hands, with a battle to be fought. To find no mention of this in Niven's books was quite inexplicable.
Further, he told his biographer Sheridan Morley (`*THE OTHER SIDE OF THE MOON',Weidenfeld & Nicholson,London*) nothing of this period with the Band and Glenn Miller. Sheridan describes a brief London meeting between the two men when they were `*introduced by BBC producer Cecil Madden'*, but this is very unrealistic - they had met years before in the Hollywood days. Niven, Madden related, was representing the British Army at a conference - but in fact he was working for the Americans at SHAEF ! Morley found the lack of references untypical; in a letter to us he said :

`*I never discovered a connection (with Miller) and it seems a little odd to me that David, who was a compulsive story-teller, didn't talk about it - if not in his book, then in long private conversations'.*

This episode appears to provide bona fide evidence of David Niven's real motives for being at Spa at the time of the Ardennes offensive - to protect Marlene Dietrich from capture,interrogation and even a trial by the Germans. Certainly, he knew her itinerary; part of his duties at Special Services involved arranging USO shows and liaising with visiting personalities. She arrived at Honsfeld (Fig.53) a few hours after the Battle of the Bulge began,to find the town under threat of immediate attack and encirclement. Marlene was hurriedly evacuated westwards in a jeep by General James Gavin of the 82nd Airborne Division, who had dated her in Paris a few days previously. We do not know what happened to her Cadillac, and her biographer Charles Higham does not refer again to her own driver Col.Robert Armstrong. Marlene was driven west by jeep to 1st Army HQ at Spa,and as nearly as we can establish she arrived around midday on Saturday December 16, after the offensive had been in progress for some 10 hours. Waiting at Spa was David Niven, who had been unsuccessful in obtaining help from Col. Hignett. It would seem probable that he was very pleased to see her.

In both biographies we find that they drove in jeeps back towards Paris (but not specifically together). Thus far, we have ample evidence to confirm the facts - but what happened next ? It seems reasonable to assume that they drove back to Paris together in convoy via Marche and Rheims, yet there is no reference to this in either biography. We wrote several times to Miss Marlene Dietrich in Paris without any response, but she is now a venerable old lady living in retirement and not given to granting interviews or replying to letters.

We found the lack of biographical cross-references to each other during this time remarkable; after all, they were very close friends, and David Niven had gone to considerable lengths to come to her rescue, perhaps even driving up overnight from Paris to Spa. Finally, there are two items of purely circumstantial interest which should be mentioned at this point. One concerns a jeep accident en route back to Paris, at which Marlene stopped to help, with no reference to the location or personnel involved. The second is the presence in Rheims US military hospital at that time of Capt.David Pecora,US Medical Corps.

We can put all these facts into proper perspective in tabulated form to encapsulate Col.Niven's movements and involvement in the mystery, making the explicit point that up to this stage we have avoided speculation or conjecture. All the foregoing, and what follows,is fact.

* Niven was effectively in charge of the AAF Band as Director of Troop Broadcasting.

* He worked closely with Glenn Miller for 6 months until the latter vanished in December 1944.

* They were already close friends in Hollywood.

* Their mutual friend was Marlene Dietrich.

* Niven chaired the November 15 `tour' conference.

* He planned and organised the Paris concerts.

* He spent a week in Paris with Miller in November 1944,before and after the conference.

* He arranged personally the Bedford Band billets.

* He knew Haynes,Col.Baessell and Gen.Goodrich.

* He was in Paris up to Thursday December 14 1944.

* So was Marlene Dietrich. He knew her itinerary.

* He planned to rescue her from the Germans but a request to Col.Hignett for help was refused.

* He and Marlene were at Spa together on December 16, and both returned by jeep to Paris that day (but not necessarily together).

* Niven was not alone at Spa, said Col.Hignett. His friend Low was probably too busy to help him.

* There are no clues to Niven's movements after he left Spa for Paris.

* He was not injured or hospitalized at that time.

* He was not contacted by Haynes in the period between Monday December 18 and December 24. Nor is he mentioned in Haynes' diaries,nor does he talk of Haynes in his post-war books.

* His books do not refer to Miller,the AAF Band,or Glenn's untimely death.

* Niven told biographer Sheridan Morley nothing of that association. This was uncharacteristic.

* David Niven told his second wife Hjordis nothing about his association with the Miller band.

* He was decorated with the Legion of Merit post-war, for his services. General Ray Barker presented the award.

While discerning readers may see in this data something resembling a pattern, it is essential to avoid undue speculation and conjecture. We have no concrete proof that David Niven met Glenn Miller when the bandleader came into Orly around 13.30 on Thursday December 14, even if the former was in Paris at that time. There are no firm grounds for believing Miller and David Niven were in Fred Payne's British Bar on the evening of Friday December 15 (despite the hearsay evidence provided by Dennis Cottam) or that Glenn's missing personal effects were lodged in Paris. While Niven possibly drove up to Spa during Friday night to rescue Marlene Dietrich, we have no reliable evidence to show that Glenn Miller was his companion on that trip (although it is generally known that the bandleader often expressed the hope he would be able to see the battlefields - evidence of Herb Miller). We have no positive evidence that Niven's jeep was the vehicle involved in the `accident' mentioned in Marlene's biography, or that a passenger was injured in the incident. It is almost certainly coincidence that Dr. Pecora was stationed at the Rheims Military Hospital at the time.

We shall never know why David Niven omitted from his books all references to his association with Miller and the AAF Band, including Miller's death, or why he was at Spa on Friday December 15 1944 when - if Haynes was to be believed, he should have been at Paris Orly to meet Miller. Nor do we know why, having arranged the Band concert programme, he found it necessary to distance himself from the action and go to Spa. Further, we could find no logical reason for his continued absence from Monday December 18 to December 24, when the news was made public. We can devise no theory to explain why he was not contacted by Haynes, and why he was not consulted about the concert cancellations.

We are left, in fact, with a mass of circumstantial details which in themselves cannot be identified positively as a resume of his activities during the period. In our view, David Niven did nothing which can be remotely construed as a slur upon his character : in fact, it seems probable that he embarked upon a long and hazardous winter journey in an effort to deliver an old friend *from the power of the dog'*. That fortunately it proved an unnecessary mission does not detract in any way from his courage in undertaking it. As his son Jamie said in a letter to us from New York, David was greatly loved in the UK and round the world. He pointed out that Sheridan Morley undertook the Niven biography without the permission of either David or himself, and that David died before Morley commenced his book. It is not surprising, therefore, that David told Morley nothing of his experiences with the AAF Band and Glenn Miller.

Col. Niven may, of course, have had his own reasons for the omissions in his own book, despite the fact that the period between July and December 1944 was probably the most exciting and rewarding in his career. We shall never know.

+   +   +

6. **SUMMATION**

The search, for the moment at least, was ended. Admittedly, we had uncovered no concrete evidence on the fate of Major Glenn Miller, but we felt reasonably pleased with the progress we had made in three years, immeasurably greater than any other researchers. We were the first group to note the typeface irregularities in MACR 10770, and first to observe the incorrect serial number in Glenn's orders for Paris. We managed to find copies of those orders, in addition to John Morgan's Service Record Card and Form 5 (flight records) all of which had been abstracted from the Burial Files before the latter were released. We were the first investigators to gain access to the Files, thanks to a personal intervention by President Ronald Reagan. We had traced Dr.Pecora through John Edwards and Jack Donnelly; by elimination we confirmed that the Norseman found by Clive Ward was, indeed, Morgan's aircraft. We were the first to confirm that Morgan took the easterly route around London to Dymchurch. Most important of all we exposed the existence of a cover-up at a very high level in SHAEF, designed to conceal the fact that no one knew what had happened to Glenn Miller. We have demonstrated beyond doubt that Haynes' diaries were largely fabricated, and we obtained much new taped and documentary evidence.

We have no doubt that certain people in various parts of the world have further important information which would be invaluable - for example, some surviving members of the AAF Band and perhaps Miss Marlene Dietrich. It is not beyond the bounds of possibility that someone somewhere knows what did happen to Glenn Miller after he stepped to the ground from the shuttle C47 on that winter afternoon in December 1944, but for reasons of his own, prefers to remain silent. All that remains now is to summarise the evidence and review the conclusions drawn on the basis of that evidence.

+   +   +

SIX

THE MILLERGATE COVER-UP

1. THE PICTURE EMERGES

We were able to draw the following general conclusions :

* The Haynes account was unviable and misleading.

* Glenn Miller travelled by shuttle Dakota to Orly on Thursday December 14 1944 and vanished. The passenger handling proce-dures at Bovingdon made it possible to travel unrecognised.

* He was last seen alive at 02.30 that morning outside the Milroy Club, Stratton Street, Mayfair, where he had spent the evening with Sqn.Ldr.Bartley and others.

* Haynes and Morgan, also there, left before midnight to return to Bedford.

* None of Miller's personal effects were ever found.

* Glenn would not have to report to SHAEF for a week.

* Don Haynes on arrival at Paris on Monday December 18 made no effort to report Glenn as missing in the Norseman. Instead,he searched Paris for two days.

* Haynes reported to Gen. Barker at 18.00 Tuesday, when the Norse-man story emerged for the first time.

* Gen.Barker delayed all reporting procedures,arranged for a con-firmatory signal to be sent from 8th AFSC and cancelled the second and third Paris concerts.

* The MACR was delayed 9 days, and was despatched to Wash-ington December 23. Adjutant Capt. Ralph S.Cramer refused to sign it.

 * A facsimile Report No. 10770 was fabricated at Maxwell AFB, Alabama, dated March 26 1946 and released in November 1948. It was certified and guaranteed as genuine by the National Archives in Washington for 44 years, while the unsigned `ORIGINAL' MACR was suppressed.

* No official investigation was made in 1944, and Don Haynes was never questioned or interrogated. After Helen Miller pressed the AG Department again in 1946, they arranged a superficial inquiry in Europe, but in his subsequent reply to Helen, Col. Donnell deliberately omitted important information on the aircraft route.

* To support the Non-Recoverability Board inquiry in 1947, Washington AG Department supplied information to Major Morrow of Isolated Burials, Europe, which he sent back to the NR Board in the United States.

* General Ray Barker at SHAEF may have believed the Don Haynes story. Alternatively, he may have known it was false but went along with it, in the lack of any other options. Lastly, he may have developed the plan himself, but we have no firm evidence of that. His actions after Lt. Haynes reported to him suggest that he knew Miller had arrived in Paris but was out of touch.

* The actions of Gen.Barker's ADC Major May, such as amending the Norseman's take-off time, tend to support that conclusion.

* The post-war policy of restriction of access to the Burial Files by various archival departments in the United States is self-evident from the correspondence set out in an earlier chapter.

* Only two conclusions are possible : that Glenn Miller either died in Paris from causes unknown, but because his body was never discovered, foul play cannot be ruled out, or he was sent back to the USA injured but unrecognised, due to misidentification.

2. THE DON HAYNES CONNECTION

* No official report or narrative of his account was ever released by any United States governmental or military agency.

* All references to his account in official documents can be traced to his interview with General Barker.

* He was never questioned or interrogated, despite some reports that he was interviewed by Provost Marshals in Paris. There is no official record of an 8th AF inquiry on January 15 1945.

* The account contains numerous inconsistencies, errors and anomalies indicating that it was falsified as from the entry for Wednesday December 15 1944. Haynes used extensive data from

the November 8 flight to give his December 15 account some authenticify.

* The account is diametrically opposed to MACR No.10770 and the `ORIGINAL' in reference to route, departure and destination airfields,take-off time,etc. He is not named as the `*person with last knowledge of the aircraft'* and he made no eyewitness statement to the compiling officer.

* Both Don Haynes' account and the MACRs are contradictory to the evidence in the Burial Files and Morgan's own Service Records.

* Haynes' actions on arrival in Paris confirm that he was aware that Miller had arrived in Paris but was out of touch temporarily.

* Inexplicably, he omits all reference to his superior officer, Lt. Col.David Niven.

3. THE DOCUMENTARY EVIDENCE

Missing Aircrew Report 10770 (Figs.12/13)

* Circulated for 44 years as genuine by the National Archives. The unsigned `ORIGINAL' was suppressed.

* The National Archives denied there was any other MACR and refused to allow experts to examine it.

* It was fabricated at Maxwell AFB Alabama on March 26 1946, because the `ORIGINAL' report was unsigned.

* Capt. Cramer's signature was forged. He had refused to sign the `ORIGINAL' and would hardly sign a forgery.

* Cramer's name and rank were erased on all the released copies of Report 10770, making his identification difficult.

* At least two different machines were used on several occasions to type Report 10770.

* A trial version (the `SAMPLE MACR) was compiled at Maxwell AFB, and was found in the Burial Files.

* The 10770 format follows closely the `ORIGINAL', which was used as a template.

* The Ansell Report confirms its fraudulent nature.

* A false `date/time' arrival stamp was used to suggest the Report did not reach Washington until January 22 1945. No such stamp is seen on the `ORIGINAL'

* Report 10770 was included in the numerical file of MACRs, made possible because 44-70285 was not included in the Cumulative Loss Listing until 1947 - after the fabricated Report was produced. Report N-19 (the `ORIGINAL') is not listed in the MACR File.

THE `ORIGINAL' MACR N-19 (Figs.14/15)

* While stamped `ORIGINAL', it is an extract from some complete document, which has never been located.

* Its existence was never suspected until access was gained to the Burial Files.

* Page 1 was in Miller's File. National Archives stated there was no Page 2. But it was found subsequently in Morgan's File.

* It specifies `A42' as the first destination and `Twinwood' as the location the plane was last seen. The weather and engine number are quoted as `unknown' but were available.

* Lt. Haynes is not named, and there is no eyewitness statement from him.

* There is no Washington `date/time' arrival stamp.

* It bears the same compilation date as 10770, December 23 1944 - nine days after the Norseman was lost.

* It is unsigned but the identification details of the compiler, Capt. Ralph S.Cramer are clearly legible.

* National Archives refused to comment on the Report and falsification of 10770, saying they did not comment on Files.

`SAMPLE' Missing Aircrew Report (Fig.16).

* An obvious attempt to simulate the `ORIGINAL', but is annotated as a `copy of 10770' !

* There is no Page 2.

* An error at Para.12 made the document unviable.

* The depressed `B' in `Bordeaux' confirms its origin as Maxwell AFB in 1946.

Confirmatory Signal December 20 1944 (Fig.46)

* Sent at Gen.Barker's request to get the Haynes story on record.

* Omits Haynes' name as take-off witness.

* Not released officially until November 1948.

AG Letter to Helen Miller (Fig.32).

* The first identifiable communication from the AG.

* Triggered by her previous letters, and the USFET/USAFE investigation in 1946, leading to the fabrication of Report 10770.

* Deliberate omission of any reference to an intended landing by Morgan at A42 Villacoublay.

* Confirms that Morgan was cleared directly from Abbotts Ripton to France `via Twinwood Field'.

Press Memo and Release (Figs.41/42)

* Confirms an official policy of delay until the last possible moment (1 hour before the broadcast to America).

* Required correspondence to be returned to originator.

* No subsequent Press Releases or statements.

Finding of Death Documents (Figs.22,28,30)

* Originated December 16 1945.

* Gives the destination of all three men as Bordeaux.

* All `Circumstances of Disappearance' entries appear to coincide precisely. Possibly photocopied.

Report of Death Documents (Figs.23,27,31)

* All confirm no investigation made in 1944.

* Dated differently for Miller, Morgan, Baessell.

* The 1948 version shows Morgan as a `Battle Casualty', which was amended in 1952.

Letter from Gen.Davis to Gen.Eisenhower (Fig.34)

* Davis delayed 6 days before advising Eisenhower in an `official' letter. Why ? Did `Ike' already know ?

* Dated December 23 and triggered by Casualty Report, it confirms an official delay policy and a deadline imposed by the Christmas Eve broadcast to the United States.

* Fails to identify Haynes by name as prime witness.

* But quotes Haynes' story from the Casualty Report. An MACR had not yet been compiled !

Morgan's Service Record Card (Fig.28) and Forms 5

* Both documents had been abstracted from the Burial File. One was sent to us anonymously by an employee in National Archives.

* Totally refutes both the MACRs and Haynes' story.

* Confirms true destination was B42 Beauvais.

* Confirms that Morgan was at Honington on November 8 but not on December 15.

Major Miller's Orders for Paris

* To travel `*on or about December 16'*. Flexible.

* In name of `*Alton G.Miller'*.

* Incorrect serial number `0606271' unidentified.

* Missing from the File copy provided by Archives.

New Jersey Letter

* An alleged typing error, it states that `*Alton Glenn Miller died in Ohio in December 1944'*.

* Information confirmed after second check of records.

* Claims letter gave `birth details' instead of `death' i.e `Born in Ohio December 1944'. Glenn Miller was born in Iowa in 1900.

Special Services Letters in Burial Files

* From Major J.Hayes to SHAEF,providing confirmation that Mr. Ted Gower was resident BBC engineer from November 24 1944.

* Gower told John Edwards he travelled in the seat behind Miller on a shuttle flight to Paris after that date.

* Checks on Miller's movements indicate that his only possible flight date was Thursday December 14 1944.

* Col. Niven was involved in finding transmitters for the Paris concert tour.

Burial File Letter - Miller's Personal Effects

* Confirms that no effects were ever returned to Helen Miller.

* No effects were found in UK.

* For 6-week tour Miller would take at least 3 bags.

* Haynes took no Miller effects to Paris with the Band and refers to only 1 bag in the Norseman story.

* Logical assumption is that Major Miller took all his effects with him to Paris on Thursday December 14 1944.

4. AFTERMATH OF INVESTIGATION

When our inquiry closed we wrote to Memorial Services in Alexandria in summer 1987, commenting on the various papers and documents in the Burial Files. The ever-helpful Mr.John Manning replied :

`*The* (Miller) *case has been thoroughly reviewed, including your previous correspondence. We feel that many of your concerns relate to attempting to interpret information contained on copies of documents, instead of actually examining original documents, or carbon copies of the original documents...We feel that a visit to our office would be beneficial - examining actual records in the Miller File and comparing with other individuals'.*

This, we felt,was all very well - but the truth was that we had not been shown genuine original documents at all. Not the important ones,certainly : the MACR 10770 was a forgery and they had declined to confirm it via expert examination. The `ORIGINAL' MACR N-19 had been concealed and suppressed, while several documents had been abstracted from the Files and never released officially,including Miller's orders and Morgan's Service records. When we learned that Page 2 of the `ORIGINAL' was missing, National Archives said emphatically that there was no Page 2 - yet we found it in another File ! Was that because it was unsigned and also bore the complete identification of Capt.Cramer - a witness we would dearly like to have interviewed ?

Further, all these things provoked a sense of unease. Had the Archives tampered with or suppressed other items which we had never seen ? How could we be certain we had received all the File contents ? Many items were duplicated and included in all three Files - why ? To `pad out' the contents and display an impressive bulk of documents ? It may well be true that, if we had visited Washington to examine the original typed MACR 10770, we may have found the vital identifying details about Capt.Cramer clearly legible - but they had been erased on all normal-sized copies of the MACR we could trace; further, when Archives sent us the `blown-up' copy we requested, the details were erased in the copy also !

We were extremely uneasy about the frequent attempts to deny us access to the Files. They had been variously lost, misplaced,destroyed in a fire and mis-filed. We know from a further letter that other relevant Files may exist, which we cannot request because we know no other details. But we must stress that lower-echelon heads of departments were in the main helpful and cooperative; they may not have known what was in other Files, and Mr.Manning's letter of November 6 1986 demonstrates a lack of cooperation between various departments of National Archives. The official policy of delay, denial and obfuscation clearly emanated from top level, as evinced recorded telephone comments of Mr.George Chalou. Such a policy must have been authorised by a directive from the State Department, the Adjutant-General or the Attorney General, and we must ask why even today there is a motivation to conceal the truth about events which occurred almost half a century ago.

What had been done was done undoubtedly to conceal from the general public the attempts by senior officers at SHAEF to explain the inexplicable - why a senior officer of the United States Army Air Force,and a VIP to boot, had vanished from human ken while under the care and jurisdiction of the US Armed Services. No doubt it was an error of judgement on the part of SHAEF staff to decide that a false explanation was preferable to no explanation at all, but once that decision was taken, there was no going back, and all other events followed in train : the fabrication of MACR 10770, the total suppression of the unsigned `ORIGINAL' MACR, concealment of the identity of Capt.Cramer until it was too late to trace and interrogate him.

We can cite the lack of an immediate official investigation, the covert search of Paris for Major Miller, the failure to interrogate Don Haynes, the lack of any official version of his story, the efforts of Col. Donnell of the AG's Department to conceal vital information from Helen Miller - the list is endless. It cannot be coincidence that almost every researcher, including John Edwards, Henry Whiston, Dennis Cottam and the late Sqn.Ldr.Jack Taylor were all approached and `warned off' by polite but insistent Americans - or that our telephone was bugged for a period of a year during the inquiry. It cannot be coincidence that Elaine Everley of National Archives `forgot' to tell us about the Press cutting in the Burial Files dated 1973, referring to the discovery of a C64 Norseman which had been identified as Morgan's aircraft ! Or saying that Mr.Rodd at Maxwell AFB had told us about the engine numberplate being already removed and stored in the National Archives `as a joke' ! This was at the time we were preparing an exploratory dive on the Clive Ward aircraft...

+   +   +

And so we come to the end of our story. Our extraordinary success in locating new information was little consolation for our failure to account for Major Alton Glenn Miller's disappearance. But as long as his kind of music retains the popularity it has today (and one cannot envisage a future time when this will not be the case) the search will go on, year after year, because it is a challenge that will not go away. As Mr.Winston Churchill said at the Mansion House in London on November 10 1942 :

>   `This not the end... It is not even the beginning of the end. But it is perhaps the end of the beginning'.

All over the world, faithful Glenn Miller fans deserve to know the truth of the matter. Most of all, the world owes the man himself a debt of gratitude for the pleasure and enjoyment he has given us, from those dark wartime days to the present, and on into the 21st Century.

END

Wilbur Wright
Southampton,England
1986-1990

REPORT OF MICHAEL ANSELL MA
No. 861205
in the matter of
MISSING AIRCREW REPORT
15 January 1987

Introduction

I hold the degrees of B.A. and M.A. at the University of Oxford, and I am experienced in the scientific examination of documents and handwriting, having retired from the post of Deputy Head of Documents Section of the Metropolitan Police Forensic Laboratory in October 1983. During my 14 years exclusive experience I have examined tens of thousands of documents on behalf of the Police, Government Departments, Banks, Building Societies and other companies, as well as for private individuals. During part of my time at the MPFL I was the British representative on the Interpol Committee for identification of typescript.

On 4th December 1986 I received by post from Wilbur Wright of Southampton a number of photocopy items as listed below.

1. Missing Aircrew Report – 2 pages.
2. Fig. 33 (later renumbered 17) Blow-Up of Item 1.
3. Fig. 31 (later renumbered 18) Classification Change.
4. Fig. 12 Record Card of Flight Officer Morgan.
5. App. 13 Non-Battle Casualty Report (Glenn Miller).

I have examined these.

Assumptions

I have taken these items to be true copes of their originals except where they have been reasonably edited or enlarged in order to illustrate certain points in the text of the book.

Instructions

I have been asked to express an opinion as to:-
(a) Whether the route details were typed by a similar model but different machine to that used in the rest of the Report.
(b) Whether, if (a) be correct, the same other machine was used to type the Classification Change Certificate.
(c) Whether either of these machines was used on both first and second pages of the Report, such that a falsified first page could have been attached to a genuine signed second page.

Observations

There are two restrictions to my examination. Firstly, the examination of photocopies is never as good as the examination of originals for a number of reasons, and secondly because the type of machine(s) used here, as is often the case with Government machines, particularly of that period, were of poor quality having a number of loose characters.

The first limitation means, for example, the colour of ink and depth of impression cannot be seen. The second means that, for example, the same machine can easily type a raised 'B' on one occasion and a lowered 'B' on a different occasion. This means that two apparently-different, in regard to defects, entries may in fact be by the same typewriter and vice versa.

However, the impression is given here that the Missing Aircrew Report was printed or duplicated in some way, albeit from a possibly-typed original which incorporated the word 'pilot' as part of the original document. The particulars 'Morgan, John R.S., F/O, T-190776' and 'Missing' appear to have been typed by one machine which I designate 'A'. The particulars 'Passenger' against 2 and 3 appear to have been made by a different machine which I designate 'B'. The remaining particulars for the two passengers and the three entries ',AC' including that against Pilot appear to have been typed by machine B but on a different occasion.

I also notice that the number of passengers '2' and total '3' have a peculiar 'thick' appearance as if they may have been typed more than once. I also note that the 'B' is consistently lowered in 'Bordeaux' in the route details. This also occurs in the words 'Norseman' and 'Morgan' but not 'Norman' or 'Major' against Passenger details.

Conclusions

It is difficult to reach any firm conclusions because of the combination of the photocopying process and variable and poor quality of the typescript. It is not possible to tell, for example, how many of the details at the top right were typed, and how many stamped. However, I am able to comment that the following are likely to have taken place:

A.   The Pilot's particulars (Para. 11-1) except ',AC' were typed by machine 'A'.
B.   The words 'Passenger' (Paras. 11-2 and 11-3) were typed by machine 'B'.
C.   All other passenger details including the three words ',AC' were typed by machine 'B' but on a different occasion.

I am unable to account for the peculiar appearance of the figures '2' and '3' for the number of passengers and total. The words 'unknown' on each sheet all appear to have been typed by the same machine, therefore I think it unlikely that the first sheet was a complete substitution unless it was by a different person with access to the same machine. However, I do think it possible that the whole Report was prepared for Pilot only and the number of passengers and their details added later, for whatever reason.

M. Ansell M.A. 15th January 1987

`Appendix `A'
The Ansell Report

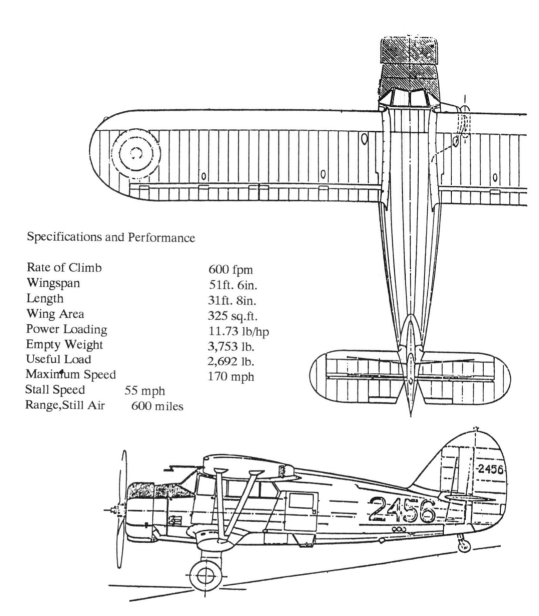

Specifications and Performance

Rate of Climb	600 fpm
Wingspan	51ft. 6in.
Length	31ft. 8in.
Wing Area	325 sq.ft.
Power Loading	11.73 lb/hp
Empty Weight	3,753 lb.
Useful Load	2,692 lb.
Maximum Speed	170 mph
Stall Speed	55 mph
Range,Still Air	600 miles

NOORDUYN UC64A NORSEMAN

With acknowledgements to `AIR PROGRESS'

Manufactured by Noorduyn Aviation Ltd.
Montreal, Canada.

Appendix `B'
Leading Particulars - C64A Noorduyn Norseman

APPENDIX `C'

`LANCASTER BOMBS KILL GLENN MILLER'

1. INTRODUCTION

Reports began to circulate during 1987 that an ex-R.A.F. Lancaster navigator, Fred Shaw, claimed to have seen a UC64A Norseman aircraft destroyed by heavy bombs jettisoned into the English Channel from a force of 137 Lancaster bombers returning from an aborted raid on Siegen, near Cologne. This occurred, Shaw said, on December 15 1944, and it has been discussed in detail on P.58 *et seq*, and also on Pp.82 and 89. Our main interest in the story was that it appeared to assume that Morgan took the `long-way-round' route west of London, via Bovingdon and Beachy Head, but we had already identified a number of valid reasons supporting the shorter route east of London (P.83 *et seq*) which we repeat here for convenience :

* Morgan was cleared direct from Abbotts Ripton to France. (Evidence Fig.32).

* The weather was fair,with at least 3000 foot cloudbase,visibility 1 mile+ and no rain. (Fig.39). He could fly `contact'.

* He did not land at Twinwood Farm (evidence of three surviving Twinwood Farm personnel, a Form 540 (Station Daily History, his Service Record Card and Haynes' flawed evidence about Honington).

* Morgan could not have departed from any other airfield but Abbotts Ripton (Record Card, Form 5,Fig.32).

* Flight times from Abbotts Ripton to Beauvais,overflying Bovingdon, effectively prohibited any flight west of London from arriving before dusk :

Bovingdon/Guildford/Beachy Head/Beauvais	2hr.30m.
Same route + 1 hr flight plan/clearance Bovingdon :	3hr.30m.
Bovingdon/Guildford/Cap Gris Nez/Beauvais	3hr.30m.

and

Abbotts Ripton/Dymhurch/Beauvais direct	2hr.10m.

Dusk at Beauvais was 16.22. Taking off at 13.25, Morgan could not make Beauvais before dark taking any route west of Bovingdon involving landing there for clearance, or overflying the airfield and using the `iron compass' rail line via Ashford. The only feasible route to make Beauvais before darkness fell was direct from Abbotts Ripton-Dymchurch to Beauvais, arriving at 15.35 with half an hour safety margin.

* A single-engined aircraft was reported crossing out at Dymchurch at a time compatible with a departure at 13.25 from Abbotts Ripton. The sighting was reported to General Barker at SHAEF.

* The `Diver' Gun Box was inactive on December 15, permitting all aircraft to fly through the area. The 137 Lancasters from East Anglia flew through it around noon en route to Amiens and Siegen.

* At approximately 14.40 Morgan would be several miles west of Le Touquet - the exact location in which Clive Ward discovered a Norseman in 1980.

* That aircraft, by simple elimination, has been identified as John Morgan's Norseman.

* Two surviving Norseman pilots who flew this route several times confirm that they regarded the Beachy Head-Dieppe-Paris route as unsafe,particularly in the winter period, because the Norseman was single-engined and ditching in winter seas was fatal. They briefed Morgan to use the safer shorter route from Dymchurch-Cap Gris Nez.

However, we decided that the `bomb' story merited a closer examination and analysis, because while all the evidence suggested that Glenn Miller was not aboard the Norseman, and that Morgan took the easterly route around London on December 15, it was perfectly clear that Fred Shaw had, in fact, seen some aircraft destroyed. Extensive research showed that, other than Morgan's Norseman, no USAAF or R.A.F. single-engined passenger aircraft had been reported missing that day. One P51 Thunderbolt was lost on a daylight attack on German positions around Dunkirk (which may have been the aircraft reported by John Edwards' three witnesses).

Mr. Roy Nesbitt has written an article on the Channel sighting in `THE AEROPLANE' magazine, in which he assumed that Morgan had chosen to overfly Bovingdon and use the long (65-mile) crossing from Beachy Head to Dieppe, and he also made the assumption that Morgan was bound for Villacoublay, to drop off Glenn Miller. Mr. Nesbitt, of course, did not have our advantages in regard to the contents of the

Burial File, the Service documents of John Morgan or our proof that the MACR 10770 was fraudulent. He sought to prove mathematically that the Norseman could have been in the Channel Bomb Jettison Area at the same time the returning Lancasters jettisoned their bombs.

To determine that time, we must examine the history of the Siegen Raid on December 15 1944.

2. THE LANCASTER FLIGHT PROFILE

In the first two weeks of December 1944, the 1st US Army in the Ardennes had no accurate indications of an impending offensive by the Sixth Panzer Army, other than scenarios put forward by a few alert Intelligence officers based on unconfirmed and possibly `scaremongering' reports from forward patrols about noises of heavy armoured vehicles moving in the fog-bound forests. The weather had grounded Allied reconnaissance aircraft, but Bomber Command Intelligence learned of extensive movements of troops and armour through many rail junctions around Cologne, such as Trier and Siegen. Accordingly a daylight raid of medium size involving 138 Lancasters of No. 3 Group in East Anglia, was organised for December 15. (One aircraft aborted take-off). Participating units included Nos. 15 and 149 Squadrons from R.A.F. Methwold (including Fred Shaw's crew). The group was told a force of USAAF P51 Mustangs would be in support all the way to the target.

Daylight raids were always hazardous and the route was planned to involve the minimum time over enemy territory - low level at 2000 feet direct to Tunbridge Wells, flying through the inactive `Diver' Gun Box to Beachy Head from whence the formation would climb on track to 20,000 feet over Amiens, France, pick up their escort and head due east into Germany. Most of the aircraft carried `cookies', large cylindrical bombs with thin skins that were notoriously dangerous when landing. Aircrews were briefed to dump such bombs in an area due south of Eastbourne in mid-Channel (Fig.51) before they returned from an aborted raid. The safe jettison altitude was 6000 feet, and if they were in cloud the navigator would jettison on a pre-calculated time and position. The bomber stream was some 30 miles long and would take 8 minutes to pass over the centre of the Jettison Area - it was a circle 20 miles in diameter. Flying at 240 mph, each bomber would take 5 minutes to cross the widest point.

The danger period, therefore, was 4 minutes on either side of the time the Norseman was calculated to be at the central point in the area. On the day, the fighter escort was grounded by inadequate visibility and Bomber Command sent the Recall Signal to all aircraft to abort the mission.

Having access to some of the navigational logs and recollections of crews taking part in the operation, and knowing the time at which the `Recall' signal was received, we were able to identify the force's position at the time and we constructed a flight profile for one of the attacking aircraft, flown by Flt.Lt.French and his crew.

It is necessary to remember that any co-incident event involving two aircraft must be assessed on the basis of a common timebase. Mr.Nesbitt sought to prove that an apparent 1-hour variation between the times that Morgan and the Lancasters were in the area was due to the difference between GMT (Greenwich Mean Time) and BST (British Summer Time). BST was GMT + 1 hour, used by both the general public and armed forces in Britain and France in the winter of 1944. It was called `military time' and written as `18.00A' by American forces. The exceptions were aviation and marine navigators, who used GMT to conform with their navigational star tables. Normally, an `A' suffix was unused except in correspondence and radio signals, so that when the R.A.F., USAAF and general public referred to `13.25' it meant 13.25 BST, i.e GMT + 1 hour. While the R.A.F.navigators wrote GMT or `Zulu' times in their logs and charts, other crew members were using BST in completing their flight log books and signing the Flight Authorisation Book which recorded flight times. Both Morgan in the Norseman and the Lancaster crews were using the same time base throughout.

Our flight profiles use the following abbreviations :

DIS	Distance in nautical miles.	AR	Arrival Time.
IAS	Indicated Airspeed,mph.	MW	Methwold.
TAS	True Airspeed,mph.	BH	Beachy Head.
ALT	Altitude,feet x 1000.	AM	Amiens.
GS	Ground Speed,mph.	RP	Recall Point.
DEP	Departure Time.	JP	Jettison Point.

Lancaster Flight Plot

	DIS	TAS	ALT	GS	TIME(m)	DEP	ARR
MW - BH	110	170	2,000	155	42	11.15	11.57
BH - AM	100	150	to 16,000	150+	40	11.57	12.37
AM - RP	30	150	to 20,000	170	10	12.37	12.47
RP - JP	90	200*	to 6,000	240	22	12.48++	13.10

Notes :

1. Fred Shaw's take-off time was `12.00 approximately'. This is reasonable - it was not unusual to take 30 minutes to get two squadrons of 16 aircraft each airborne. The time lag was made up en route to the `assembly area'. Flt.Lt French and crew were in the first wave.

2. The IAS-TAS equation requires explanation. At sea level,IAS = TAS (ignoring instrument error). With increasing altitude and less-dense

air, the IAS indicator underreads and IAS falls below TAS. At 20,000 feet, 170 mph IAS may represent 240 mph TAS. TAS was calculated using a Dalton computer.

3. At `150+' we assumed that increasing IAS would offset the known southerly wind vector of approx. 12 mph.

4. At `200*' we took IAS 200 mph from Shaw's taped narrative in which he said : `We wanted to get home for lunch and stuffed the nose down...'

5. At `12.48++' we allowed 1 minute for a left-hand turn to 335 degrees from 090 degrees, heading for the Jettison Area. Shaw describes this as a `10-mile radius turn' but in the author's experience, the general reaction to a `Recall Signal' was a split-arsed turn and full-throttle dive for home ! Note that `Recall Point' was calculated empirically from the time Recall was received.

This profile places the Lancaster force passing through the Bomb Jettison area between 13.06 and 13.14.

3. THE NORSEMAN FLIGHT PROFILE

Notes :

1. We assumed TAS as 120 mph at 2,000 feet, and that Morgan overflew Bovingdon but did not land. Also, a 12 mph headwind would cancel the IAS-TAS variation at 2,000 feet. We assumed he departed from Twinwood Farm at 13.55.

2. Dieppe, liberated September 1, was not a hazard area.

3. `JPA' below represents the centre of the Jettison Area.

The Norseman Flight Plot.

	DIS	TAS	ALT	GS	TIME	DEP	ARR
TF - BH	90	120	2000	105	51	13.55	14.45
BH - JPA	35	120	1000	105	10	14.45	14.55

The Norseman would take 10+ minutes to pass through the area's maximum diameter, ie 14.50 to 15.00. The last Lancaster would vacate the Jettison Area at 13.14, and the earliest time the Norseman would enter is 14.50. This is a time gap of more than an hour and a half, and the last of the bombers would be back on the ground before Morgan departed Twinwood Farm at the MACR time of 13.55. Even with a 1-hour variation caused by the use of GMT by the navigators, there is still a time gap of 34 minutes.

Applying the same reasoning to a take-off time of 13.25 from Abbotts Ripton, distance to JPA would be 160 miles = flight time 91 minutes, ETA at JPA 14.56, only 1 minute later than the Twinwood time ! The time gap remains unbridged. The possible time of an incident would be between 13.06 and 13.14 - before Morgan left either Twinwood or Abbotts Ripton. Further - in order to enter the Jettison Area after leaving Beachy Head, Morgan would have to be flying some 40 degrees off his course for Dieppe, ten minutes after a good pinpoint !

4. CONCLUSIONS

The sum does not add up. We investigated the possibility of a jettisoned `cookie' heavy bomb detonating after delayed action, an hour after it was dropped, but information from the R.A.F. Museum at Hendon revealed that the thin-skinned weapons usually detonated after breaking up, which activated the fusing mechanism. There is one other point - the weather in the Channel. Actual observations (Fig.39) confirm that the cloudbase over the Channel was a full-cover layer of stratus at 1500 feet, going up to 2,000 feet, such that Morgan would be flying at low level over the sea, probably under 1,000 feet. This would also preclude any possibility of the Lancaster crews observing a small aircraft, painted in wartime camouflage, more than a mile below against a leaden sea - much less identify it as a Norseman, but we must accept the possibility that there were breaks in the cloud, through which the sea may have been visible from 6,000 feet.

If Fred Shaw did see a Norseman surrounded by bomb explosions on December 15 1944, it was almost certainly 43-5367 (see Pp.56-59,85) destroyed en route to its base in France from Grove Field.

In the face of this strong evidence, we were obliged to discount the `Lancaster bombs' theory, as a cause of the death of the late Major Alton Glenn Miller.

+ + +

INDEX

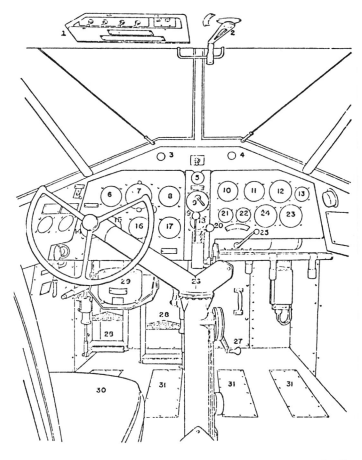

AIR PROGRESS

UC64A NOORDUYN NORSEMAN
COCKPIT LAY-OUT
(Right hand seat and controls omitted for clarity)

1. Switch Panel
2. Flap Control
3. Carburettor Heat Control
4. Oil Temperature Shutter Control
5. Propeller Control
6. Airspeed Indicator
7. Artificial Gyro Horizon
8. Rate of Climb Indicator
9. Ignition Switch
10. Tachometer
11. Manifold Pressure Gauge
12. Cylinder Head Temperature Gauge
13. Ammeter
14. Clock
15. Altimeter
16. Gyro Compass

17. Turn and Bank Indicator
18. Oil Pressure Gauge
19. Throttle
20. Mixture Control
21. Oil Temperature Gauge
22. Fuel Gauge
23. Air Temperature Gauge
24. Blank extra gauge fitting
25. Nose Shutter Control
26. Control Column
27. Elevator Trim Control
28. Rudder/Brake Pedals
29. Magnetic Compass
30. Pilot's Seat
31. Metal Heel Plates

Fig.59

VETERANS ADMINISTRATION
Insurance Form No. 1662 (Revised)
Form prescribed by
Comptroller General, U. S.
April 12, 1944

Clf. ....
XC- .. 6 036 049
N- 12 859 933

DETERMINATION OF LIABILITY AND CERTIFICATION
BY THE COMMITTEE ON EXTRA HAZARDS OF SERVICE
NATIONAL SERVICE LIFE INSURANCE

Name of insured .... **John R. S. Morgan** .... Date of death ... **12/15/44** ....

Entered active service .... Active service terminated .... Date of application for insurance ....

Face value of policy, $ **10,000** Plan **5 LPT** Effective Date **6/1/43** Age at Issue **21**

Changed to $ ....

Premiums paid to .... Date of total disability .... Due date of first premium covered by waiver ....

Date for application for premium waiver .... Does total disability continue? .... If not, date terminated ....

Disease or injury causing disability or death and statement of facts:

**Missing when aircraft failed to arrive at its destination in France.
Officially declared dead.   On transport mission.**

(IF ADDITIONAL SPACE IS REQUIRED USE REVERSE OF FORM)

On the basis of the evidence recited above, it is the decision of this committee that the disease or injury resulting in the above-numbered claim is traceable to the performance of duty in the military or naval service and that said disease or injury is traceable to the extra hazards of such service. Accordingly, by virtue of the authority conferred upon the Administrator of Veterans' Affairs it is authorized and directed that transfer be made pursuant to the provisions of Section 60 of the National Service Life Insurance Act of 1940 from the National Service Life Insurance Appropriation to the National Service Life Insurance Fund of

☒ an amount which, when added to the reserve of the policy will equal the then value of such benefits under above policy.

☐ an amount sufficient to cover the premiums on the policy for the period while the payment of premiums by the insured is waived by reason of the total disability of the insured.

FOR THE ADMINISTRATOR OF VETERANS' AFFAIRS:

IL/ejp   COMMITTEE ON EXTRA HAZARDS OF SERVICE

.... _____ Member. _____ H. N. _____ Member.

Date .... **MAR 1 2 1946** .... _____ vice Chairman.

I CERTIFY that in accordance with Section 607 of the National Service Life Insurance Act of 1940 the calculations the above-numbered claim are as follows:

.... Monthly premiums of $ .... $ ....

From .... to ....

Commuted value of policy .... $ ....

Reserve .... $ ....

Amount to be transferred .... $ ....

Date ....

Insurance Accounts Section, Finance Servi

U. S. GOVERNMENT PRINTING OFFICE   16—89483-1

Fig.60

John Morgan's Insurance Document